SUMMER MATTERS

ALA Editions purchases fund advocacy, awareness, and accreditation
programs for library professionals worldwide.

SUMMER MATTERS

MAKING ALL LEARNING COUNT

ELIZABETH M. M^cCHESNEY
and the Chicago Public Library

BRYAN W. WUNAR
and the Museum of Science and Industry

with illustrations by
STEVE MUSGRAVE

An imprint of the American Library Association

CHICAGO | 2017

© 2017 by the City of Chicago and the Museum of Science and Industry

Extensive effort has gone into ensuring the reliability of the information in this book; however, the publisher makes no warranty, express or implied, with respect to the material contained herein.

ISBN: 978-0-8389-1561-5 (paper)

Library of Congress Cataloging-in-Publication Data
Names: McChesney, Elizabeth M., author. | Wunar, Bryan W., author. | Chicago
  Public Library, author. | Museum of Science and Industry (Chicago, Ill.),
  author.
Title: Summer matters : making all learning count / Elizabeth M. McChesney
  and the Chicago Public Library, Bryan W. Wunar and the Museum of Science
  and Industry ; with illustrations by Steve Musgrave.
Description: Chicago : ALA Editions, an imprint of the American Library
  Association, 2017. | Includes bibliographical references and index.
Identifiers: LCCN 2017014889 | ISBN 9780838915615 (pbk. : alk. paper)
Subjects: LCSH: Libraries and museums—Illinois—Chicago—Case studies. |
  Children's libraries—Activity programs. | Summer reading programs. |
  Libraries and community. | Science and the arts—Study and teaching
  (Elementary) | Education, Elementary—Activity programs. |
  Interdisciplinary approach in education. | Libraries and education.
Classification: LCC Z716.9 .M385 2017 | DDC 027.62/5—dc23 LC record available at
  https://lccn.loc.gov/2017014889

Cover design by Alejandra Diaz. Images courtesy of Chicago Public Library and Museum of Science and Industry. Text design and composition by Karen Sheets de Gracia in the Malaga, Claire Hand, and Gotham typefaces.

♾ This paper meets the requirements of ANSI/NISO Z39.48–1992 (Permanence of Paper).

Printed in the United States of America
21 20 19 18 17   5 4 3 2 1

To the children of Chicago

CONTENTS

- - - - - - - - -

FOREWORD

Summer in America is a special time. In the best of circumstances, families are able to use the months away from school to rest, relax, and recharge. At the same time, however, the summer months present a unique set of challenges around child health and well-being, the availability of affordable child care, and, of course, the phenomenon that researchers have dubbed the summer slide.

A friend of mine once described summer learning loss as an epidemic. "Think about it this way," he argued, "millions of American children experience it on an annual basis. It damages academic performance by dragging down skills and test scores. It hits young kids and poor kids the hardest, and it costs taxpayers tens of millions of dollars each year in lost learning."

It's a persuasive argument, and he may be right. Indeed, researchers tell us that the learning loss that occurs during the summer compounds year after year—in other words, there is a long-term "drag" that occurs when children fall back summer after summer after summer.

Libraries, of course, have a long and impressive record of championing summer reading. From my own experience, I remember going to the Fairfax County (Virginia) Library on a blistery hot and humid day in the late 1970s because I was excited by the possibility of checking out what my father gently described as way too many books.

Today, more libraries across the nation are running bigger and better summer reading programs than ever before. These programs hold the promise of not simply curbing the problem of summer learning loss but, equally importantly, sparking children's interest in the pleasures of nonschool reading.

In 2013 the eighty-branch Chicago Public Library System revamped its thirty-seven-year-old Summer Reading Program. Librarian Elizabeth McChesney and museum educator Bryan Wunar led the effort with innovative thinking, strategic partnerships, and a clear and ambitious vision.

Whereas Liz and Bryan may be too modest to brag about the success of their work, the truth is that their program has proven itself as a model for our field. They established a partnership between Chicago Public Library and the Museum of Science and Industry, incorporated STEM/STEAM activities, created play-based and hands-on learning for students of all ages, made smart use of online technologies, and expanded the role of volunteers.

Today, Chicago Public Library partners with community-based organizations to offer a Summer Learning Challenge in every neighborhood across the city and twenty-four hours a day through online and take-home content—and it is the collective power of partnerships that Bryan and Liz emphasize as the key to their success. I'm proud to say that my organization, the National Summer Learning Association, recognized their program's extraordinary innovation and impact by presenting them with our first Founder's Award for Excellence.

Liz and Bryan have now turned their extraordinary talents toward sharing the lessons they've learned through their work. I am delighted to present this new and important book by them, and I expect that you will find *Summer Matters: Making All Learning Count* to be both easy to read and useful. As you will discover, the book provides practical, hands-on guidance for both librarians and museum educators. With the Chicago program as a template, the various chapters walk the reader through the ways in which libraries and museums can leverage partnerships to develop sustainable community-wide programs for kids and families and provide readers with dozens of easy hands-on STEM activities that directly link to children's literacy activities.

Enjoy the book—and thank you for the time and effort you are putting into creating innovative, sustainable, and just plain fun summer learning programs.

DR. MATTHEW BOULAY
Founder and Chairman of the Board
National Summer Learning Association

PREFACE

- - - - - - - - - -

I ONLY WANT TO DO WHAT I WANT TO DO

In the summer of 2012, we toured some of our branch libraries during the Summer Reading Program. It was a great experience to see kids reading books, reporting on them, and attending programs. In one branch library, I started asking a group of kids about six years old what they liked to do at their library and what was the most fun for them. One fidgety little boy looked me squarely in the eye and said: "I only want to do what I want to do." Well. I found that to be a profound truth for our libraries. Kids need and deserve a place to do what they want to do. To read, to discover, to play, to create . . . on their own terms.

And public libraries have long been the place of choice for children in their communities. The library doesn't tell you what to read or how to read it or even, really, if you should read it or not. We are one of the only places in the community where kids can actually choose their own individual pathways and find collections and activities that match their interests. And as the times change for libraries, so does the definition of choice. Libraries are adding play spaces and maker spaces, and redefining service and programs, but something that will always stay the same is how we keep our patrons at the center of the choice. I love that about public libraries.

I don't know about you (but I can guess you're just the same), but in Chicago it has always been important to us to make our libraries as welcoming, joyous, and intriguing as possible. Part of our priority is that we want our libraries' children's rooms to not "feel" like a school, but instead to be a noisy and interesting neighborhood learning laboratory where kids and families can cook up all sorts of interesting ideas and projects. We want a place where youth will find inspiration by pursuing their interests and learn for fun or just because the spark of curiosity has taken hold of them. We recognize that reading is learning and that other learning has been going on in our libraries, too. Learning because it is fun is at the heart of Chicago Public Library's redesigned Rahm's Readers Summer Learning Challenge. Our program tagline, "All Learning Counts," recognizes that every child's unique path should be celebrated and nurtured. We accomplish this through our partnership with the Museum of Science and Industry (MSI), which introduced informal science concepts and experiential learning into the program. Bryan and the MSI Community Initiatives Team helped teach us how to focus on "one big idea" of science each week, opening doors to learning and experimenting for kids and families. Together, we believe that every child in Chicago deserves high-quality opportunities outside of school time. Aligning our summer program to current research, customer feedback, our library's own evolving strategy, and a strong partnership between the library and museum was a great place to start. We hope you think so, too.

LIZ McCHESNEY
Director, Children's Services
Chicago Public Library

BRYAN WUNAR
Director, Community Initiatives
Museum of Science and Industry

ACKNOWLEDGMENTS

--- --- --- --- --- --- --- --- --- --- ---

Together we would like to thank the many people who have encouraged and supported this work throughout the last five years. This transformation would not have been made possible without the support of Mayor Rahm Emanuel and his staff; the vision, unflinching support, and leadership of Commissioner Brian Bannon and the Board of Directors of Chicago Public Library (CPL) led by Linda Johnson Rice; and the leadership of President David Mosena and the Board of Directors at the Museum of Science and Industry. Thank you to CPL First Deputy Commissioner Andrea Sáenz for her acumen and support, and to MSI Vice President of Education, Andrea Ingall. We are grateful for the perseverance and humor of CPL Deputy Commissioner Baronica Roberson, and for the support of the Chicago Public Library Foundation staff led by Rhona Frazin and their Board under Bob Wislow, as well as the many funders who have supported this work. Thank you also to the entire senior staff of Chicago Public Library for supporting the Summer Learning Challenge and to the Museum of Science and Industry leadership team and staff for their vision and support. Thank you to the National Summer Learning Association for your support and important work, led by Dr. Matthew Boulay, whose foreword appears here. A special shout-out to Sarah Pitcock, past president of the National Summer Learning Association, for believing in Chicago's work for kids.

~ LIZ AND BRYAN

First, to the kids and parents of Chicago who participate in this adventure with us each summer, thank you for trusting us to bring you fun and high-quality learning, and for all your hard work each summer. I would also like to thank the entire staff at Chicago Public Library, especially the committed and dedicated System Wide Children's Services staff who have been "rivers" through this major change. Your dedication to kids throughout the city of Chicago inspires me each and every day. Andrea Telli, Assistant Commissioner of Neighborhood Services and my very dear friend: I am humbled by your support of me and of Children's Services. Thanks to the Marketing and Press Office and especially Patrick Molloy, Mary Beth Mulholland, and Scott Mitchell. Thank you to the brilliant Liz Huntoon and the incredible Bernie Nowakowski who developed and built the Children's Services Department at CPL and created a bedrock of service for children. I was lucky enough to be mentored by these two remarkable leaders in our field, and it shaped my career. There are so many staff who were instrumental to this work at its inception and have now moved on from our team. You all helped move this forward: Elizabeth Basile, John Glynn, Elaine Kaneshiro, Andrew Medlar, Sarah Tansley, and Robin Willard. To Margy Dunne, Mary Jo Godziela, Rose Powers, and Sherri Stroebel, CPL alums: you've taught me what I know about being a good children's librarian; I love and thank you. Mary Dempsey and Amy Eshleman: thank you for leadership and never-ending support. Ruth Lednicer: thank you, my friend, for always believing in me and my work—you pushed me to do better and I am so thankful. Patty Seibert: thank you for all your support of all of my ideas. To all the library leaders who have pushed the conversation about the importance of summer learning: the staff at the American Library Association, the Public Library Association, and the Urban Library Council. And then there's my team. More family than coworkers, these are the people I am proud to stand side by side with each day. Although you are listed here as contributors, you own this work. No longer small, but always mighty: you guys amaze me, and I am so honored to work by your side. Katherine Bence, Caroline Broeren, Cristina Camargo, George Coleman, Jason Driver, Josh Farnum, Shilo Halfen, John Mangahas, Noemi Morales, and Rebecca Ruidl, thank you for your contributions. Katie Eckert, Lori Frumkin, and Alexa Hamilton of the Children's Services team: you are the true holders of this book, and I thank you for your amazing work on this thinking, the project, and this manuscript. Chad Weiden, you inspire me by your example to lead with an equal mixture of intellect and heart; and for the ways in which you advocate for kids every day; you are my hero. David Hoyt and Claire Hassel, thank you for "puzzling us" each summer: your gifts to the program and to kids are so deeply appreciated. To Steve Musgrave, you bring an elegance and thoughtfulness to this project that is braided together with a child's sense of playfulness. Each year your illustration is a gift to Chicago, and it is my deep privilege to create this program with you annually. And to my partner and valued friend, Bryan

Wunar: I am proud to be your colleague and call you my friend. You've taught me how to launch rockets, drop eggs, blow things up, but most importantly, you have shown me how to never, ever give up, how to stay focused on the "one big idea," and have fun in the process. I'm fortunate to continually learn from you; I admire your integrity, and I'm proud to share a vision with you that both pushes us and drives our work for youth. Thank you. And last but certainly not least, thank you to my family—Steve, who always believes I can do anything; Fred, whose devotion and humor makes everything better. And last and most important of all: to my daughters, Maren and Phoebe: you guys are my inspiration for absolutely everything.

~ LIZ

I would like to thank the entire Museum of Science and Industry community. A special thank you to the staff of the Center for the Advancement of Science Education who are so dedicated to making science accessible, relevant, and fun for all of our audiences every day. David Mosena, President and CEO of the Museum of Science and Industry, thank you for supporting my ideas and allowing many of them to become a reality through our continual institutional change and growth. Andrea Ingram, Vice President for Education and Guest Services, thank you for being the constant advocate for the children and youth we serve. Thank you to Nicole Kowrach, Director of Teaching and Learning, for being my partner in all things education and for being my sounding board every step of the way. To Kevin Frank, Director of Government and Foundation Relations, you have played such a strong role in ensuring that informal science education is recognized as a major contributor within the education field, and to all the members of the External Affairs staff, thank you for working tirelessly to ensure that we have the resources to do this wonderful work. A special thank you to Julie Parente, and the members of the Marketing and Public Relations team for being a creative force to expand the Summer Brain Games and for your impact on summer learning. I would also like to acknowledge the efforts of the Science Minors, Science Achievers, and Farrell Fellows; the teens who have brought our work to life over the years, who never fail to inspire me, and are among the best ambassadors for science learning in our communities. I must acknowledge my colleagues and friends in Community Initiatives; you are the ones who put this all into practice. You are an amazingly passionate team who always find a way to make an impact on the children, youth, families, and communities we serve. To Brett Nicholas and Marvin McClure, my two right hands, who always remind me that this is not just what we do, but it is who we are. To my dear friend and collaborator, Liz McChesney, who opened my eyes to the power of libraries, taught me that all learning counts, and challenged me to reinvent the role that museums can play in the lives of children. Together, we have found a way to make fifty-two weeks of summer learning a reality. My final thanks go to my family, for your never-ending support, and especially my fearless children, Beatrix and Baxter, who are always willing to try anything. Thank you.

~ BRYAN

Designing a new visual identity for this program each year is a privilege. I would like to thank Liz McChesney and the Children's Services staff at Chicago Public Library for consistently providing a creative and collaborative working environment. Liz encourages an open discussion of ideas while making sure the message stays on point. I also want to thank the children's librarians, the kids, and the parents who participate in the programs. I am always inspired by the librarians' dedication to the program and the kids' enthusiastic response.

~ STEVE

And last but certainly not least, to the brave and brilliant Jamie Santoro, friend and editor and a tireless advocate through the process, thank you from the bottom of our hearts for believing in us, championing this work, and never giving up on making this book live.

~ BRYAN, LIZ, AND STEVE

LETTER FROM COMMISSIONER BRIAN BANNON

- - - - - - - - - - - - - - -

Summer is an important time at Chicago Public Library for patrons of all ages. While Rahm's Readers Summer Learning Challenge is aimed at children, a strong library system recognizes that a well-run summer program impacts most every kind of user we serve. This program is one of the largest of any in which the system will invest, execute, or evaluate. It has a reach that very few other programs in the public library can have: it touches the youngest children through teens and very often features an adult component. It serves parents and caregivers, and teachers and other adult child-care providers in a strategic way. At Chicago Public Library, it has the broadest reach across age groups of any program we conduct.

For us in Chicago, the Rahm's Readers Summer Learning Challenge became an important tool to signal change in the library. The restructuring of this program underscored the shift in thinking about summer learning in Chicago, and exemplified this shift for both patrons and staff in Chicago's libraries. For our staff, it was important to focus on twenty-first-century learning skills and experiential learning through library programs, work on the changes as a team, and execute the program. The Children's Services team continues in its iteration of the process to this day. For our patrons, the beloved Summer Reading Program became a new and even more reinvigorated experience as it was transformed into the Summer Learning Challenge. We asked children for the first time to create their own individual pathways for summer learning success.

Participants in Rahm's Readers Summer Learning Challenge 2016

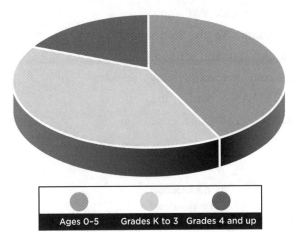

Ages 0–5   Grades K to 3   Grades 4 and up

Cross-sector support is essential to the strength and success of the Rahm's Readers Summer Learning Challenge. We receive indispensable support from our city's mayor, for whom the program is named. Mayor Rahm Emanuel is the biggest champion of our work. Each year he challenges the children of Chicago to a different learning goal. His support and that of the staff at City Hall allows us to be successful. Working within the context of your municipality will help posit your program and library in the citywide conversation.

For us, the relationship with the Museum of Science and Industry is critically important. This partnership gives us the foundation we need to build healthy STEAM habits with our librarians and to implement the best thinking in informal science education in the nation today. The Rahm's Readers Summer Learning Challenge allows the museum to extend its reach into each of our eighty communities. They take their thinking and best practices and accomplish their own goals within our library system, and therein we also deepen our ability to deliver high-quality STEAM in our communities.

The Rahm's Readers Summer Learning Challenge would also not be possible without generous private support from the Chicago Public Library Foundation. This public/private partnership allows CPL to use philanthropic donations to leverage public investment, supporting innovative programs like our Summer Learning Challenge. When the philanthropic visions of corporations in Chicago can support our work, we become united in building a stronger city.

The strength of our program also depends on rigorous evaluation, which bears out that participants make academic strides in math and reading through sustained participation in summer reading programs. Program attendance throughout the summer is high and is part of the value proposition of the library within the greater community. Surveys of participants, caregivers, and child-care providers all show an extremely high rate of customer satisfaction in this program. We also know through careful analysis that this is also a program that is fun for staff and good for internal morale. The staff all come together each year around our theme and enjoy decorating their library branches, experimenting with related STEAM activities, and supporting Chicago's kids. I am sure that the value of a Summer Learning Challenge within your library will be rich and multilayered, too.

BRIAN BANNON
Commissioner
Chicago Public Library

LETTER FROM MAYOR RAHM EMANUEL

‑ ‑

Keeping our children engaged and learning year round is attainable! Summer break is a time of leisure, fun, and relaxation, but it can negatively impact our children's ability to keep up when they return to school if they are not kept engaged in brain-stimulating activities. Summer learning loss can and does happen when children are out of school. It means that kids can lose up to three months of what they learned during the school year. We can do better. No city can afford to have our children slip. We need our kids to make gains, stay engaged, stay encouraged, and be prepared for success when school resumes in the fall.

In Chicago, we've worked to build learning opportunities by maximizing the library system to support children across the city. The strength of our library system has become a powerful way to bridge the learning gap by keeping kids engaged through our award-winning Rahm's Readers Summer Learning Challenge. The Summer Learning Challenge leverages partnerships with Chicago's generous cultural institutions and with service providers who help us scale the program in every neighborhood across our beautiful city.

The groundwork for the success of the Summer Learning Challenge was laid in 2013 when Chicago Public Library redesigned what had traditionally been its summer reading program. By developing a partnership with the Museum of Science and Industry, the summer program incorporated STEAM activities, which are geared toward helping students get excited about learning over the summer. Since this redesign, the program has experienced a 50 percent increase in participation, and we're seeing data indicating that the Summer Learning Challenge not only mitigates learning loss, but actually improves academic performance.

A recent analysis by Chapin Hall at the University of Chicago revealed that, on average, children participating in the Rahm's Readers Summer Learning Challenge have demonstrated 15 percent greater reading gains and 20 percent greater math gains over and above their peers who did not participate in the program.

This sustainable model employs partnerships and relationships that act as a web across our City of Learning and deepen our work on behalf of kids.

Investing in your library's summer program and services to children lays an important foundation in your city. I have taken this step to ensure that summertime is learning time with this unique and fresh approach to library service. I am proud of our Rahm's Readers Summer Learning Challenge for the way in which it invigorates learning, encourages children and parents to learn together, invests in neighborhood libraries, and engages communities in a way that strengthens our neighborhoods.

Each year I challenge the children of Chicago to read, learn, and create even more than the year before. And each year the kids of Chicago answer that call. Now I challenge all of you to support your own library in this ambitious and worthwhile program for your readers and learners.

HONORABLE MAYOR RAHM EMANUEL

CHAPTER 1

RATIONALE FOR CHANGE

For years, like many libraries across the country, Chicago Public Library enjoyed hosting a popular and successful Summer Reading Program. In its last iteration, the traditional program encouraged children to read either 25 picture books or 10 chapter books over the summer to earn a prize. Each summer, over 50,000 children signed up and read at least one book, and many children reached their goals over the course of the summer. Children's librarians throughout the system were fond of the program, which functioned as a well-oiled machine, but in the spring of 2012 we began to think bigger.

It started when we took a closer look at the program. We asked ourselves: are we reaching everybody in a meaningful way? This became the central question of the redesign. Sure, the program was successful and well-liked, but how was it impacting kids? What were they getting out of it? Chicago Public Library is a large library system with eighty branch libraries in a diverse city that is changing all the time. How could the program become even more valuable across the city?

At the same time, the effectiveness of traditional summer reading programs had been evaluated in *The Dominican Study: Public Library Summer Reading Programs Close the Reading Gap* (2010). The study looked at whether public library summer reading programs did in fact reach their stated goals of creating and sustaining a love of reading in children and preventing the loss of reading skills over the summer. The study showed that "students who participated in the public library summer reading program had better reading skills at the end of third grade and scored higher on the standards test than the students who did not participate." However, and of special interest to Chicago Public Library, "students who participated in the public library summer reading program included more females, more Caucasians, and were at a higher socioeconomic level than the group of students who did not participate" (Roman, Carran, and Fiore 2010, 1–2). How could Chicago Public Library enhance its program to reach more youth than the traditional summer reading program's participant demographics?

Representatives of the Children's Services team at Chicago Public Library had these questions on their minds as they attended the National Summer Learning Association (NSLA) Conference for the first time in 2012. Although not many libraries were represented at the conference at this time, they were struck by research surrounding the "summer slide," which is the tendency for students, especially those from low-income families, to lose some of the achievement gains they made during the previous school year. Our central question resonated even stronger now—might the library's summer program reach more children in a way that could also help mitigate the summer slide?

As Children's Services was considering a shift in summer, the senior management team at CPL was working to define the system's impact and the social enterprise of the library. While CPL's timeless mission remains unchanged, the strategic plan developed for 2015–2019 would respond to the current and evolving needs of patrons trying to learn, thrive, and grow in the twenty-first century by nurturing learning, supporting economic advancement, and strengthening communities. With the support of the library's commissioner and a new strategic plan, CPL's Children's Services team set out to create a program that would combat the summer slide and thus would better serve children and families in Chicago. Pulling together research and trends from a variety of fields, we began to explore what an effective and engaging summer program should look like.

NATIONAL SUMMER LEARNING ASSOCIATION

Since our trip to the NSLA annual conference proved to be one of the key inspirations in redesigning our summer program, we began our research by looking at their publications and resources. The National Summer Learning Association is an independent organization that provides resources, guidance, and expertise to the summer learning community. In particular, two published reports exploring the achievement gap and youth access to knowledge became invaluable.

In 2009 the NSLA published an interview with Karl L. Alexander, a Johns Hopkins University sociology professor whose research shows that low-income youth suffer significantly from a loss of academic skills over the summertime (see figure 1.1). Summer after summer, as kids' skills diminished, so did their academic achievement. When asked if summer programs can help close the achievement gap, Alexander stated that he believes children need "strategically planned, structured

School-Year Cumulative Gains

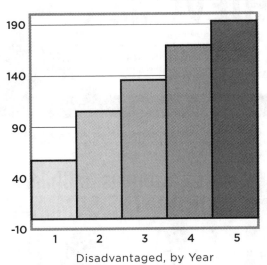

Disadvantaged, by Year

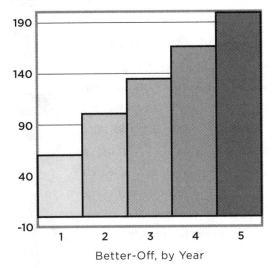

Better-Off, by Year

Summer Cumulative Gains

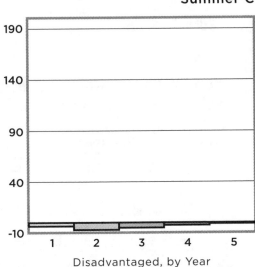

Disadvantaged, by Year

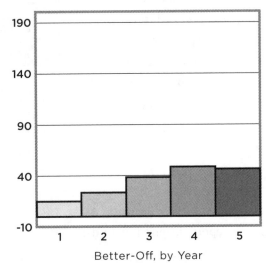

Better-Off, by Year

FIGURE 1.1

Summer Learning and Its Implications

From "Summer Learning and Its Implications: Insights from the Beginning School Study," by Karl L. Alexander, Doris R. Entwisle, and Linda Steffel Olson, 2007, *New Directions for Youth Development*, no. 114, p. 18. Reprinted with permission from Wiley.

summer experiences, and that's especially true for those who don't have access to enriching, home-based learning. . . . Summer programs can be an important part of that strategy by providing a variety of experiences that challenge children, develop their talents, keep them engaged, and expand their horizons" (National Summer Learning Association 2009c, 2).

Also, in a report published by the NSLA in 2009, Susan Neuman discussed how the work she and her colleagues did studying how people access public library resources, including computers, in both low-income and middle-income neighborhoods affects summer programming. Neuman believes "the idea that we can close the knowledge gap by just providing access to computers is a terrible fallacy." Her research indicates that during the school year there's at least some leveling in terms of technology education, with children from all income groups learning and gaining skills, but during the summertime the gap between these income groups widens even further. In a statement that is all too familiar to those of us working in public libraries, Neuman's research showed that "low-income youth lack options in the summer, and sometimes come to the library just to hang out or because it's air conditioned" (National Summer Learning Association 2009a, 2). Neuman's call for kids to be able to access educational opportunities every single moment of every day, especially in the summer, helped steer the multimedia aspects of our redesigned program.

SUMMER SLIDE

The National Summer Learning Association's reports inspired us to dig a little deeper into the summer slide (see figure 1.2). As far back as 1996, researchers were looking at the summer slide in relation to socioeconomic factors. That year, Harris Cooper, a professor at the University of Missouri-Columbia, and his colleagues analyzed thirty-nine studies and found that "kids do forget over the summer. Across the board, all kids lose some math skills. In reading, the middle class holds its own, but the poor lose reading and spelling skills, and that pattern emerged as a possible explanation for the academic achievement gap between those who have financial resources and those who don't" (National Summer Learning Association 2009b, 1).

Eleven years later, Karl L. Alexander and his colleagues showed a direct link between summer opportunities and academic achievement during the school year. "During the school year, lower-income children's skills improve at close to the same

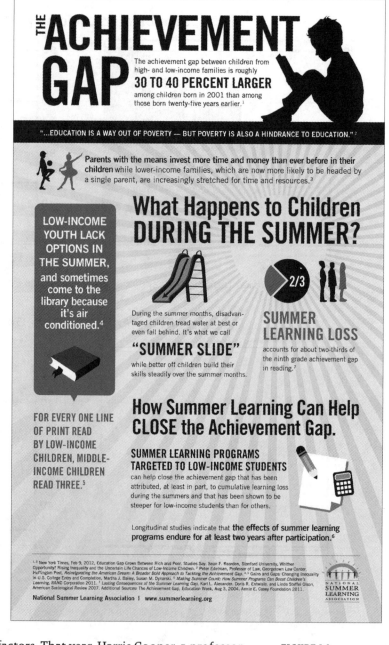

FIGURE 1.2

Summer Slide and Achievement Gap

Used with permission from the NSLA.

rate as those of their more advantaged peers. Over the summer, middle- and upper-income children's skills continue to improve, while lower-income children's skills do not" (Alexander, Entwisle, and Olson 2007). Alexander and his team point to more opportunities for summer enrichment activities like camps, vacations, and classes for middle-class children compared to their lower-income peers. These early out-of-school summer learning differences substantially account for achievement-related differences in high school-track placements, high school dropout rates, and four-year college attendance.

Thus, research about the effects of the summer slide proves that it affects all children, but children in lower-income families are more severely impacted. About 85 percent of the Chicago Public Schools' students receive free or reduced-price hot lunches, which is an indicator of poverty. With this in mind, we set out to redesign a program to include more enrichment opportunities that would help mitigate the summer slide for all of Chicago's youth, using this research to leverage support for the program.

MUSEUMS, LIBRARIES, AND TWENTY-FIRST-CENTURY SKILLS

Since the start of the new millennium, global leaders have been asking questions about what sort of skills are needed to support productive participation in a new twenty-first-century workforce. Today's economy requires the ability to perform nonroutine, creative tasks, such as app development or sustainable energy solutions, which has heightened the need for individuals to master twenty-first-century skills like creative thinking and problem-solving. In response, the Partnership for 21st Century Skills (P21), a nonprofit coalition sponsored by education, business, and community organizations, created a widely accepted framework that defines "21st century skills." The P21 framework has been adopted by numerous states, organizations, and associations, including the National Education Association and the American Association of School Librarians.

Museums and libraries play a critical role in helping build twenty-first-century skills, especially for children. With that in mind, the Institute of Museum and Library Services (IMLS) considered the list of skills commonly referred to as "21st century skills" and modified it slightly to better align with library and museum priorities:

Learning and Innovation Skills
- Critical thinking and problem-solving
- Creativity and innovation

- Communication and collaboration
- Visual literacy
- Scientific and numerical literacy
- Cross-disciplinary thinking
- Basic literacy

Information, Media, and Technology Skills
- Information literacy
- Media literacy
- ICT (Information, communications, and technology) literacy

21st Century Themes
- Global awareness
- Financial, economic, business, and entrepreneurial literacy
- Civic literacy
- Health literacy
- Environmental literacy

Life and Career Skills
- Flexibility and adaptability
- Initiative and self-direction
- Social and cross-cultural skills
- Productivity and accountability
- Leadership and responsibility

(Institute of Museum and Library Services 2009, 3)

The IMLS also suggested that the twenty-first century has changed *how* and *when* we learn, blurring the lines between formal and informal learning experiences. We see this expressed especially in a growing interest in self-directed learning. The IMLS report quotes Dr. Dennie Palmer Wolf, a leading researcher in the area of children's out-of-school-time learning: "Goal-directed free-time activity in safe, supportive environments with responsive adults and peers makes sizable contributions to learning, social skills, and mental health" (Institute of Museum and Library Services 2009, 11). From this exploration of societal needs in the twenty-first century, Chicago Public Library began to consider a self-directed, goal-oriented model for its summer program.

The IMLS pointed out that patrons now expect higher levels of interactivity and programs specific to their individual needs and interests. In particular, patrons increasingly expect museums and libraries to act as "partners to enhance (in mission-appropriate ways) the learning systems across a community" and create "flexible, co-created, immersive experiences" (Institute of Museum and Library Services 2009, 13). CPL already had a history of successful partnerships with numerous city and cultural partners (see chapter 3: "Partnerships: Stronger Together"), but in response to this community expectation, CPL looked to create a deeper and richer partnership with Chicago's Museum of Science and Industry.

The IMLS's stress on twenty-first-century skills heavily influenced CPL's frame of reference as we looked at shifting from a summer reading program into something more dynamic. The IMLS issues this call to action:

> All libraries and museums—and the people they serve—stand to benefit from becoming more intentional and purposeful about accommodating the lifelong learning needs of people in the 21st century, and doing this work collaboratively in alignment with community needs. Therefore, it is critical that we envision, define, and implement library and museum approaches that integrate 21st century skills in more tangible, visible ways.
>
> (Institute of Museum and Library Services 2009, 6)

CPL's traditional summer reading program was decidedly a twentieth-century program that wasn't meeting all of the needs of a new generation of children. If the NSLA's research helped CPL staff prove the need for a redesigned program, it was the IMLS's 21st Century Learning Skills that provided the spark of inspiration we needed to get going.

KEEPING BOOKS AND READING THE CORNERSTONE

We knew that reading would continue to be the cornerstone of the redesigned program. Our traditional summer reading program was well-loved and effective, and a successful redesign that kept some aspects of the old program would stand the best chance of being embraced by families and staff. Also, research shows that reading is a key component in addressing the summer slide. *The Dominican Study* showed that "students who participated in the public library summer reading program had better reading skills at the end of third grade and scored higher on the standards test than the students who did not participate" (Roman, Carran, and Fiore 2010). Research on information literacy and children's reading habits helped steer the literacy aspect of the summer program's redesign.

Research by Dr. Nell Duke in 2000 showed that students have access to a very small amount of informational text, and classroom instruction rarely focuses on informational literacy materials. In the study, 20 first-grade classrooms were observed, 10 from high socioeconomic status (SES) schools and 10 from low SES schools. The amount, type, and use of informational text in low SES schools was significantly less than in higher SES schools (Duke 2000). In thinking about reaching all of the children in Chicago, CPL staff considered this disparity in access and exposure to informational texts and thought a redesigned summer program could be the perfect place to address this issue.

Informational texts are a key component of the Common Core State Standards for the language arts. These learning goals outline what a student should know and be able to do at the end of each grade. The standards were created to ensure that all students graduate from high school with the skills and knowledge necessary to succeed in college, career, and life, regardless of where they live. As of this writing, forty-two states, the District of Columbia, four territories, and the Department of Defense Education Activity have voluntarily adopted and are moving forward with the Common Core (Common Core State Standards Initiative, 2016). Common Core State Standards tie in directly with 21st Century Skills and work together as a student progresses through school. Because of this, the standards place emphasis on students' exposure to informational texts and media literacy skills.

Dr. Susan Neuman explains that "in our knowledge-based economy, students are not only going to have to read, but develop knowledge-based capital. We need to help children use literacy to develop critical-thinking skills, problem-solving skills, making distinctions among different types of evidence . . . To ensure they are career and college ready, we have to see students as lifelong learners and help them develop the knowledge-gathering skills they will use for the rest of their lives" (Sparks 2012). We live in an information age in which most of the reading and writing that adults do is information-based, so it seemed appropriate to incorporate informational text into a redesigned summer program. We wanted children to explore and engage with informational text in the same way that they already did with fiction.

However, how much should participants read? A set quantity of titles? A set number of minutes spent reading? Research suggests that the more time students spend reading independently, the higher their gains will be in reading achievement. Multiple long-term studies have also shown that reading volume is directly connected to reading success for all students, regardless of ability. Cunningham and Stanovich note, "Although there are considerable differences in the amount of reading volume in school, it is likely that differences in out-of-school reading volume are an even more potent source of the rich-get-richer and poor-get-poorer achievement patterns" (Cunningham and Stanovich 1998, 4). Researchers analyzed the correlation between reading percentile, the amount of time spent reading per day, and the number of words read per year (Anderson, Wilson, and Fielding 1988). We can see the connection in table 1.1.

Of course, we want to encourage children to spend as much time as possible reading independently outside of the classroom. However, table 1.1 shows an interesting leveling off of achievement gains when compared to independent reading.

Students who read about 20 minutes per day were ranked in the 90th percentile for student achievement, but students who read more than twice that amount—65 minutes per day—showed only minimal gain in student achievement scores over those who read more than 20 minutes per day. Reading about 20 minutes a day seems to be the perfect sweet spot to encourage children to maximize achievement when reading independently, whether during the school year or in summer.

Thus, CPL planned to keep reading, both fiction and informational text, as the cornerstone of the program and use a suggested amount of twenty minutes of reading per day in the redesigned program.

REFLECTION: CLOSING THE LEARNING LOOP

Just as we wanted to keep reading as the cornerstone of a redesigned summer program, we also knew that reporting and reflection would continue to be key aspects of our summer learning program. For many years, "reporting" played a huge role in CPL's summer reading program. Participants were asked to report back to library staff or a teen volunteer about the reading they did as part of the program. Staff and volunteers asked open-ended questions to help guide the reporting. For example, if a school-aged child shared that she read a *Junie B. Jones* book, staff might ask, "What was your favorite part?" or "Who would you recommend this book to and why?" as opposed to "Did you like it?" For younger children or children who felt shy, we also encouraged reporting in the form of drawing or writing about what participants read. We saw that when children were asked to share more about what they read, it created a deeper and more meaningful summer reading experience.

This type of reporting is a form of reflection, an aspect of learning that scholars cite as a key step in helping youth get into the habit of linking and constructing meaning from their experiences. In the book *Learning and Leading with Habits of Mind*, Arthur L. Costa and Bena Kallick explain that "reflecting on work enhances its meaning" and "reflecting on experiences encourages insight and complex learning. . . . Reflection was not a time for testimoni-

TABLE 1.1

Variation in Amount of Independent Reading

%	Independent Reading Minutes per Day	Words Read per Year
98	65.0	4,358,000
90	21.1	1,823,000
80	14.2	1,146,000
70	9.6	622,000
60	6.5	432,000
50	4.6	282,000
40	3.2	200,000
30	1.3	106,000
20	0.7	21,000
10	0.1	8,000
2	0	0

Republished and adapted with permission of John Wiley & Sons—Journals, from "Growth in Reading and How Children Spend Their Time Outside of School," by Richard C. Anderson, Paul T. Wilson, and Linda G. Fielding, *Reading Research Quarterly*, vol. 23, no. 3 (Summer 1988); permission conveyed through Copyright Clearance Center, Inc.

als about how good or bad the experience was. Instead, reflection was the time to consider what was learned from the experience" (Costa and Kallick 2008).

Reflection is also a valuable tool in helping children embrace key aspects of twenty-first-century skills. For example, if a child is participating in a stomp rocket launch challenge and the rocket flies only two feet, the child will need to consider what changes he could make to his rocket to get it to fly further. Reflection factors into this process by helping to redefine and redirect mistakes or failures. "Many of us grow up thinking of mistakes as bad, viewing errors as evidence of fundamental incapacity. This negative thinking pattern can create a self-fulfilling prophecy, which undermines the learning process. To maximize our learning it is essential to ask: 'How can we get the most from every mistake we make?'" (Gelb and Buzan 1994, 68).

This research on the importance of taking time to think about learning reinforced the value of reflection as part of a summer learning program. Asking youth to think about the reading and learning activities in which they take part throughout the summer allows for opportunities to reflect on failures and successes, make connections to other parts of their lives, and complete their learning.

REACHING DIVERSE LEARNERS

The theory of multiple intelligences encourages us to ask questions about how children think and learn. The theory of multiple intelligences comes from Dr. Howard Gardner of Harvard University. He suggests that the accepted notion of intelligence is too limited. He theorizes that there are eight different intelligences to describe the "human potential" in children and adults. These intelligences are linguistic intelligence, logical-mathematical intelligence, spatial intelligence, bodily-kinesthetic intelligence, musical intelligence, interpersonal intelligence, intrapersonal intelligence, and naturalist intelligence (Armstrong 2012). Gardner explains that "we all have the multiple intelligences. But we single out, as a strong intelligence, an area where the person has considerable computational power" (Gardner 2013).

The theory of multiple intelligences encourages us to learn as much as we can about each child, and teach each individual in ways that he or she finds comfortable and learns effectively. In this way, we can reach youth who have different strengths and build a bridge from what they are interested in to our programming. The theory of multiple intelligences inspired us to think about making a summer program more youth interest-driven. Additionally, it offered a great opportunity to approach this shift with our staff. In asking the staff, "How do you learn? What are your interests? What is your strength? How do you go about solving a problem?" and looking at how each was different, we were able to set up the idea of making the program more individualized for each of our participants.

FAMILY ENGAGEMENT

Parents are often in the library with their children, but our traditional summer reading program did not make family engagement a priority. Would stronger family engagement make our redesign more effective? We looked to research conducted by James Kim, assistant professor of education at Harvard University. Kim looked at different approaches to summer reading and found that voluntary summer reading programs (such as traditional library programs like CPL's) can work, but they work best when adult caregivers get involved by helping youth to choose appropriate books and employ simple techniques to improve their skill and understanding.

> In our first study, we surveyed 2,000 kids in fourth and sixth grade and asked what they read over the summer. We found that the kids who read the most over the summer did better in the fall—but that didn't tell us why. Do books lead to comprehension or do good readers just have more books? . . . Even having teachers encourage kids to read appeared to have no impact on comprehension. But we saw a significant difference when we provided books and adults were involved to guide reading skills and understanding.
>
> (Kim 2008, 2)

The National Center for Family and Community Connections with Schools synthesized additional research. They concluded that no matter what their income or background, when families are involved in their child's learning, the child will be more likely to

- Earn higher grades and test scores, and enroll in higher-level programs
- Be promoted, pass his or her classes, and earn credits
- Attend school regularly
- Have better social skills, show improved behavior, and adapt well
- Graduate and go on to postsecondary education

(Henderson and Mapp 2002, 7)

This research proved the importance of engaged adults (particularly parents and caregivers) in helping combat the summer slide and improve children's lives in a variety of ways. Clearly, when families learn together, everyone benefits. This research informed new parental engagement components in our redesigned summer program.

SUMMARY

A lot of formal and informal research helped support Chicago Public Library as we began to build a new summer learning program. In looking at all we had reviewed, we knew that our program would need to do the following:

- Align with our strategic plan and city priorities
- Combat the summer slide
- Be self-directed and goal-oriented
- Promote twenty-first-century skills
- Keep reading as the cornerstone of the program
- Enhance access to books that match readers' interests, including informational texts
- Encourage reading for at least twenty minutes a day
- Help youth participate in individualized ways, with many different opportunities to learn
- Embrace dynamic partnerships with other cultural organizations
- Incorporate opportunities for reflection
- Increase parental and family engagement

THINK ABOUT IT

A mission statement is essentially a proclamation that describes the purpose of your program's existence and your long-term goals. Think of it as the banner that you wave proclaiming who you are and what your intent is with this program. A mission statement is concise and helps everyone understand and communicate the objectives of the project. It can be useful for developing your program over time, and when done well, it can help you get support from your municipality, potential funders, and your partners.

A vision statement is a road map of your vision for the program. Imagine that you are looking into the future. What do you see your program accomplishing for your library kids? This is different from your mission statement in that it talks about what the program will do when you have perfected the activities and are seeing successes. Think of it as the light at the end of the tunnel! In Chicago, our vision statement is:

If we achieve what we want, we will have a fully sustainable summer learning program which attracts kids of all ages and their parents/caregivers to us each and every summer. Through robust participation in our engaging themes, children will read, conduct STEAM activities, and engage in design challenge that allows both Chicago Public Library and Museum of Science and Industry's educational goals to be met. We will nurture learning and strengthen communities through this robust and rigorous and fun program.

To develop your mission statement, we have broken it down into four essential questions you will want to include in your statement. These are included in the chart below. At Chicago Public Library, our program mission statement is:

Provide awesome and excellent programs and services for children birth to age 13 in summer that help Chicago kids and families beat back summer slide, accelerate summer learning, start school prepared, and joyfully embark on 21st Century learning through partnerships across Chicago.

Now you try it.

- - - - - - -

MISSION STATEMENT: Foundational Statement That Describes the Purpose of Existence and Our Long-Term Goals

What do we do?	How do we involve our partners?
Whom do we do it for?	What value are we bringing and to whom?

VISION STATEMENT: An Image or Description of What We Aspire to Become in the Future. "If we achieve what we want, it will look like this . . ."

The Summer Learning Challenge of 2025 will:

CHAPTER 2

THE ROLE OF STEAM

After taking a close look at the research that supported our summer redesign, we realized that we needed a context through which we could embrace twenty-first-century skills at the library. Science, technology, engineering, and mathematics (STEM) has become a hot topic among educators, policymakers, and business leaders over the past few years. We felt that the skills developed in STEM learning could be the perfect lens to focus our redesigned summer program. Rather than simply following the latest educational trend, we wanted to explore and understand why STEM was so important and what iteration would work best both in the library setting and for our intended audience.

Looking across the educational landscape, we learned very quickly that a universal definition of STEM does not exist and, as a result, there are many different variations of STEM. Technical definitions of STEM emerged from the scientific community, which were intended to address the academic pipeline and prepare the future workforce. The STEM acronym can be traced back to Judith Ramaley, former director of the National Science Foundation's (NSF's) Education and Human Resources Division from 2001 to 2004 (National Science Foundation, 2012b). She called for the realignment of the previously existing acronym of SMET (science, mathematics, engineering, and technology). This shift from SMET to STEM emphasized the increasing role of technology in our society.

The NSF is instrumental in expanding the definition of STEM. Today when we think of STEM, it includes subjects in the fields of chemistry, computer and information technology science, engineering, geosciences, life sciences, mathematical sciences, physics and astronomy, social sciences (anthropology, economics, psychology, and sociology), and STEM education and learning research (National Science Foundation 2012a). Arts have now been added to the acronym to create STEAM. STEAM education instills the skills needed to solve problems, evaluate information, and think creatively. STEAM proponents identify the need to educate the whole child to become a global citizen (Jolly, 2014) and look for formal ways to connect the subjects together within the context of our global socioeconomic world. For example, Yakman's definition of STEAM treats engineering and art as interpretive elements and reads "Science and Technology, interpreted through Engineering and the Arts, all based in elements of Mathematics" (STEAM Education, 2016). Other variations range from the inclusion of religion (National Catholic Educational Association, 2016) resulting in STREAM or the addition of robotics and multimedia to emphasize the development of information technology skills through STREM (STREM HQ, 2016). The Museum of Science and Industry's historical scope of content includes science, technology, medicine, and engineering (Wunar and Kowrach, 2015).

We ultimately decided that the label doesn't matter. The types of learning experiences and the range of resources we can provide to serve youth and families are more important than an acronym. We chose to use the term STEAM, emphasizing that STEAM-based learning encourages youth to be active thinkers. By incorporating STEAM-based learning into our library program, we are able to facilitate summer learning that effectively combats summer slide, builds on our goals of nurturing twenty-first-century skills, and meets the needs of a diverse set of learners, all in a fun, literacy-rich environment.

These objectives may seem daunting, but STEAM-based learning actually fits in with the mission and culture of many libraries, even if it may not seem that way at first. Libraries have long been places where lifelong learning is celebrated and encouraged (see figure 2.1). As a librarian, you may see some similarities between conducting a successful reference interview and participating in the scientific process. The scientific method and the engineering process encourage asking questions, digging deeper, testing out solutions, and reevaluating as you go, just like a reference interview. Librarians may not see themselves as scientists or science teachers, but they don't have to be either to explore STEAM in the library. John Y. Baek calls a librarian who is not formally trained in the sciences, but who is meeting this need in an informal setting, an "accidental STEM librarian." He states that "STEM is no different than what the library has always done, which is provide learning opportunities that help [patrons] fuel new interests, support career development, and engage in lifelong learning" (Baek 2013, 11).

FIGURE 2.1

Lifelong Learning in the Library

SUPPORT FOR STEAM IN INFORMAL SETTINGS

Strands of Science Learning: Overall, research about STEAM in informal settings tells us that places like libraries and museums have incredible potential to support STEAM and science learning. In 2009, the National Research Council issued a report on *Learning Science in Informal Environments* to examine the range of informal science activities and outcomes specific to informal learning. The report found that informal environments provide a context in which to successfully learn science.

Ultimately, six strands of learning were developed that describe "science-specific capabilities supported by informal learning environments" (National Research Council 2009, 3). The strands are useful to help guide library STEAM practices and provide practical goals for science programming and activities. Learners in informal environments

Strand 1: Experience excitement, interest, and motivation to learn about phenomena in the natural and physical world.

Strand 2: Come to generate, understand, remember, and use concepts, explanations, arguments, models, and facts related to science.

Strand 3: Manipulate, test, explore, predict, question, observe, and make sense of the natural and physical world.

Strand 4: Reflect on science as a way of knowing; on processes, concepts, and institutions of science; and on their own process of learning about phenomena.

Strand 5: Participate in scientific activities and learning practices with others, using scientific language and tools.

Strand 6: Think about themselves as science learners and develop an identity as someone who knows about, uses, and sometimes contributes to science.

(National Research Council 2009, 4)

The report emphasizes an informal learning environment's ability to build excitement around science and allow children to really see themselves as scientists. The self-guided structure and choice associated with library programs help accomplish these goals. Libraries allow children to express themselves and explore based on their own interests, which is key to encouraging science learning.

Next Generation Science Standards: In 2011 the National Research Council published *A Framework for K–12 Science Education*, which provided an evidence-based foundation for the development of new education standards. The *Framework* was based on scientific research, including how students learn science effectively, and it outlines the science that all K–12 students should know. It describes types of learning that were consistent with how many places, like museums and science centers, have historically supported learning, and as a result, the informal science education community embraced it. The *Framework* has since served as the foundation for the state-led process to develop the Next Generation Science Standards released in 2013.

The Science and Engineering Practices represent the greatest advance over prior standards, emphasizing the development of habits of mind employed by scientists and engineers. Learners engage in the practices to construct, deepen, and apply their understanding of the Disciplinary Core Ideas and Crosscutting Concepts (see sidebar for more information about Crosscutting Concepts). The Next Generation Science Standards provide an exciting new educational opportunity to support students in exploring the content of science, making the connections between the scientific disciplines, and thinking like scientists and engineers. Whether guiding topic selection, promoting complementary literacy and science skills, or determining linkages between in-school and out-of-school learning, these standards can provide a useful context when creating or coordinating STEAM-based activities at the library.

Design Thinking: Design thinking is generally defined as "an analytic and creative process that engages a person in opportunities to experiment, create and prototype models, gather feedback, and redesign" (Razzouk and Shute 2012, 330). For example, NASA employed design thinking to orbit John Glenn around the earth, testing a variety of strategies until they were sure he would return home safely. When children attempt to solve a problem using design thinking, they will make several attempts and adjustments to reach their goal, supporting scientific and engineering principles. These principles include defining a problem, harnessing inspiration to find a solution, and working through numerous iterations to make improvements.

At Chicago Public Library, design thinking has influenced us in a variety of ways, from providing a framework for institutional growth to the development of activities encouraging youth to solve problems. When youth develop a solution that does not work properly the first time, they use this iterative process to make it work. This process empowers youth to refine their work and hone in on ideas in a sharper way. We remind youth that there can be multiple solutions to a single problem and that the old adage, "try, try again" is really valid for all learners. They learn that problems are not a bad thing; instead, problems are the starting point for new discovery.

THINK ABOUT IT

Consider your own library's role as an informal learning environment. Think of a program you already do at your library. Which strands of science learning, if any, are supported in this program? Are there ways you could emphasize additional strands?

_____

_____

_____

_____

_____

MUSEUM OF SCIENCE AND INDUSTRY'S SUMMER BRAIN GAMES

The National Research Council recognizes that "from their inception, informal environments for science learning should be developed through community-educator partnerships and whenever possible should be rooted in scientific problems and ideas that are consequential for community members" (National Research Council 2009, 6). Chicago Public Library realized that having a partner with a tradition focused on science education would help us integrate STEAM into our program. Our partnership with the Museum of Science and Industry has allowed us to work within the community to develop meaningful, engaging, and successful science programs.

One way that we have built programs relevant to our communities is through the Summer Brain Games: these are family-friendly, accessible science projects developed by the Museum of Science and Industry that are carried out at the museum, in the library, and at home. These activities, designed by the museum's science educators, are developed to be successful in diverse communities using easily accessible materials. They support informal science learning around a single key concept and develop scientific thinking through fun, hands-on activities (see figure 2.2 for sample activity sheets).

One family favorite at the library is the Egg Drop Challenge (see figure 2.3). In this activity, children explore engineering and physics by designing a way to drop raw eggs without breaking them. The activity encourages families to test ideas, make observations, and solve problems. Youth plan their design, and then work together to improve it. They act as scientists and engineers do, learning and having fun along the way. This type of activity can be used within the context of a broader STEAM theme. For example, we adapted this activity as part of a space exploration theme, challenging participants to design a lander that would safely deposit their

Crosscutting Concepts are big ideas that have applications throughout science disciplines, including

1. Patterns
2. Cause and effect
3. Scale, proportion, and quantity
4. Systems and system models
5. Energy and matter
6. Structure and function
7. Stability and change

(Next Generation Science Standards 2013b, 1)

The Science and Engineering Practices describe what scientists do to investigate the natural world and what engineers do to design and build systems, including the following eight practices:

1. Asking questions (for science) and defining problems (for engineering)
2. Developing and using models
3. Planning and carrying out investigations
4. Analyzing and interpreting data
5. Using mathematics and computational thinking
6. Constructing explanations (for science) and designing solutions (for engineering)
7. Engaging in argument from evidence
8. Obtaining, evaluating, and communicating information

(Next Generation Science Standards 2013a, 1)

FIGURE 2.2

Summer Brain Games Activity Sheets

Egg Drop (top left), Stomp Gliders (top right), Balloon Racers (bottom)

For a selection of Summer Brain Games activities, go to www.alaeditions.org/webextras.

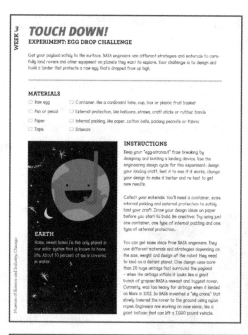

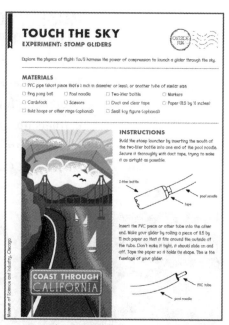

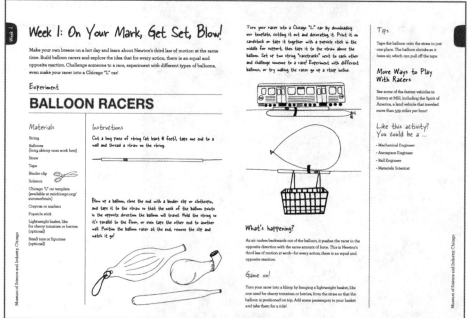

"egg-stronaut" on the surface of Mars. Activities like the Egg Drop Challenge support the six strands of science learning and can be done in a variety of spaces. We even dropped eggs in the rotunda of our main library: this was an exciting and unique experience for children, parents, and staff.

In the Stomp Gliders Challenge, children explore the physics of flight and design a simple glider that, when shot into the air, flies across the room or the lawn (see figure 2.4). Children use models to understand concepts of flight and in the end are able to communicate what worked and what didn't. At the conclusion of this activity, children often share what they created and proudly show what their

FIGURE 2.3

Egg Drop Challenge

(left)

FIGURE 2.4

Stomp Gliders Challenge

(right)

design can do. This activity is a perfect example of how hands-on learning at the library can easily support the science and engineering practices described in the Next Generation Science Standards. Each step creates an exciting and valuable learning experience: asking questions about flight; planning and experimenting regarding the effects of specific variables on their glide; and reflecting and communicating what they learned.

Some Summer Brain Games are really open-ended. The Parachute Challenge explores aerodynamics by designing and testing a parachute that will safely land a passenger. In this case, the passenger is a metal washer. Youth use coffee filters, string, and other everyday materials to construct a parachute canopy. They test their designs and make adjustments until they can land their "passenger" safely on a target. This is a great example of design thinking. Instead of being disappointed if their parachute isn't immediately successful, youth are encouraged to learn from every attempt until they achieve their goal.

Summer Brain Games have been instrumental in our success at integrating STEAM at Chicago Public Library. Our partnership with the Museum of Science and Industry has given us the content, skills, and confidence to engage with informal science and make STEAM education a regular part of our programs, which continue to highlight books and literacy (see chapter 5: "Giving It Context with Books").

IMPACT OF STEAM

Our work with the Museum of Science and Industry showed us how important informal STEAM education is and the impact it can have on youth and families in our libraries. The museum's science educators showed us that informal science exploration is similar to how real scientists and engineers actually do their work. Scientists work together to construct explanations and solve real-world problems, testing their ideas over and over again. They fail and try out new solutions, learning and improving along the way. Scientists are motivated by what they see and experience in the world around them and use observations and context to help them explore. When exploring real-world problems in a library, youth do the same thing, working independently, with their peers, or as a family unit. At CPL we now encourage STEAM activities that are relevant and interesting to youth. Because of this relevancy, the concepts stick with them and can be applied in new situations. They are acting as scientists, architects, and engineers in the library.

Informal STEAM learning also promotes curiosity. Children are natural scientists, and are interested in what they observe around them. We can build on that natural curiosity. Formal school settings and their required outcomes can limit youths' curiosity, but the library setting allows for self-directed learning and open exploration. Children who visit the library are not graded and do not have specific grade-level expectations. Regardless of their age, gender, race, or socioeconomic status, we meet them where they are and encourage their natural wonder. By providing access to STEAM experiences in a supportive environment, libraries can provide opportunities for youth from backgrounds that have traditionally been underrepresented in science-related fields to succeed. All children can make choices about what they do and learn in the library and can take ownership of their learning. Children who may struggle in school, either academically or behaviorally, can be successful in an informal setting. It is amazing to see what children can create and accomplish when they are inspired by their own curiosity and truly enjoy learning.

Libraries are in the perfect position to support the next generation of leaders and learners. STEAM learning teaches us how to create solutions in a changing landscape with new and complex problems: how to think critically, how to solve problems, and how to be a team player. Whether he or she grows up to be an engineer, a politician, an athlete, or a writer, every child needs these skills. Setting out to redesign our summer reading program felt daunting, but incorporating STEAM has focused our efforts and served as a guide. Moreover, it's made our program more meaningful. Our Summer Learning Challenge is stronger because a focus on STEAM allows us to engage a diverse group of learners to prepare them for success in the twenty-first century.

LIBRARIAN'S CORNER
THE JOY OF LEARNING AT THE LIBRARY

Libraries provide an amazing opportunity to reintroduce joy in learning. Where a school-teacher must facilitate learning for thirty or more students at a time and stick to a curriculum, a librarian is free to explore at a gentler pace, often with smaller groups, and with a greater freedom to allow the child to shape the learning experience.

This freedom allows us to give children experiences they otherwise might never have the luxury to try, from pleasures as simple as choosing their own reading material or deciding how to spend their computer time to more in-depth investigations such as looking for microorganisms in lake water, identifying tracks in the snow of the Reading Garden, or designing a model city of the future from LEGOs.

While the primary focus of libraries is and continues to be literacy, we foster multiple literacies—not just the ability to read words, but the ability to interpret pictures, comprehend instructions, and interpret complicated texts. Additionally, I believe it has become more important than ever that we help children gain science literacy and the ability to reason, plan, and tinker—skills that are not always nourished in the atmosphere of a school's science or math class, but which form the foundation of scientific reasoning. The public library is a space devoted to independent learning and inquiry, and it also has the advantage of not being an academic environment and hopefully not evoking the fear of assessment that many children struggle with in school.

Unfortunately, fear is not exclusive to children, and sometimes part of the battle for children's librarians is overcoming our own discomfort or unfamiliarity with the principles of engineering, math, and science, or overcoming prejudices of our own about science programming. We are afraid that it may be hard to attract kids, time-consuming to plan, and just plain boring. We also fear appearing foolish if something does not work.

In fact, failure may be an opportunity to show the progress of our own inquiry, and to rely on our skills as librarians to help students find answers rather than giving them answers. The scientific method is a process by which one moves from ignorance to knowledge. It is okay to not know the answer going in.

Without denying those fears, I can also say that every one of the most popular and fun programs I have run at my library has had its basis in science, engineering, or art, and that, in particular, engineering programs are among the easiest ways to engage children, often requiring far less preparation than traditional library programs.

As children's librarians tend to prefer practical advice to pedagogy, these are the elements that I consider most central to having a successful science or engineering summer program at your library. Build each program around a single specific challenge or activity. Do not provide models or examples, but do try it out yourself prior to the class. Promote directly to the child using the goal, not the scientific concepts you hope for her to acquire (i.e., "build a rocket," not "principles of aeronautics"). Gather your materials ahead of time in a dedicated space such as a cart or bin. Use terminology and introduce concepts as part of the learning process, instead of introducing them beforehand. Have a secondary challenge in mind for groups that finish quickly. Gather feedback and ideas from participants and use them to shape future programs. And finally, budget time for cleanup and make it part of your time together.

Fear no formula, and go forth and do science.

—MS. KENDRA, **Greater Grand Crossing Branch**

CHAPTER 3

PARTNERSHIPS
STRONGER TOGETHER

Partnerships are the topic of much conversation in libraries. How do we form rewarding partnerships in our libraries? How do we frame partnerships in the context of our libraries' missions? How do we know what makes the right partner for us, and perhaps even more importantly, how do we make sure we are strong partners in return? How do we create a partnership that can be sustained over the long term? The conversations around these questions help define ideal partners, set expectations, and grow partnerships.

A partnership is an alliance in which organizations come together to work toward a common goal or set of goals. No matter what the extent of the partnership, it always requires a jointly agreed-upon outcome connected to a program or project. When starting a partnership, consider capacity; whether you can commit to a short-term partnership; and what your shared institutional goals may be.

One of the first things to consider when looking for a partner is capacity. Some partners have greater capacity than others. For example, in the summer, one partner may be able to work deeply with you on developing content using their subject expertise, while others may only be able to host you for field trips. You will have to work with the staff in your partner agency in order to understand both their abilities and their limitations. Just because your partner is a large institution doesn't mean they will have the capacity to partner in an all-inclusive way. Also, consider your own capacity for partnership. We have found that it's easy to promise the moon, but we are most successful when we set realistic and attainable goals.

Some partnerships are temporary and others continue for a long time. Meaningful long-term partnerships can grow out of these short-term partnerships. Deeper partnerships involve sophisticated sets of overlapping goals obtained through multiple strands of programming with specific outcomes. Partnerships only work if both partners are dedicated and dependable. When both partners do what they are going to do, a story hour at the Nature Center can morph into a Nature Club or even a Summer Learning Challenge. Like in any relationship, trust is built over time. If you are just starting to work with others in your communities, it is always best to start small; consider capacity; have clearly identifiable, shared goals that you set together; and create a strong, successful project.

The strength of an institution lies in its mission. Look for ways your mission may overlap with that of a potential partner. Finding a shared goal is key. It is important that both partners talk openly about their institutional goals in order to find a shared mission that matches both institutions' priorities. You need to be able to see where each other's goals lay in order to create a plan to help each other.

THINK ABOUT IT

What might a new short-term summer collaboration look like for you?

Here are a few ideas:

- Offer a sign-up time for your summer program at a local pediatrician's office.
- Take a field trip to your local supermarket and ask them to talk about how they receive produce and check it for freshness.
- Ask a police officer to show kids how they "dust" for fingerprints.
- Think about people in your community who can talk about the science in your neighborhood.

- _____
  _____
- _____
  _____
- _____
  _____

PARTNERING WITH A CULTURAL INSTITUTION: CHICAGO PUBLIC LIBRARY AND THE MUSEUM OF SCIENCE AND INDUSTRY

In Chicago, like many cities, we enjoy a long and rich tradition of creating and maintaining deep, meaningful relationships with museums, parks, zoos, and other organizations that serve children. For Chicago Public Library's Children's Services team, this tradition began with a 1988 grant, NatureConnections. This grant linked the library to Chicago's robust museum communities to provide nature lessons and increase museum exposure for the children of Chicago. Its approach to bringing cultural organizations together around the library was groundbreaking. Nearly thirty years later, this grant has morphed into a project called ScienceConnections, making STEAM as relevant now as it was then. The relationships between libraries and museums built by this grant laid the groundwork for our partnership with the Museum of Science and Industry in the Summer Learning Challenge and provided the credibility to develop a STEAM-based approach to summer learning.

Build basic literacy	Build digital, information, and cultural literacy	Advance critical thinking and problem-solving	Advance creativity and innovation	Foster communication and collaboration
• **Pre-K patrons who are ready to read** • Patrons who have improved reading and writing skills • Patrons who have improved English-language skills	• **Patrons who have improved technology skills** • Patrons who have improved information literacy skills • Patrons developing cultural literacy • Patrons who have improved job search skills • Patrons referred to workforce development programs	• **Patrons who have improved critical thinking and problem-solving skills** • Patrons who have completed job-related training • Students engaged in out-of-school-time learning	• **Patrons who have improved creativity and innovation skills** • Patrons referred to entrepreneurial programs	• **Patrons with a sense of connectedness and belonging as a result of the library** • Patrons participating in civic or community groups • Patrons exposed to mentors or role models

FIGURE 3.1

Chicago Public Library Areas of Impact

Chicago Public Library and the Museum of Science and Industry share a goal of serving kids and families. Our experience developing partnerships has taught us that the best ones come from a simple shared mission. For CPL and MSI, the moment when we jointly said "we're serving the same kids" stands out as the point in which we crystallized the purpose of working together and cemented our partnership. From this conversation, we realized that the goal of our work centered on harnessing the power of both institutions to serve youth in the summertime.

For example, to assess our original needs and goals, we shared overarching strategies for Chicago Public Library (figure 3.1) and the Museum of Science and Industry (figure 3.2).

Using our individual missions as a jumping-off point, CPL and MSI were able to agree on several key objectives that aligned with our institutional strategies. These include

FIGURE 3.2

Museum of Science and Industry's Center for the Advancement of Science Education Steering Wheel

- Maximizing our summertime reach into Chicago's communities
- Providing high-quality experiences for children in STEAM
- Having an MSI-trained staff at CPL who can effectively deliver high-quality STEAM programs for children across the city

Just like finding a common goal in your mission, leveraging each partner's strengths makes a partnership more effective. MSI's expertise helps CPL incorporate STEAM and science literacy into traditional library work with the goal of building twenty-first-century learning outcomes. CPL's reach and credibility within Chicago's communities allows MSI to extend beyond its walls and serve children in every neighborhood.

Formalize shared goals and plans by writing them down in a "memorandum of understanding" (MOU) (figure 3.3). A memorandum of understanding is a formal, cooperative agreement that lays out the terms of collaboration and is co-signed by both partners or institutions. If you are just starting a partnership, your MOU might be a friendly letter that simply lays out the steps for collaboration. This document keeps both partners on track and helps set a priority for the institution, the departments, and the project leaders. The MOU makes expectations explicit, creating intentionality around the partnership. The MOU between CPL and MSI, revised annually, is part of our planning process, and leaders of both the library and the museum renew this letter annually. In fact, our next MOU will look much different from the first one. This is the ultimate goal: to grow your relationship by working together, learning about each other, and defining new goals and targets using that knowledge.

THINK ABOUT IT

Who are your potential partners? What do you want to achieve from working with them? What can you do for them?

_____

_____

_____

_____

_____

_____

_____

_____

_____

_____

_____

_____

MEMORANDUM OF UNDERSTANDING

Building long-term partner relationships takes time and energy. In our partnership with the Museum of Science and Industry, we prioritize setting aside time to plan and evaluate over the course of the partnership. CPL and MSI evaluate our work year-round and are always thinking of the future. As we often say, it's always summer in Chicago. This evaluation and preparation have been an essential part of the process as we continue to refine our programmatic offerings, deepen our mutual understanding of each other's institution, and set overarching goals.

Memorandum of Understanding

[your library name] and [partner name]
For [name of program partnership]

This memorandum of understanding (MOU) establishes a partnership between the two aforementioned institutions for the [insert program name here] program.

1. Mission: List your program mission statement and your institution's mission statement here
2. Partner institution's mission or vision statement here

Together both parties enter into this MOU to mutually promote the efforts of the [insert program name here]. Accordingly, both organizations operating under this MOU in these ways:

Purpose:
1. List why you are forming a collaboration
2. Who is the targeted population
3. How does the target population benefit

Scope:
1. List the activities that you will jointly plan, conduct, evaluate and disseminate
2. Describe the staff who are involved
3. Detail the effects of this work

[Your institution] will:

[LIST ACTION ITEMS HERE]

_____

[Partner institution] will:

[LIST ACTION ITEMS HERE]

_____

Terms of Understanding: The term of this MOU is for [list duration of project term] from the effective date of this agreement. It may be extended upon mutual agreement between the two Institutions. It shall be reviewed annually. Either organization may terminate this MOU upon 30 day written notification with no penalities or liabilities.

Signed:

_____   _____
Your Library Name   Partner Organization Name

_____   _____
Name   Date   Name   Date

_____   _____
Title   Title

_____   _____
Organization   Organization

FIGURE 3.3

Sample Memorandum of Understanding

LIBRARIAN'S CORNER
WHAT HAS PARTNERING WITH A SCIENCE MUSEUM MEANT FOR ME IN MY BRANCH?

Partnering with a science museum has meant a boost in confidence and a change in perspective for me, and wonderful family-friendly science programs for kids and families in my branch library. I don't come from a science background, so when we were asked to increase our STEAM programming, it was initially quite daunting. Would everyone see that I am not "a scientist"?

The staff of the Museum of Science and Industry provided us with hands-on training on their amazing Summer Brain Games. They walked us through these science experiments step-by-step and gave us tips on how to do them with a group, answering our questions and addressing our concerns. It was soon clear to me that having a thorough understanding of scientific concepts was not as important as my ability to create an environment in which kids feel safe to problem-solve, to fail, to dig in and try new things.

I took my newfound confidence back to my library and tried my first STEAM program with families: "The Egg Drop." Kids were asked to construct something that would prevent an egg from breaking when dropped from a high ladder. I was concerned that they would look at me and say, "I don't know how!" Instead, they used the materials provided, worked together, and built fantastic parachutes. Everyone learned from each other's mistakes and successes, and it was easily the proudest I've ever felt after a program.

Now I take pleasure in interspersing science moments into any program I offer, from color-mixing in toddler storytime to making hot-air balloons with tweens. I love to see kids' faces light up with wonder at what they've accomplished or awe at what they've discovered. Thanks to our partnership with MSI, I can offer kids experiences I never would have felt confident enough to try before.

—MS. JESSIE, Rogers Park Branch

By nurturing the relationship, a strong collaboration can present new opportunities for both organizations. In addition to increased available content resources and expanded audience reach, a partnership can have important fund-raising implications. In Chicago, we did not base our partnership on the requirement of new financial resources, but leveraged elements of our existing budgets to support our work together. However, as we began to see signs of success, each organization shared information about the impact of our partnership with funders. We soon realized that we had mutual funders who were willing to consider not only their support for each institution, but also were interested in expanding their investments to support the work of the partnership. We have broadened our collaboration to now include the development of joint grant proposals that are intended to sustain the work of the partnership for the foreseeable future.

PARTNERING WITH DIRECT SERVICE PROVIDERS

Outreach Services: Outreach to groups or organizations that care for children during out-of-school times provides a unique avenue for partnership. Wherever children are in summer, be it a park, private camp, or day care, you can provide library services to them. These outreach partnerships allow the library to serve a more diverse set of children throughout the community who may not be regular library users or have access to high-quality out-of-school-time programs. Plus, your cultural partners have an opportunity to extend themselves into the community in a way they may not have otherwise been able to accomplish.

Before contacting an outreach group, you will want to check with your manager and your staff to ensure that you can visit the outreach site. Then talk with the coordinator at the outreach site to establish your shared goals for the outreach. To support summer outreach at CPL, we have created documents with tips for working with large groups (see text box on page 32) as well as a group agreement form that our staff use to clearly define these relationships. (See appendix A.)

THINK ABOUT IT

Imagine that you are going to reach out to a local nature center. They are small and not very well funded, but they have a beautiful nature trail. What can you suggest to them about working with you and the library? What can you do to show them you are a credible partner? List five ideas here that you might suggest to this partner that would highlight their resources and serve your patrons.

_____

_____

_____

_____

_____

_____

Bonus Round

Be a good partner. Share your expertise. What are five children's books you could have on display at your library that would help promote the nature trail? What is a science- or STEAM-related activity that would pair with these books? Here are some examples:

- *In the Tall, Tall Grass* by Denise Fleming: Make a terrarium using recycled materials.
- *Look Up! Bird-Watching in Your Own Backyard* by Annette Cate: Make binoculars out of cardboard tubes.

TIPS FOR WORKING WITH LARGE GROUPS OF CHILDREN AND THEIR CAREGIVERS

Planning

- Talk to the group coordinator and explain the logistics of the program.
- Schedule a planning meeting with the coordinator.
- Plan an in-service training with all adults/volunteers who may be participating.
- Inquire into how you can send home summer program flyers or promotional information with the children.
- Ask to tour the camp or school and look for places and ways that your coloring sheets, fact sheets, and flyers can be displayed.
- Explain how to use a logging sheet and/or other program materials. Where can this sheet be displayed for easy logging?
- Create a special place for storing all summer program paperwork for each separate group at the site.
- Use branch calendars to schedule programs you will hold in the branch.
- Explain your branch's cancellation policy (example: if they must cancel, please do so twenty-four hours in advance).
- Communicate plans to your supervisor and/or staff.

Implementation

- Get library card applications to the group two weeks before their first visit to the library.
- Get logging sheets, flyers, and/or other program materials to the group before they begin the program.
- Make sure you have a roster of participants by the end of the first week in which the group meets.
- Visit the site and conduct the actual reporting process with the group leaders.
- If you are providing a program element at the group's location, communicate all expectations for the group: the group will be assembled when the librarian arrives, ready to hear stories, getting ready to report on learning, and so on.
- Make yourself available to the group leaders so that all questions can be answered: leave your business card and a branch map with all who will be conducting this program.
- If you can find space, be sure to include the group in a display or hang their coloring sheets or STEAM projects in the children's room. This makes their experience in the library feel more integrated and helps welcome them to the branch.
- At the end of the summer, make sure you have a plan to collect the group's statistics in a timely fashion.

Follow-Through

- Make every effort to get groups to visit the library. Consider adding a letter home to parents to ensure they are aware of their child's participation and invite the parents to visit the library with the child.
- Check in with your groups periodically to see if they have any questions or concerns.

At the end of the program, evaluate with the coordinator. Some questions you may want to ask the leaders are:

1. How successfully do you feel you were able to incorporate the library's summer program materials into your summer program?
2. What would have made this easier for you?
3. What elements of the program did the kids like?
4. What elements of the program did you like?
5. How can we best continue to work with you?

Based on a resource originally developed by Chicago Public Library

FIGURE 3.4

Summer Learning Challenge Outreach Poster Log

(left, top right)

FIGURE 3.5

Summer Learning Challenge Outreach Poster Log in Action

(bottom right)

Outreach Tracking: Tracking information from outreach groups is a monumental challenge. To address this challenge, CPL created an Outreach Poster Log (figure 3.4) to track groups of children. Teachers and camp leaders can display these Outreach Poster Logs at their sites and use them to track the progress of an entire group. In doing this, we have helped create a collaborative learning culture with our groups. Youth love to log their groups' daily reading and activities together (see figure 3.5). At the end of the summer, the groups return their Outreach Poster Logs to the library where staff compile the data.

School Services: School administrators and faculty have an intrinsic interest in children's learning throughout the summer. This is a natural place for partnership. Teachers and principals recognize the importance of beating back the summer slide. In many communities they assign reading, homework, or experiential learning over the summer. In Chicago, we are working very carefully with teachers in our public school district, the Chicago Public Schools, to align the Summer Learning Challenge with Common Core State Standards. Through completion of our activities, school faculty can see what standards their kids have met when they return in the fall. Chicago Public School Principal Chad Weiden was the first principal to partner with his elementary school in the redesigned program. Of the partnership and summer learning, he says:

SIZZLING SIXTY-SECOND SCHOOL VISIT IDEAS FROM CPL LIBRARIANS

- **DRESS YOUR THEME:** Nothing grabs kids' attention like a grown-up in a costume. What is your theme? Find a great hat, cape, or other costume element to help you grab kids' attention when you walk into the classroom!

- **ADD A LITTLE RAZZLE DAZZLE:** You need to redirect the kids' attention quickly and efficiently as you walk into the classroom. What can you do to catch their attention immediately and appropriately signal you are there for fun? Throw a beach ball into the audience, or throw a handful of confetti up in the air as you toot a horn or come in playing a kazoo. Partnering with a zoo? Pull a rubber snake out of your bag and toss it into the rows of desks—this is fun every time.

- **MARKET YOUR COLLECTION:** Bring along themed joke books, show them off, and read a couple of jokes to the class. Show off interesting, gross, or amazing science facts with a beautifully illustrated informational text or read a funny poem to help whet the appetites of the kids.

- **BUNDLE YOUR INFORMATION:** Before arriving at the school, think through what materials you will take to promote the summer learning program. If it's a flyer or postcard, be sure to bundle them into the approximate number each classroom will need. That way you won't have to take the class's time to count out flyers at the end of your visit.

- **YOU CAN'T OVERSELL:** Be sure they know you're from the library and that you have a really fun summer planned. Tell them the name of the library's summer learning program and as you are leaving say, "Be sure to see you where?" and have them shout out the . . . LIBRARY!

When children show fidelity to the Chicago Public Library's Summer Learning Challenge, we see positive results when kids come back to school in the fall. Engaged readers and academically prepared students are crucial outcomes that can come from summer learning at the library. I have found that teachers spend the first 2–3 weeks reviewing content and skills that were taught the previous years as a result of the "summer slide."

To combat this, in my school, we partner with the local library each year to promote the menu of options the library provides for kids in the summertime and recognize kids who come to school in the fall and have participated in the program. Schools and public libraries together are a powerful weapon to help beat back the summer slide. Libraries are important partners with schools in a child's learning ecosystem.

Partnering with a school is similar to partnering with any other organization. You need to create a plan, establish common goals, and consider capacity. Once you've determined the framework for your school-library partnership, build a connection with the school through school visiting. The ideal way to do this is to arrange a day and time for your visit to the school through the principal's office. If that's tricky, connect where you can, with teachers, library media specialists, or secretaries. Then get ready for your visit: plan, plan, plan. Think of this visit as a summer infomercial. Be quick, informative, and fun. Find a way to motivate youth to come into the library. Here are some things to think about:

- What do you want youth to know?
- How can you communicate the theme of your program?
- How can you make it fun?
- Is there a central place where you can leave summer information?
- How can you get word of your program into the newsletter or e-mail blast to parents?

OUR FIVE FAVORITE PIECES OF ADVICE ABOUT PARTNERSHIPS

1. **GIVE MORE THAN YOU EXPECT TO GET:** Be a good partner. Go above and beyond to meet the terms of your partnership. Being a generous partner, always offering to help, and really listening to your partner go a long way when you're building a relationship between organizations.

2. **PROVE YOURSELF EVERY STEP OF THE WAY:** In other words, do what you say you are going to do. Be true to your word and deliver what you promise. There is nothing more disappointing than setting up a program with someone and having one side that doesn't follow through. To this end, it's important not to take on more than you can deliver. You can grow your partnership as you go, but be sure to check yourself each time so both you and your institution's integrity remain intact.

3. **IT'S A JOURNEY, NOT A DESTINATION:** A good partnership evolves over time. It starts with an idea for working together and can evolve as successes are proven and new ideas

emerge. You will not necessarily end up where you start out in a partnership, which can be a very good thing.

4. **TRY, TRY AGAIN:** Evaluate and be truthful with each other about what works and what doesn't work for you both. Remember that both institutions need to see benefits—not just one of the partners. Hang in there and try again. It can benefit everyone to go through several cycles together and iterate solutions.

5. **YOU CAN'T ALWAYS GET WHAT YOU WANT:** Sometimes partnerships don't reap the big-picture results you want right away. You and your partner may not have communicated all the nuances properly, or perhaps both partners have different views of what success really looks like, or something else has happened along the way. It's important to evaluate as you go and get together at the end of your first collaboration. And sometimes the partnership moves in a new direction that is organic and useful to you.

ROAD MAP FOR PARTNERSHIP DEVELOPMENT

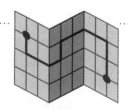

DECIDE TO TAKE THE TRIP TOGETHER. Like carpooling, taking a programmatic journey with a partner helps you share resources.

- Share your institutional strategy and goals.
- Share project goals and talk about how you can work together.
- Decide your "route" or your path to success.

PLAN FOR A SAFE TRIP. The more you can do to plan ahead of time and prepare for success, the better off the partnership and outcomes of the program will be.

- Create a framework for your program together. This allows you to "buckle into place" your plan and your schedule.
- Create a memorandum of understanding to ensure that everyone shares the same expectations.
- Map out how you will communicate and when. And be good to your word.

BE PREPARED FOR SETBACKS. Setbacks in a partnership can and will happen. Be prepared to pick up for one another and accommodate as nimbly as you can.

- Expect some setbacks along the way. Be creative and be clear and concise when communicating a "pothole" in your path.
- Sometimes one institution can navigate around a roadblock the other one can't get through. This can help both sides of the partnership.
- Communicate when a problem or setback does happen so the other partner understands what is happening.

MONITOR THE TRIP. Be sure to watch and assess as the program planning, implementation, and evaluation progress.

- Set time to check in with each other. Remember: there's no such thing as over-communication.
- Share evaluations openly and candidly.
- Tweak your program along the way.

Find out if the classes you are visiting are prepared for you to "interrupt" their day. Remember, the school day is a busy and well-oiled machine and even a three-minute visit can feel like a major disruption. Be respectful of what's happening in the classroom. When you knock on the classroom door, be sure to introduce yourself, reiterate why you are there, and then use your plan to "wow" the class.

Being able to promote specific programs or highlight special times of the year in schools can reap big rewards at the library. A good relationship with a school in your service area is critical to library success all year-round, not just in summer. Having a dynamic interaction while promoting summer learning can lead to increased collaboration throughout the year.

PARTNERSHIPS WITH BUSINESSES

Are there companies near your library that help support and fund your summer learning program? In addition to a monetary contribution, how can businesses engage in the civic dialogue of the library's mission? Many companies and corporations care deeply about giving back to the community. Involving corporate donors in the development of your summer library program can move the relationship between giver and grantee to a collaborative partnership. For example, businesses can help share expertise on the subject area you are exploring with kids; provide speakers for in-service trainings or career development programs; offer to volunteer or mentor children in your program; and leverage other relationships within the business community in order to strengthen your program.

FIGURE 3.6

Kiffle the Kangaroo, KPMG's Family for Literacy Mascot

Chicago Public Library partners with KPMG, a global professional services company that provides audit, tax, and advisory services. The library's sustained commitment to children's literacy and learning in the summertime in Chicago matched KPMG's community investment strategy.

KPMG's community investment strategy focuses on youth and education, helping to ensure that all children have opportunities to acquire the skills they need to become successful adults. The cornerstone of our strategy, KPMG's Family for Literacy, operates with the understanding that literacy is the foundation of learning and that the ability to read has a profound effect on a child's success in school and life. Not only do we share these values with the Chicago Public Library, we believe that the public library system is perhaps the most effective way to achieve impact in terms of scale and mission across our community. Community libraries are an established brand, resource, and asset in the community and we proudly work with them in Chicago to help us invest and engage where support is needed most—in the neighborhoods (see figure 3.6).

PAT CANNING

Managing Partner, KPMG | Chicago

Additional corporate donors not only fund our program, but also offer support for our program in other ways. Boeing developed content for our Explorer's Guide; corporate human resources departments trained teen volunteers in pre-employment skills; and corporate volunteers lent their time at citywide summer programs. Just as with all partnerships, considering the expertise of corporate donors can mean they benefit your program in more than just a financial way.

Partnerships make us better together. Partnerships channel the strength of cultural institutions, the breadth of neighborhood service partners, the richness of our school districts, and the force of our business community to build the ultimate outcome for children and families: successful summertime and out-of-school-time learning. Summer is a great time for the public library to start the work of partnerships that can be extended into year-round, sustainable practices. Strong partnerships will reap strategic rewards for your ultimate goal: serving youth effectively.

CHAPTER 4

ALL LEARNING COUNTS

Using an evidence-based approach and looking at the research we compiled, Chicago Public Library created a new model for a Summer Learning Challenge that we call the "All Learning Counts" model. This approach is goal-oriented but still self-directed and interest-driven.

Participants are asked to

READ: Read for twenty minutes a day to a set goal. Read a book, magazine, article, e-book, or anything else you want—all reading counts. Or listen as someone reads to you.

DISCOVER: Discover by doing. Complete a set number of activities. Try attending a library program, visiting a museum, completing a STEAM activity such as a Summer Brain Game, or visiting an interactive learning website.

CREATE: Make something new. Complete a set number of activities. Try completing a design challenge, making art, cooking a new recipe, writing a story, recording a song, or building a new structure.

These three tracks of learning address aspects of the summer slide, 21st Century Learning Skills, STEAM learning, multiple intelligences, and continued reading as the cornerstones of the program. Participants can choose to engage with the tracks of learning in any way they want for a self-guided summer of reading, discovering, and creating. This model offers children who might not consider themselves readers a welcoming pathway to the program. It's deceptively simple.

CHICAGO BEST PRACTICES

The "All Learning Counts" model is adaptable for any size library system and allows for customization of the reading goal based on community, age, or whatever

FIGURE 4.1

Summer Learning Challenge Kickoff Meeting

other factors are present. Make it work for you! Chicago Public Library asks participants to read to a goal of 500 minutes, which is about three weeks of daily reading, because we have found that's a fair amount to balance reluctant readers with more prolific readers. We set a goal of completing one Discover activity and one Create activity. Most children log more than the minimum number of minutes and activities, but we have found that these goals make the program accessible to the widest audience possible. Children share what they have read, discovered, or created by coming back to the library and reporting on it. Staff and volunteers are trained to ask open-ended questions to help youth reflect and close the learning cycle.

In Chicago, each Summer Learning Challenge has a theme and a name (just like a traditional summer reading program), and often the suggested tracks of learning incorporate ideas which tie to that theme. The theme is chosen in collaboration with our cultural partner, the Museum of Science and Industry, and reflects their content specialty. We take a deep dive into that theme with all of our librarians at our annual Summer Learning Challenge kickoff meeting in March (figure 4.1). Librarians share ideas for summer including school visiting tips, program plans, decoration ideas, STEAM activities, and thematic collection tie-ins. Whatever the size of your staff, bringing them together for a fun and productive kickoff meeting will build excitement for summer.

READ, DISCOVER, CREATE

One of the key things about our three tracks of learning is that we were already reading, discovering, and creating all along. Now we're emphasizing discover and create activities alongside reading and are tracking all three of these activities. There is a lot of overlap: you can read while you're discovering or create and discover at the same time. All learning counts.

Though the program is open-ended and youth can read, discover, and create however they choose, we make sure to provide opportunities for all three tracks of learning in the library through

- Thematic book promotion
- Programming
- Performers/educators
- Summer Brain Games
- Activity guides
- Family engagement

Thematic Book Promotion: Enhanced collections help youth get into the theme. We refresh book collections to include themed books for all ages, from preschoolers up through parents. We highlight diverse books that reflect our communities. These refreshed collections inform programming and are integrated into every aspect of the Summer Learning Challenge.

We promote these collections with print and online book lists; feature them in blog posts; give book talks to teachers and outreach coordinators; bring the collections to school visits; and use them to create book displays. We truly believe that "all learning counts" and so we encourage personal choice by also highlighting websites, magazines, and databases. We also prioritize giving away books to help participants build home libraries.

Programming: All of our programs are tied to the content of our summer theme and collections. CPL offers two types of programs that children and families can attend to complete a read, discover, and/or create activity: librarian-led and outside performers and educators.

Librarians plan a variety of programs using the template in figure 4.2:

- *Storytimes*: Traditional year-round storytimes incorporate the summer theme during the Summer Learning Challenge. Librarians also add STEAM content whenever possible.
- *STEAM programs*: Librarians use a variety of resources to design their own STEAM programs. For example, one librarian created a paper airplane target challenge that incorporated engineering and math during our transportation-themed Summer Learning Challenge.

Librarians also prepare passive programming, allowing children to explore at their own pace. Passive programming supports discovering and creating even during the busiest moments in our libraries.

- *Curiosity Kits*: Inspired by the maker movement and a program at the Exploratorium in San Francisco, Curiosity Kits are tackle boxes filled with odds and

Chicago Public Library
System Wide Children's Services
SLC Program Planning Sheet

Program Topic/Name: _____

Age/Audience: _____

Members of Planning Group: _____

READ: List at least 5 books related to your topic
(Please include "call number")

- _____

- _____

- _____

- _____

- _____

DISCOVER: List at least 2 STEM activities that relate to your topic
(Please include url/link or activity description)

- _____

- _____

WEBSITES: List at least 2 interactive websites that relate to your topic
(Please include url/link)

- _____

- _____

CREATE: List at least 2 art, writing, or design challenges that relate to your topic
(Please include url/link or activity description)

- _____

- _____

FIGURE 4.2

Summer Learning Challenge Program Planning Template

FIGURE 4.3

Kids Enjoy Making with the Curiosity Kit

ends that children can use to design and create (see figure 4.3). Any simple, accessible materials can inspire children. We often include coffee stirrers, clothespins, feathers, pipe cleaners, bottle caps, and office supplies.

- *Challenge Cards* (figure 4.4): To add deeper engagement with literacy, we created Challenge Cards to go with the Curiosity Kits. Challenge Cards present design challenges based on children's literature that can be completed using supplies in the Curiosity Kit. Challenge Cards serve as a natural hook into the books and help us make the stories come alive. They also offer meaningful problems for kids to solve.

- *Discovery Carts*: Discovery Carts serve as a learning center for children to explore thematic materials and activities. Unlike the open-ended Curiosity Kits, Discovery Carts offer guided exploration of specific STEAM topics. For example, we explored light using secret codes and colored filters.

- *Tween Deck*: The Tween Deck is a set of activity cards in a recipe box. These activities are based around our three tracks of learning—read, discover, and create—but they are more complex, offer more independent opportunities for exploration, and are more tied to pop culture in order to appeal to children of ages 11–13. These activities can also serve as inspiration for programming for this age group.

FIGURE 4.4

2016 Summer Learning Challenge Challenge Cards

Oh no! Your toy plane got caught in a very tall tree. Design something that you can use to safely get it down.

It helps to keep in mind ideas that might not work so well. You can find one of these not so great ideas in *My Friend Rabbit* by Eric Rohmann.

Have you ever heard the phrase "when pigs fly"? Most people think it's impossible for a pig to fly through the air. Invent a way to make pigs fly and prove them wrong!

Check out how one little pig learns to fly in *Today I Will Fly (An Elephant and Piggie book)* by Mo Willems.

Going on a long road trip can be a little uncomfortable. How would you design the inside of a minivan to give you the most comfortable and fun ride possible?

Raina has to take a long trip with her family and would probably want to borrow your minivan in the graphic novel *Sisters* by Raina Telgemeier.

- *Play*: We purchase a variety of themed materials that support open play in the children's room. Our libraries have generic open-play materials available year-round, like wooden blocks and Duplos, that we adapt to support our summer theme. For example, we added cars and trucks to the blocks area for our transportation-themed Summer Learning Challenge. Our Come! Stay! Play! Play Group in a Bag (figure 4.5) allows librarians to borrow a bag full of thematic play materials and scripts that can be used to facilitate a program or be used by parents to guide open play.

FIGURE 4.5

Come! Stay! Play! Play Group in a Bag

We also offer programs facilitated and created by outside performers and educators. These programs include storytelling, musical performances, hands-on STEAM, arts and crafts, puppet shows, and more. When looking for performers, we specifically ask for programs that tie into our theme. These programs are big draws to our libraries. Many of these programs can be expensive, and at CPL, we are fortunate enough to have the generosity of our private Chicago Public Library Foundation to fund these outside programmers. However, leveraging partnerships can also offer opportunities for programming in the library at no cost. For instance, Chicagoan and game inventor David L. Hoyt shares his word and math games, Giant Word Winder and Giant Math Winder (figure 4.6), with us each summer. These games promote math and vocabulary skills as well as twenty-first-century skills.

One example of partnership in-kind programming is the Museum of Science and Industry's Science Minors. The Science Minors are a corps of teens who are supported by the museum. These teens are engaged throughout the school year, exploring science concepts and learning to facilitate science activities with the museum's public audiences each week. This unique program offers teens the opportunity to be both the learners and the teacher. They learn how to work with younger children, how to teach scientific concepts, and how to engage learners in a community setting. As part of their paid summer internship, they train on the concepts and activities of the Summer Brain Games and then deliver programs each summer in library branches.

FIGURE 4.6

David L. Hoyt Plays Giant Math Winder

The Science Minors, now called the Farrell Fellows Summer Interns, have become a mainstay of the Summer Learning Challenge. Youth love having the teens facilitate the high-energy programs and librarians love the integration of the content into the library. It's a great training ground for the teens, establishing them as ambassadors for science in the community, while encouraging them to consider science- and education-related career choices. In these ways, the Science Minors help both organizations leverage existing assets and serve more children in a fun and engaging manner.

MSI Summer Brain Games: Librarians facilitate Summer Brain Game activities in hands-on programs, tying in books and other library resources. These make great family programs. During the Summer Learning Challenge, Summer Brain Games are

- Published online by the museum and linked to via the library's website
- Used in the Explorer's Guides as suggested "Discover" activities
- Facilitated by librarians as in-house programs, often paired with a book or book display
- Used by families to explore family science together at home
- Explored by various library staff departments as a training tool and for staff buy-in for the program (see chapter 7: "Managing Change")
- Modeled for youth in libraries by MSI's Science Minors

ACTIVITY GUIDES

Explorer's Guide: Every participant in our Summer Learning Challenge is an explorer. The Explorer's Guide is an activity booklet developed in-house by Children's Services librarians. When youth sign up for the program, they are given the Explorer's Guide full of puzzles, design challenges, literacy activities, and STEAM activities. The guide also features MSI's Summer Brain Games, giving us the opportunity to ensure that every participant has access to these activities. The Explorer's Guide has a loose narrative that allows learners to discover and create on their own within the summer theme (see figure 4.7). Featured activities are meant to be developmentally

appropriate for school-age children and yet broad enough that older or accelerated learners can challenge themselves, too (see figure 4.8). The Explorer's Guide functions as a road map for staff, participants, and families throughout the summer. The Explorer's Guide

- Introduces the goals of the Summer Learning Challenge
- Provides a fun, educational way for youth to engage with the theme
- Highlights print and electronic collections
- Features partner content
- Incorporates local Chicago connections
- Appeals to the wide and varied interests of our city's youth

Little Explorer's Guide: After the first year of the redesigned Summer Learning Challenge, we realized that younger children would need to take a different path throughout the summer. This resulted in what we now call the Little Explorer's Guide, an activity booklet geared specifically toward youth ages 0 to 5 and their parents and caregivers.

We promote summer learning to young children by calling out the five practices based on the ALSC's and PLA's Every Child Ready to Read 2® (ECRR2). ECRR2 is a parent education initiative which stresses that early literacy begins with the primary adults in a child's life. It focuses on five key practices—Talk, Sing, Read, Write, and Play—that are the best ways for children to get ready to read. They are

FIGURE 4.7

Scrapbooked Explorer's Guide

(left)

FIGURE 4.8

Excerpt from the 2016 Summer Learning Challenge Explorer's Guide

(right)

The 2016 Explorer's Guide incorporated Marjorie Priceman's *Hot Air: The (Mostly) True Story of the First Hot-Air Balloon Ride* to bring the history of hot-air ballooning to life.

FIGURE 4.9

Excerpt from the 2016 Summer Learning Challenge Little Explorer's Guide

(left)

FIGURE 4.10

First Iteration of Early Literacy Piece

(right)

easy to do with children at home, in the car, or anywhere a parent and child spend time together. The guide lays out one early literacy practice per page with activities families can do to achieve that practice (figure 4.9). We also link play and STEAM, as play naturally reinforces key concepts of STEAM.

Early learners read, discover, and create when they engage in the five practices, so it's a natural fit for the "All Learning Counts" model. We debated tracking reading, discovering, and creating for all age participants. However, we realized that ECRR2 is our main objective for year-round early childhood services and it was missing from our Summer Learning Challenge. We decided to highlight the five practices of early literacy in the Summer Learning Challenge to best correspond to our year-round early literacy programming.

The Little Explorer's Guide is one of many components of the Summer Learning Challenge that continues to undergo changes to improve it and meet the needs of our patrons. Each year we reassess and adapt many aspects of the program based on what we've learned. For example, our first attempt at incorporating ECRR2 involved a place mat–sized handout featuring the five practices, a handful of tips for parents, and a log to track learning (see figure 4.10). However, this piece didn't do all we needed it to do. Its size and shape limited its appeal and usefulness for both children and parents. Moreover, compared to the Explorer's Guide, it did not offer the same depth of learning opportunities for families.

Family Engagement: Family engagement makes the Summer Learning Challenge more meaningful and is a major objective of our program. We encourage

FIGURE 4.11

Families Attend a Summer Learning Challenge Program Together

CHICAGO PUBLIC LIBRARY SUMMER LEARNING CHALLENGE

RAHM'S READERS
June 20 - September 1, 2017
Win prizes, earn digital badges and have fun when you READ, DISCOVER and CREATE at your library.
chipublib.org/summer

Parent/Caregiver Family Learning Log
Here are some ways that you can help your child learn and have fun this summer.
Complete at least one **Read**, one **Discover** and one **Create** activity with your children and share what you did together.

Read Together	☐ Read books together ☐ Share music, songs or poems ☐ Ask your child about what they are reading ☐ _____	Describe activity here
Discover Together	☐ Try a Summer Brain Game or other family science activity ☐ Attend a family library program or visit a museum together ☐ Play a game together ☐ _____	Describe activity here
Create Together	☐ Create art together ☐ Draw a family tree or write a story together ☐ Cook together ☐ _____	Describe activity here

What was the best part of doing the Summer Learning Challenge with your child?
_____
_____
_____

Submit this log to a Chicago Public Library branch to receive a prize (while supplies last) and be entered to win a special technology package.

Parent/Caregiver Name _____ Branch _____
Child's/Children's Name(s) _____ Age(s) _____
Phone Number _____ Email Address _____

FIGURE 4.12

Summer Learning Challenge Family Learning Log

parents to read, discover, and create as a family. We don't want to limit our invitation to parents, since many children have other adults or alternative family members involved in their child-rearing. Looking at family involvement allows us to broaden the lens through which we view a child's community connections.

By nature, this programming model is flexible and does not have to be completed in the library. We have a number of tools to help support family engagement:

- *Family Programming*: When families attend programs together, caregivers see easy ways they can support literacy, STEAM, and learning at home (see figure 4.11).
- *Summer Brain Games*: All of these activities are designed to be family-friendly and used with easily found and inexpensive household materials. For example, the straw bridges use drinking straws and tape.
- *Parent Tip Sheet*: During the summer, we offer a specially designed Tip Sheet for adults that distills the research and benefits of summer participation as a family. This piece offers accessible ways parents can engage with their children at home.
- *Family Learning Log* (figure 4.12): Our Family Learning Log is a way to focus adults on the importance of reading and learning alongside their children during the summer. These forms also serve as a way for us to monitor the success of specific activities and program elements.

For a selection of Summer Brain Games activities, go to www.alaeditions.org/webextras.

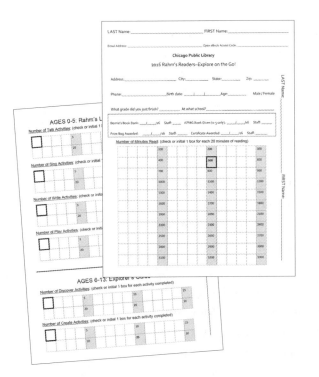

FIGURE 4.14

Summer Learning Challenge Log

FIGURE 4.14

Summer Learning Challenge Log

FIGURE 4.13

Summer Learning Challenge Registration Card

LOGGING AND REPORTING

How do we keep track of all of the learning happening during the Summer Learning Challenge? Each participant signs up for the program at their local branch library. Staff use a paper registration card (figure 4.13) to sign them up and then keep track of their learning when participants return to the library to report. Participants also receive a paper log (figure 4.14) that outlines the program goals and has room to record their learning. Participants use their own logs to track their learning, then report on it to staff and volunteers who record it on the registration card. Eventually all of the information from the registration card is entered into an online tracking system.

Each time youth walk into a library branch during the summer, they're bound to hear "Tell me about what you're learning!" They'll also visit the reporting table, a friendly and welcoming space where they can share what they have read, discovered, and created. Library staff and volunteers sit at the reporting table and ask open-ended questions. Children share what they're reading, give opinions, and make connections between what they did and the larger world. Staff and volunteers listen carefully, make suggestions, and point out real-world connections. Our goal is that children engage with their learning in a meaningful way and develop a desire to learn more after visiting the reporting table.

This process looks different when you're working with a large group of summer campers participating as an outreach group. That's why we developed the outreach poster log. Registration and logging are done on one poster-sized sheet handled by the outreach group leader. These logs spend the duration of the summer at the outreach site and are collected by the local branch librarian at the end of the summer (see chapter 3: "Partnerships: Stronger Together").

JUNIOR VOLUNTEERS

The Summer Learning Challenge has a lot to keep track of, and Junior Volunteers help with that process. Our Junior Volunteer program is mutually beneficial: librarians get help at the reporting table, and Junior Volunteers gain valuable pre-employment experience as they serve their community. Plus, younger children love interacting with tween and teen Junior Volunteers.

Junior Volunteers range in age from 12 to 17. Volunteers who participate are given an opportunity to work with children and be mentors, keep schedules, work collaboratively, gain experience in public service, and organize the complex records associated with the Summer Learning Challenge. For many of our tweens, this is the main way they participate in the SLC.

Junior Volunteers can almost always be found at the reporting table, assisting with SLC registration and reporting. In order to enhance this complicated program, Junior Volunteers are trained by their children's librarian both before and throughout the summer. Because training is a key part of the program, we create and share documents to assist librarians, including a training PowerPoint and a training checklist (figure 4.15).

Trainings cover

- How to register and record reading and learning
- The three tracks of learning and what they are
- How to engage with parents and children
- Asking open-ended questions
- Promoting the program
- Exploring thematic summer topics
- Job skills

It's a joy to watch tweens who have aged out of the program choose to stay a part of the library community by becoming Junior Volunteers.

REWARDS

You've heard it before: "What do I get if I sign up?" We know the real answer is wrapped up in the value of learning. But of course, there are physical prizes in-

Chicago Public Library

Rahm's Readers: Summer Learning Challenge 2016
Explore on the Go!
Junior Volunteer Program

Junior Volunteer Training Checklist

Can be used with SLC 16 Training PowerPoint

Materials

If this year's materials haven't made it to you yet, we recommend you use last year's as they are very similar to what you will see this year.

- ❑ Registration card (1 per volunteer, to be used to register another volunteer)
- ❑ Explorer's Guide (1 per volunteer to keep and use)
- ❑ School-age Logs (1 per volunteer to keep and use)
- ❑ Early Literacy Component (enough so all volunteers have a chance to read)
- ❑ Report forms (1 per volunteer to use)
- ❑ Raffle ticket—weekly book raffle and eReader raffle (1 per participant)
- ❑ Prize bag (1 to show)
- ❑ Prize books (a few to show)
- ❑ Parent Reflection form (1 per volunteer)
- ❑ For Teens: Teen promotional materials

Topics

- ❑ Volunteer basics
    - ❑ Scheduling
    - ❑ Signing in
    - ❑ Wearing your lanyard and badge at all times
    - ❑ What to do if you can't come in
    - ❑ What to do in case of emergency
- ❑ Registration
    - ❑ How to register
    - ❑ Registration card
    - ❑ How to use each side
    - ❑ Filing system
- ❑ Summer Learning Challenge Components
    - ❑ Read
    - ❑ Discover
    - ❑ Create
- ❑ Printed Pieces
    - ❑ Explorer's Guide
    - ❑ School-age Log

- ❑ Early Literacy Piece
- ❑ Report forms
- ❑ Reporting—Talking to participants about what they've done
    - ❑ Active listening
    - ❑ Asking questions
    - ❑ Reporting Table Scenarios (use cards)
- ❑ Prizes
    - ❑ Prize bag
    - ❑ Weekly Raffles
    - ❑ eReader raffle
- ❑ Parents
    - ❑ Parent Reflection Form
    - ❑ Parent Tech Package Raffle
- ❑ Your turn!
    - ❑ Register each other for the Summer Learning Challenge

FIGURE 4.15

Sample Junior Volunteer Training Checklist

volved. Like many libraries, we've tried a variety of rewards for summer participation. Currently, through the incredible generosity of funders and the Chicago Public Library Foundation, youth who complete the program (read for 500 minutes, and complete one discover and one create activity) receive a tote bag featuring the summer theme (see figure 4.16).

We know that receiving a new book can be a great incentive for children and can make them feel proud. Additionally, building a home library is important for children and owning books is critical to reading success. For these reasons, we also offer additional rewards for children who come into the library and report. Each time they report on their learning, they have the chance to earn a book. This is a good motivator for youth to keep learning after they receive their tote bag.

Parents can also earn a reward. Parents or caregivers who complete a Family Learning Log are eligible to receive a Family Tech Package. The Tech Package contains a laptop, tablet, and digital camera as well as other books related to the summer theme to help further the family's ability to learn together throughout the year.

We've also been exploring using digital portfolios through Chicago City of Learning, an initiative of our mayor's office to expand access and understanding of summer opportunities for youth. This initiative comes from the Digital Youth Network at DePaul University. Youth can add to their digital portfolio when they meet the program's read, discover, and create goals. This online platform connects youth to a broader learning campaign across the city.

FIGURE 4.16
Summer Learning Challenge Tote Bag

STANDARDS

With all of these moving parts, this program can feel overwhelming. To help in planning and execution, at Chicago Public Library we have a set of standards for branch staff, and librarians set individual goals. Because this program is massive, individual goals help. It is easier to plan for success if you can focus on two or three measurable objectives. For example, one branch librarian may choose to focus on increasing the number of programs and reaching at least five new outreach groups.

Along with individual goals, librarians are expected to meet specific, system-wide standards (figure 4.17). These standards help provide a common language and a vision of the scope of the Summer Learning Challenge. They help define and develop the practice of each librarian and support her as she takes on the role of

Standards for Children's Services Staff Working on Summer Program

1. Attend a minimum of two days of training offered (total of 15 hours)
2. Be able to talk about the summer program including customer segments (early childhood, school-aged, tween and families) and the program components (Read, Discover, Create) with fluency
3. Be able to talk about the summer slide and ac,hievement gap and why the summer program is important to children, families, and teachers
4. Complete weekly calendars, set goals and create program plans for overall summer
5. Share these goals with manager and branch staff by end of May
6. Discuss the program at monthly staff meetings May – September about progress of program
7. Conduct the following:
   7a. School visit each of your neighborhood elementary schools
   7b. Meet with summer camps, daycares and other outreach sites in your neighborhood to bring the program to each of them
   7c. Use Outreach Poster Logs to encourage group participation in the following:
      i. Preschools/HeadStart and other child care agencies
      ii. Camps
      iii. Rec Centers/Boys and Girls Clubs/YMCA's
      iv. Other agencies serving children
   7d. Create and conduct a minimum of two STEAM-learning based program per week for each week of the program
   7e. Host a National Summer Learning Association – Summer Learning Day program on July 14 (or create a display for your unit).
8. Make design challenge materials, challenge cards, and related books available and train all your branch staff on their purpose and use
9. Make flash cards and board games available for use during the day. These need to be accessible and available for in-house use in each library
10. Make blocks available for in-house use during the day
11. Make art supplies available during the day
12. Weed collections according to the CREED guidelines.
13. Ensure that newly purchased summer collections are labeled and on display in Children's Room
14. Decorate the branch in a thematic way using at least one bulletin board and/or display case.

CONTINUED ON FOLLOWING PAGE ▶

FIGURE 4.17

Sample Summer Learning Challenge Librarian and Branch Manager Standards

▶ CONTINUED FROM PREVIOUS PAGE

15. Ensure a minimum of 20 hours of reflection/book reporting are available to children in the branch.

16. Keep data as up to date as possible during summer using selected data entry method.

17. Evaluate yourself on success of program using summer evaluation form. This program is intended to help children and families in the summertime. How did you do? What can you do to plan or implement even better for next summer?

Branch Manager Standards for Summer Programming

1. Ensure that branch staff sponsors the summer program.
   1a. Assign a branch staff person to conduct the program if a children's services staff member is not available. Ensure assigned person receives all materials and support needed to conduct the program.
   1b. If children's services staff member is available to conduct the program, assign a back-up person from the branch staff to answer questions/oversee the program when children's librarian/associate is not scheduled or not available.

2. Schedule and send staff member to summer program trainings.
   2a. If there is no children's services staff available, select and send an appropriate staff person to the meeting.
   2b. If no one is able to attend, review meeting materials.

3. Communicate weekly with children's services staff member about plans, commitments, and resources.
   3a. Monitor program deadlines.
   3b. Discuss and co-sign Goals & Objectives Form
   3c. Discuss and co-sign summer program final evaluation

4. Communicate to all branch staff about the summer program
   4a. Ensure all scheduled program hours are posted at reference desks and front desk.
   4b. Ensure that meeting rooms and/or activity spaces are available and that program times are recorded in branch meeting room calendars.
   4c. Ask children's services staff to report at monthly staff meetings from March to September.
   4d. Check to see if staff understands guidelines for volunteers and lanyards.

CONTINUED ON FOLLOWING PAGE ▶

FIGURE 4.17

Sample Summer Learning Challenge Librarian and Branch Manager Standards (continued)

5. Oversee that all deadlines are met.
    5a. Review deadline date sheet
    5b. Sign off on Goals and Objectives Form and Final Evaluation Form.
6. Work with children's services staff member to schedule at least 20 hours of reporting time per week.
    - Ensure that children's services staff member visits assigned elementary schools before program begins. Visits can include an appointment to discuss the summer program with principals, reading teachers, teacher-librarians, local school councils, visiting assemblies, or visiting individual classrooms. A school visit DOES NOT include dropping off flyers in the office or emailing a flyer. A visit involves talking directly with students or faculty.
    6a. See that appointments are made in a timely fashion and when branch staffing permits.
    6b. See that school visits are completed before summer program begins and include in appropriate reports
7. Ensure that children's services staff conduct 2 weekly programs that reflect the summer program theme during the entire summer. A story program is defined as one that utilizes or features stories and books that relate to the theme. These programs should be over and above the scheduled system wide programs.
8. Oversee outreach efforts by the children's services staff member to community organizations' summer programs such as block clubs, YMCA, Boys and Girls Clubs, and summer schools. See that phone contact and follow-up has been made.
9. Ensure that the branch is decorated in a thematic way before the summer program begins.
10. Ensure that all summer-themed collection materials are processed and prominently displayed.
11. Ensure the branches design challenge materials, challenge cards, blocks, and art materials are on display and available for patrons.
12. Ensure that promotional materials for the summer program are displayed prominently in the branch during the entire program.
13. Ensure that branch programs are entered into the Event Calendar and are held at dates and times listed.
14. Ensure that all summer decorations are removed from the Children's Department by beginning of the school year.
15. Review these summer performance standards with branch children's librarian/associate. Include on performance evaluation of staff.
16. Ensure that Branch Evaluation is turned in to Children's Services.

Based on a resource originally developed by Chicago Public Library

administering this project. Additionally, we have found that having standards for branch managers as well as children's librarians helps create an environment that is conducive to summer learning by ensuring that all staff are on the same page.

ACTIVATE YOUR SPACE

During the summer, our libraries are transformed. We've landed on Mars! We've boarded a hot-air balloon! We've explored the tundra! At Chicago Public Library, we use decorating as a way to expound on our theme by using physical space. Creating a thematic environment within our libraries builds excitement and signals to the community that something special is going on for children and for parents (see figure 4.18). It also serves to reflect each community. In fact, we feel so strongly about activating our spaces that a well-decorated library is considered a program standard. We host a friendly decoration competition each year between our many branch libraries. This helps build enthusiasm for decorating and helps us share best practices with one another.

Along with decorating, signage is a critical element. You can't speak with every patron who enters your library doors, but signage can help do it for you (figure 4.19). We translate signs and other program materials when necessary.

CHICAGO PUBLIC LIBRARY'S TRIED-AND-TRUE TIPS FOR DECORATIONS THAT DAZZLE

1. **USE YOUR WINDOWS.** Display your decorations to anyone who passes by the library. Let anyone who passes by the library know that something awesome is happening inside. Use window markers, tissue paper, or colorful die-cut shapes with participants' first names.

2. **PUT YOUR VOLUNTEERS TO WORK.** Get your tweens and teens engaged by asking them to help make decorations out of construction paper and other library supplies. They will take this to heart, and with a little supervision, they can do a great job for you.

3. **MAKE EVERY SPACE A LEARNING SPACE.** Use all open spaces to encourage learning. Put shelf talker cards which promote the books that connect to your theme near the books in your collection. Create an animal height chart on the side of your bookshelf or make a themed game on the floor.

4. **PUT YOUR DECORATIONS TO WORK.** Don't just decorate; make your decorations functional. Make signs that show kids where to sign up and what's included in registering and participating: don't assume everyone "just knows" what happens during your summer program.

5. **INCORPORATE KIDS' ART.** This makes them feel like superstars and celebrates the kids' learning. String a clothesline or an art line through your children's room and use clothespins to hang up art or book reviews the kids have made. It also allows you to easily change your decorations, keeping your program fresh and visually interesting all summer long.

A NOTE ABOUT APPEALING TO THE AGES

Although our program is open-ended, over the years we've seen some significant differences in how children of different ages participate in the program. Our experiences have led to some major programmatic changes based on the ways we saw youth participating in the program and on age-specific research.

Preschoolers and Their Caregivers: The years from birth to age five are developmentally important. At Chicago Public Library we most often focus on aspects of early literacy, play, early STEAM, and parental involvement. Every Child Ready to Read 2 covers the majority of developmentally appropriate early literacy practices. Significant research about the power of play indicates that the role of play in a young child's life is predictive of later aptitude for twenty-first-century learning and life success. Young children are natural scientists. It's important to offer opportunities to explore, sort, build, classify, count, and manipulate. We promote these early science practices in STEAM programming with unit blocks and other materials. All

What are some ways you can inexpensively decorate your children's room to match your theme? What is one way you can acknowledge each of the youth who are participating in the program in your space? When is a good time to do this? What can you do to add visual appeal to your program through the way you decorate? Imagine you have been asked to justify why decorating is important. What key elements do you include to sway key decision-makers?

_____

_____

_____

_____

_____

_____

of these can and should be done alongside parents and caregivers for maximum impact.

School-Age Children/Middle Childhood: School-age children are a key part of our summer programming. Middle childhood is marked by a growing independence and curiosity about the world. Children aged 6 to 10 are becoming independent readers and learners. Their skills and abilities are developing as they gain confidence in their capacity to learn, try new challenges, and regulate their behaviors and emotions. This all means that they are primed for new hands-on experiences, and they are able to learn from an occasional failure as they experiment. They are able to express themselves, reflect on what they learn, and articulate plans.

At this age, the notion that they are contributing to the overall success of the library's program carries great weight; children want to contribute to the greater good and they want to see themselves as successful. Adding their time spent reading or the number of learning activities they try or complete will be important to them and good for the outcome of the program. We make sure to offer school-age

LIBRARIAN'S CORNER
WHAT ABOUT THE NOISE, WHAT ABOUT THE MESS?

When I first heard that the Summer Reading Program was transforming into the Summer Learning Challenge, I had a few discouraging thoughts. Everything from "How am I going to manage all of this new stuff on top of working the reference desk, planning for storytime, dealing with patrons, and all the other duties that my job requires?" to "Are the children we serve really going to be into this?" But the biggest question I had was "How am I going to do this when I am not a teacher—especially a science teacher?" Now I know that I had no need to worry myself with these questions. Liz, our director of children's services, often reminds us that "we are a river" and as that river ebbs and flows, I too adapted and changed my thinking over the three years since the program has changed.

It was never easy to be a children's librarian, but it was a lot less noisy and messy before we made the switch to the Summer Learning Challenge. For the first seven years I worked at Chicago Public Library, the Summer Reading Program involved the children reading a specific number of books based on their reading level and visiting the library to report to the librarian. Children visited the library and spoke to the librarian about their favorite parts of their books, and then the librarian would record the titles of the books read. In addition, librarians led storytimes and book clubs and hosted professional performer shows during the Summer Reading Program.

In 2013, the Summer Learning Challenge was born and our tasks got harder. The new SLC brought early literacy, play, and STEAM to the forefront. With the new program, the high tide of noise and mess just came in and has never receded. I never thought that children should remain completely silent in the library because they are developing their socialization skills. As long as other children are able to concentrate on their reading or schoolwork and staff are able to concentrate on their work, I have always allowed children to be a little noisy. However, when the Summer Reading Program changed to the Summer Learning Challenge, that level of noise became a din. And with the chaos that comes with working at the busiest branch in the North District of the Chicago Public Library system, this din was almost too much to handle.

But with all of my 21st Century Skills professional development trainings, provided by the Children's Service's Department, I am able to remind myself that this noise needs to happen in order for those children to develop the collaboration, communication, problem-solving, and critical thinking skills needed to compete in this global marketplace. Let me tell you that the mantra "We are a river" flows through my mind often during these times and has helped me to relax when the stress flows in.

With the love and support of our system-wide Children's Services team, the Chicago Public

CONTINUED ON FOLLOWING PAGE ▶

► **CONTINUED FROM PREVIOUS PAGE**

Library Foundation, and our continuing partner, the Museum of Science and Industry, what felt like the choppy waters of the Summer Learning Challenge have become smooth sailing. Our STEAM and play programs are fully supported with fact sheets and lesson plans, which include the background topic knowledge and materials for each branch library to do several programs. As children's librarians, all we have to do is take time to peruse the lesson plans and conduct a run-through of the projects before presenting them. I read the lesson plan ahead of time and then explore the project for the first time with the children. This process opens up the opportunity for a discussion on failures and how to succeed; the children see that you are not perfect. What about that mess created by conducting a STEAM or play program? After our programs are finished, the children are more than happy to help me clean up.

What do the children think about this new reading program called the Summer Learning Challenge? They LOVE it! You can see it in the data—the attendance at the Edgewater library branch has increased yearly from approximately 400 in 2014 to 800 children in 2015 to over 1,000 children in 2016. And you can see it in who is participating. Children who regularly come to only use the computer at my library began to do the Summer Learning Challenge in 2015 after I visited their school, and they were excited to participate in 2016, too. Many of my regular Summer Learning Challenge participants ask about specific STEAM programs, like our Preteen Science Zone. The Summer Learning Challenge may be noisy and messy, but it's all worth it to see these children enjoying and asking for STEAM and play.

—MR. STU, Edgewater Branch

children a wide variety of hands-on STEAM activities, opportunities to interact and collaborate as a team, and the chance to try new things.

Tweens: Many children aged 11 to 13 no longer see themselves as part of the "children's department" but are not yet ready to graduate to the teen area in the library. These children, often called tweens, are developmentally distinct from youth still in middle childhood. These early adolescents are very social and they need opportunities to interact with their peers, especially at the library. At this point in their lives, their identity is group-based and they are looking to their peers for guidance. They are pushing away from their families and developing their own mind-sets. How they see themselves and how they interact with the world is changing. Programming for this age group needs to be flexible to serve this quickly changing segment of our population (Nagaoka et al. 2015).

CHAPTER 5

GIVING IT CONTEXT WITH BOOKS

Librarians always use books as the backbone of all library services. At Chicago Public Library, our Summer Learning Challenge focuses on developing twenty-first-century skills by encouraging active learning and STEAM, but books remain the backbone of the program. Books, when tied into a robust and active learning environment, can inspire, support, and enhance the goals of the SLC.

Your collection is a great starting point to begin working toward making change. Keeping twenty-first-century skills in mind when you choose books for storytime is an easy way to start incorporating these skills into your traditional library programming. A good book can help build critical thinking when used in tandem with dynamic library programming.

We use STEAM as a lens to support twenty-first-century learning skills at the library during the Summer Learning Challenge (see figure 5.1). There is a national movement to emphasize STEAM, and there are many new titles that can be used to enhance programming. Books can be the foundation for a program, the background for exploring a STEAM concept, or they can serve to broaden a child's experiences.

Program Foundation: In program development, you can use fiction and nonfiction content as a starting point. For example, *The Boy Who Harnessed the Wind* by William Kamkwamba (Dial, 2015) could inspire a fun science program where children use found materials to try and create wind energy. Or the simple picture book *Blocks* by Irene Dickson (Candlewick, 2016) may inspire you to host an engineering program where preschoolers play with blocks. Books have always been a great source for program inspiration, but looking at them through a STEAM lens offers an even broader perspective.

Some books provide you with all the tools you need to create an engaging program on the fly. Imagine that a group of ten-year-olds is coming into the library

in an hour and you don't have a program planned. Open up *The Flying Machine Book* by Bobby Mercer (Chicago Review, 2012) and choose a flying machine category. You'll have all the information you need to do the program, and don't worry, most of the materials in this book are everyday office and craft supplies.

Folktales can also be the foundation for a program that integrates STEAM. For example, you can tell the story of the three little pigs and then host an engineering program to see whose house can stand up to a fan.

STEAM Background Content: You might not be a STEAM expert, but you don't have to be. There are countless nonfiction books and series that explore STEAM concepts. Content created for children has already distilled STEAM concepts into kid-friendly language that is easy to understand. If you want more information on a concept you don't understand, try a database for kids or look to your science fair collection. We like *Try This!* by Karen Romano Young (National Geographic, 2014), a book that offers suggested science activities paired with simple and clear scientific facts and explanations.

Broadening Children's Experiences: Some kids come to your library because they love books. Other kids may have a great time in your programs but don't see themselves as readers. For both groups of children, books can open up a whole new world. Your readers may want to participate in a STEAM program that relates to a book they've read. Your reluctant readers may be inspired to pick up a title related to something they loved in a library program.

FIGURE 5.1

STEAM and Twenty-First-Century Learning Skills in Action

?THINK ABOUT IT

What is one of your favorite picture books to use in storytime? We bet there is STEAM in it. Do you remember the first time you understood what happened to Peter's snowball in *The Snowy Day* by Ezra Jack Keats (Viking, 1962), or what it meant that Max's dinner was still warm at the end of *Where the Wild Things Are* by Maurice Sendak (Harper and Row, 1963)? What is a corresponding title from your science or math collections?

_____

_____

_____

_____

_____

_____

FIGURE 5.2
Building a Straw Bridge
(top right)

A good book can frame a STEAM program and encourage even the most reluctant young scientists to take part. Consider the straw bridge activity (figure 5.2). In this activity, youth are asked to build bridges out of straws and tape and test the bridges' strength by adding weight. You can use lots of things to add weight, like washers, marbles, or pennies. This activity can easily be connected back to fiction titles in your collection. You could frame the activity around a Harry Potter theme: "Imagine you're a member of the Order of the Phoenix and you want to steal Bellatrix Lestrange's galleons from Gringotts Bank but the dragon has burned down the bridge. Try and build a bridge that is strong enough to hold all the galleon coins." Or make it a pirate-themed activity. Tie this into *The Pirate Who Is Afraid of Everything* by Annabeth Bondor-Stone (HarperCollins, 2015). In finding these new elements to enhance and underscore children's learning, we actually deepen the relevance of books.

STEAM and active learning can be the entry point to books for those kids who *think* they don't like reading. As librarians, we know there is a book out there for everyone. Hands-on STEAM activities can get kids excited about a topic, and you can harness that excitement with a great book recommendation. For those kids who love gross stuff (and this means *lots* of kids), you can make a batch of slime together and discuss the basic science principles of polymers. Then slyly make the connection to the hilarious book *Stink and the Attack of the Slime Mold* by Megan McDonald and illustrated by Peter H. Reynolds (Candlewick, 2016). And just watch: children will be motivated to read a corresponding book after learning about a STEAM concept.

PUTTING IT ALL TOGETHER

Promoting compelling books about STEAM can be fun (see figure 5.3). Kids may not even realize that the book they pick up is STEAM-related. They may just love the illustrations, the story, or some other feature. When we are recommending titles, books serve as an opportunity to showcase STEAM in a unique way. For example, Steve Jenkins brilliantly shows the link between artistic beauty and biology in *Living Color* (Houghton Mifflin, 2007).

And now, for a kind word about math. Math books get a bad rap with many kids, but publishing has done a great job of incorporating clever math concepts in beautiful and compelling ways. *How Many Seeds in a Pumpkin?* (Schwartz and Wade 2007) is a story featuring estimation with a perfect fall programming tie-in. You could have a pumpkin-decorating contest and incorporate estimation of the number of seeds in your pumpkins. And there you have it.

By incorporating books of any and all types into STEAM programming, you will be creating an experience that appeals to multiple modalities of learning, deepens the understanding, motivates the learner, and delights and inspires our kids. So what pairing will you create first?

FIGURE 5.3

Youth Enjoy a Story in a STEAM Program

LIBRARIAN'S CORNER
FINDING GOOD STEAM BOOKS

Most of the specific books mentioned in this chapter come from trade publishers, meaning they're created for the general marketplace. Yet there is no shortage of STEAM titles produced specifically for the education market. The plethora of series nonfiction from educational publishers often felt massive and unmanageable even before the Common Core State standards. Now the potential opportunity to connect to this huge educational initiative has led to the growth of even more informational texts in series. While often overwhelming, this new pool of titles can be beneficial in the STEAM sphere.

For summer programming, regardless of one's thematic focus, a series can usually be found to fit it. One key to finding the right series is in the series name. For example, the Lerner Publishing Group's "Exploring Physical Science" series offers an easy tie-in to a wide variety of STEAM programming. A prominent tool in navigating informational series books, and finding those series titles, is the BISAC Subject Headings (Book Industry Study Group 2016). The BISAC Subject Headings is a classification system developed by the Book Industry Study Group for both print and digital items for juvenile materials. This can be useful as a starting point because within the very broad categories of Juvenile Fiction and Juvenile Nonfiction they do break down to more specific categories. You can't rely on these headings exclusively, however, since they are sometimes overly general and this diminishes their practical assistance. For example, there is no identifier for fiction books with mathematics themes.

When attempting to think more about the big picture when it comes to locating STEAM titles, it's also important to understand that the same fiction book with a mathematics theme offered by a major online vendor could have a purchase rank of anywhere from, say, 68 to 168,000 depending on which category is searched. Likewise, tagging in library public-access catalogs can range widely in accuracy and consistency. Further complicating this navigation is the fact that not only are not all series created equal, but neither are all entries within a series. Thus, a vital resource to keeping on top of these thousands of options is *Booklist*'s Spotlight on Series Nonfiction, which cuts through much of this noise in targeting quality practical titles.

Another resource for making your book/STEAM pairings is the work that has already been done for you by the Association for Library Service to Children (ALSC) with their Building STEAM with Día Booklists. Día, which is short for El día de los niños/El día de los libros (Children's Day/Book Day), as well as an acronym for Diversity In Action, is a national initiative founded by author Pat Mora and administered by ALA-ALSC. The fact that Día's work, which "celebrate[s] children and connect[s] them to the world of learning through books, stories and libraries," has recently focused on STEAM is not only testament to this connection between books and STEAM throughout the year, but it also highlights the need to combat the well-documented lack of diversity within the fields of science, tech, engineering, and math (American Library Association 1996–2015). You'll also find that Día is a source of professional development support—and relief!—as you're curating this part of your collection.

—ANDREW MEDLAR,
Assistant Chief, Department of Technology, Content and Innovation, Chicago Public Library

CHAPTER 6

EVALUATION, ASSESSMENT, AND CONTINUOUS IMPROVEMENT

Stories are powerful. They convey meaning and create a common language. Evaluating your summer learning program may sound overwhelming, but it's really just a way for you to tell the story of your program. Evaluation allows you to share the strengths of your program, advocate for library services, improve your program, and set goals. When we plan our programs with a focus on the intended outcome, and then measure the outcome, we get a much deeper and truer sense of what we're doing right.

Libraries have a history of counting the number of people who show up for a program and measuring success based on that number. But simply counting heads does not give us the feedback we really need to make our programs the best they can be. How can we tell if the programs we spend so much time planning and conducting are really beneficial for the kids and families we serve?

There is new and increased interest in how to evaluate and assess programs, and how to do it well in the library world. At Chicago Public Library, outcomes-based evaluation has changed the way we create and evaluate programs. In this chapter, we will walk you through how we evaluate and assess programs and how it has changed the way we look at our own programs.

A good evaluation process can help you identify important strategic thinking about your program in a variety of ways, including the following:

- Better describe what your program is doing, or "tell your story"
- Identify the strongest elements of your program
- Support program improvements or changes
- Identify appropriate outcomes
- Help you define what success looks like, now and in the future

? THINK ABOUT IT

Look to your library's strategic plan or mission to help create a priority list for service in your library. Then consider what data you already collect and what data you wish you had that might help illuminate the items on your priority list. Do you count the number of children who participate in your programs and services? Do you count the number of adults? Why or why not? What would help you "sell" your program to your board or trustees or to the school district?

Use the Data Wish List here to name the things you suspect your program does for kids but don't yet have data to back up for yourself.

My Data Wish List, or What I wish I could tell people about the library's summer program:

Example: I wish I had data to show that our summer reading program impacts academic success.
Example: I wish I had data to show that the library is at its busiest when children's programs are being conducted.

_____

_____

_____

_____

_____

_____

In 2012, Chicago Public Library set out to answer some key questions about the services we were providing during the summer and focus on what we were trying to do. During this time, plans were being developed for the 2015–2019 CPL strategic plan, and we developed these five areas of strategy that allowed us to best serve our community:

- Basic literacy
- Digital, information, and cultural literacy
- Critical thinking and problem-solving
- Creativity and innovation
- Communication and collaboration

DEVELOPING YOUR LOGIC MODEL

To start the evaluation process, you will want to develop a system to formally set goals and objectives for your program. At CPL, we use a logic model as part of our planning process for the Summer Learning Challenge (figure 6.1). A logic model is a graphic organizer for your program that allows you to see all of its elements; sets out a path for how to deliver desired outcomes; and provides a framework for evaluation. A logic model allows you to think deeply about staff resources, staff development, and patron response. The logic model helps you to take stock of all that goes into your program and keep your goals at the forefront. Once you complete your logic model, you can use it to design an evaluation strategy for your program.

While it can seem overwhelming to think about creating a logic model, it really is just an inventory of all the moving parts of your program. Since summer library programs have so many components, it's a great program to practice with as you learn about evaluation.

To be useful, the logic model must answer questions such as:

- What large-scale problem am I trying to solve; for example, summer slide, keeping kids active, summer meals?
- What activities are required to get to this outcome?
- What resources are needed to deliver these activities?
- How will I know if I am meeting my goals?

A logic model can help you do the following things:

- Identify the intermediate and ultimate outcomes of the program and the ways through which your activities create these outcomes.
- See the relationship between the components of the program.
- Guide you and your director as you incorporate this logic model more deeply into your library's strategy.

Logic models take many forms, but essentially there are five main parts:

- *Goals*: What problem are you trying to solve? In a perfect world, what you would like to achieve in your summer program?
- *Inputs*: All the things you and your staff contribute to the program
- *Activities*: Everything the program does
- *Outputs*: What specifically comes out of your program (the things you can count)?
- *Outcomes*: Short-term outcomes are the things you see kids and families achieving immediately. Intermediate outcomes are how the knowledge gained in the short term influences behavior in the near future. Long-term outcomes are the way you hope to move or shape social, economic, civic, and environmental factors over the long haul for your communities.

Other elements of logic models may include impact, indicators, assumptions, and external factors (W.K. Kellogg Foundation 2004).

GOALS

- Encourage, facilitate, and promote literacy and STEAM-based learning for children 0–13 years to mitigate the summer slide
- Support parents' and caregivers' involvement in children's reading and learning.

INPUTS

- CPL Staff
- Volunteers
- Interns
- Time
- Money
- Collections
- Supplies
- Space
- Training
- Equipment
- Partners
- Marketing

ACTIVITIES

What we do

- Staff Training
- Programs
- Program materials
- Create learning environment at all branches
- Educational content
- Book and web lists
- Field trips
- Outreach
- Reader's advisory
- Book talks
- Reflection times/interactions
- Online content

Who we reach

- Children ages 0–13
- Teen volunteers
- Parents/caregivers
- Teachers
- Community partners

OUTPUTS

- 4 staff trainings
- 337 visiting programs
- 50,000 activity guides
- 6,300 prize books

OUTCOMES

Short-term

- Staff and volunteers successfully facilitate STEAM based programs to participants and their families.
- Preschool-aged participants take part in the five ECRR2 literacy practices.
- Parents and caregivers of preschool-aged children are aware of early literacy practices and their importance.
- School-aged participants read 20 minutes a day and participate in discovery and creativity-based activities.
- Parents and caregivers are aware of family learning opportunities during the summer months.
- Families will learn specific activities that they can engage in to help build their children's literacy.

Intermediate

- Parents/caregivers and preschool-aged participants actively practice five ECRR2 literacy practices at home/outside of the library and incorporate them into their daily routines.
- School-aged children increase participation and enthusiasm for STEAM-based learning, including critical thinking, problem-solving, creativity, and inter-disciplinary STEAM content.
- Participants and parents are engaged in reading and learning activities together.
- Families attend cultural events and utilize museums and other resources.
- Parents are informed and active participants in their children's reading and learning.
- Children will strengthen out of school time reading and learning practices and show improvements in academic areas.

Long-term Impact

- Summer learning loss in children of Chicago is mitigated.
- Children will have improved confidence and be ready to start or return to school.
- Strengthen community of library users.

FIGURE 6.1

Sample Summer Learning Challenge Logic Model

THINK ABOUT IT

Now you try it. Consider the goals that you, your staff, and your director have set for the program. Think about them as the reason why you do what you do. Why *do* you create a summer learning program each year?

List your reasons here:

_____
_____
_____
_____
_____
_____
_____
_____
_____
_____

Goals: Goals are aspirational and should address a need in your community. They are meant to define what all your work is really about. For example, CPL has two goals for the Summer Learning Challenge:

1. Encourage, facilitate, and promote reading and STEAM-based learning for children 0–13 years old to mitigate the summer slide.
2. Support parents, caregivers, and involvement in children's reading and learning.

Your goals are the things you hope to achieve over the life of the project. They should be ambitiously optimistic, and they may not be measurable.

Inputs: You will need to brainstorm a list of all the elements that are invested in your program. What are the "parts" that go into making your program? It's a summer learning program, so it will certainly include the books you promote and all the resources that go into the program. Think of all the resources that go into the elements you work on every year. Inputs include:

- Human resources: time and staff
- Fiscal resources: municipal funding, donations, grants, in-kind partnerships

- Materials and facilities: supplies, space, equipment, collections, marketing
- Partners
- Knowledge base: research, training

(McCawley 2001)

Activities: Activities are the things you do with your inputs to reach your desired outputs (quantifiable measures) and outcomes. Activities help connect your inputs to your outputs. This section is where you list your actions, or all that you and the staff actually do to make the program work.

To complete this section, you will need to brainstorm a master list of all the actions associated with summer. We include items like training, programs, outreach, content development—the list goes on and on. In our logic model, we also include a list of who we reach.

Outputs: Outputs are the quantifiable, direct products of program activities. For example, you may list staff trainings under "activities." Under "outputs," count the number of trainings and participants.

Look at the activities you have listed and think about all the things you can count: number of kids registered, number of parents, number of programs, number of kids attending programs . . . and that's just the beginning.

Outcomes: Outcomes are the desired results of the program. They show that your program has made a difference. In any library program, there are immediate changes and things that happen over time. Think about a preschool storytime. After one session, you notice that the child knows more about the "sh" sound than she did before she came to storytime. This skill development is a *short-term outcome*. If a child continues to come over time, you may notice she is using the literacy skills from storytime in her everyday life. This change in behavior is an *intermediate outcome*. As a result of the *short-term* and *intermediate outcomes,* this child is more prepared for school and is more successful in her education. This is a *long-term outcome*.

Short-term outcomes include changes in:

- knowledge
- skills
- attitude
- awareness

Intermediate outcomes include changes in:

- behaviors
- practices
- policies

Long-term outcomes are changes in economic, social, and political conditions that stem from short-term and intermediate outcomes.

USING YOUR LOGIC MODEL AS AN EVALUATION TOOL

Logic models can be used as a tool for your evaluation process. It's the next "logical" step. Determining indicators can help you connect your logic model to the evaluation of your program.

Indicators are measures used to determine whether you have achieved your stated outcomes. Don't feel like you need to track every outcome. Think about what is useful and feasible to track. For example, one of Chicago Public Library's desired outcomes is that school-age participants read twenty minutes a day and participate in discovery- and creativity-based activities. The indicators used to measure this outcome are the number of minutes spent reading, the number of discover activities, and the number of create activities.

After determining the indicators, you are ready to choose a specific evaluation method. Once you decide what you want to evaluate, you can determine what data you need to collect and how you want to measure it. In the above example, the data we want is the numbers of minutes spent reading and the numbers of discover and create activities completed. The best way to collect this data is simply to compile participant records. Your evaluation methods will be different depending on the data you want to collect as determined by your indicators. Other evaluation methods we use include focus groups, surveys, checklists, and formal observation (Coffman 1999).

GATHERING AND SHARING INFORMATION

One of the most tried-and-true methods of evaluation at Chicago Public Library involves surveying a variety of stakeholders. At a selection of branches, we survey parents of early learners (figure 6.2), parents of school-aged children (figure 6.3), school-aged children (figure 6.4), Junior Volunteers, and staff (see appendix B). We use indicators to determine what questions to ask on our surveys. These surveys are effective because we make them as accessible as possible by using everyday language, keeping questions short, and translating them into other languages as needed.

You can get even more out of your data if you analyze it alongside other relevant information. You could use census data, school enrollment data, free and reduced-price lunch data, graduation rates, and kindergarten enrollment. Though connecting with school districts can be a challenge, when successful, sharing data

Chicago Public Library—Summer Learning Challenge

Early Childhood Parent/Caregiver Survey

Library Branch: _____   Age of child: _____

I am a: (Circle one)   parent/caregiver   teacher/instructor

Please check the box that most applies (Agree, Disagree, or Don't Know) for each of the following statements.

Statement		Agree	Disagree	Don't Know
While participating in the Summer Learning Challenge, I became aware or more aware of the five early literacy practices (Talk, Sing, Read, Write, Play) recommended by the American Library Association.				
While participating in Summer Learning Challenge, I did some of the five early literacy practices (Talk, Sing, Read, Write, Play) with my child/group outside of the library.				
Once the Summer Learning Challenge is over, I will continue to do the five early literacy practices (Talk, Sing, Read, Write, Play) with my child/group outside of the library.				
After participating in the Summer Learning Challenge, I am more aware of learning opportunities for children during the summer months.				
After participating in the Summer Learning Challenge, I read and learned more with my child/group.				
Receiving free books to take home from the library encouraged me and my child/group to read more together.				
The Summer Learning Challenge helps my child/group be more prepared to start/return to school.				

FIGURE 6.2

Survey for Parents of Early Learners

Chicago Public Library—Summer Learning Challenge

School-Aged Parent/Caregiver Survey

Library Branch: _____   **Age of child:** _____

I am a: (Circle one)   **parent/caregiver**   **teacher/instructor**

Please check the box that most applies (Agree, Disagree, or Don't Know) for each of the following statements.

Statement		Agree	Disagree	Don't Know
My child/group wrote or talked to someone about what they read or learned this summer.				
My child/group enjoyed doing the Summer Learning Challenge.				
The Summer Learning Challenge sparked a new interest in STEM (science, technology, engineering, and math) in my child/group.				
My child/group took part in learning activities with the Summer Learning Challenge.				
After participating in the Summer Learning Challenge, I am more aware of learning opportunities for children during the summer months.				
After participating in the Summer Learning Challenge, I read and learned more with my child/group.				
Receiving free books to take home from the library encouraged my child/group to read more.				
The Summer Learning Challenge helps my child/group be more prepared to start/return to school.				

Please choose one or more activities that your child/group did in this summer:

- ❏ Library or museum program
- ❏ Explorer's Guide activity
- ❏ Brain Game
- ❏ Curiosity kit challenge
- ❏ Science Minors with Museum of Science and Industry
- ❏ None of these

FIGURE 6.3

Survey for Parents of School-Aged Children

Chicago Public Library —Summer Learning Challenge
School-Aged Child Survey

Library Branch: _____   Age: _____

Please answer the following questions by checking the box for Yes, No, or Not Sure.

Statement		Yes	No	Not Sure
Did you talk to someone about what you read or learned this summer?				
Did you have fun doing the Summer Learning Challenge?				
Did you learn anything new?				
Did you attend any special events with the Chicago Public Library, the Art Institute of Chicago, or the Museum of Science and Industry?				
Did the Summer Learning Challenge make you feel more ready or confident to go back to school?				

Which activities did you do this summer?

❏ Library or museum program
❏ Explorer's Guide activity
❏ Brain Game
❏ Curiosity kit challenge

❏ Science Minors with Museum of Science and Industry
❏ None of these

FIGURE 6.4

Survey for School-Aged Children

HOW DO I TRACK THIS DATA?

Data and paperwork are a surprisingly large part of a summer learning program. Whether you are in a branch library or a large system with multiple sites, you need a way to collect, manage, and share data.

1. Collect different types of data, such as program participation, attendance at events, minutes spent reading, activities, completion, and personal information (age, grade school, etc.).
2. Transfer the data to an online data management system. We currently use Cityspan, which is a system used by other City of Chicago agencies. Cityspan, and other tools like it, allow for anonymized data sharing. Microsoft Excel is also a great tool because it is flexible, easy to use, and widely available. We use Excel to track our group data and surveys.
3. Share your data. We run reports, create Excel summaries, and share infographics.

can be extremely beneficial for both parties. You could take it even further by working with other organizations that have access to information which may not be in the public record.

For example, in Chicago, we have a data-sharing partnership with Chapin Hall, a research and policy center at the University of Chicago that is focused on improving the well-being of children, youth, families, and communities. CPL shares information about our participants' read, discover, and create activities and Chapin Hall looks at it alongside the Chicago Public Schools' student-level school data. In this way we are able to analyze the relationship between school grades and library summer participation, while controlling for other social variables. In so doing, the first year's data showed results that were astounding to us: children who participate in the Summer Learning Challenge show a 20 percent increase in math scores and a 15 percent increase in reading scores.

How do you share all the data you collect? You can create a video, an executive summary, or an infographic. An infographic can be a great way to visually represent your program in an accessible way (see figure 6.5). Infographics are an illustration of your data and can help tell your program's story quickly and effectively. Free infographic websites with software to guide you through this process work well, or you can create one with desktop publishing tools.

ASSESSMENT AND CONTINUOUS IMPROVEMENT

In Chicago, we've been running a redesigned summer program for a few years, we have an evaluation plan in place, and you might imagine that by now, the program

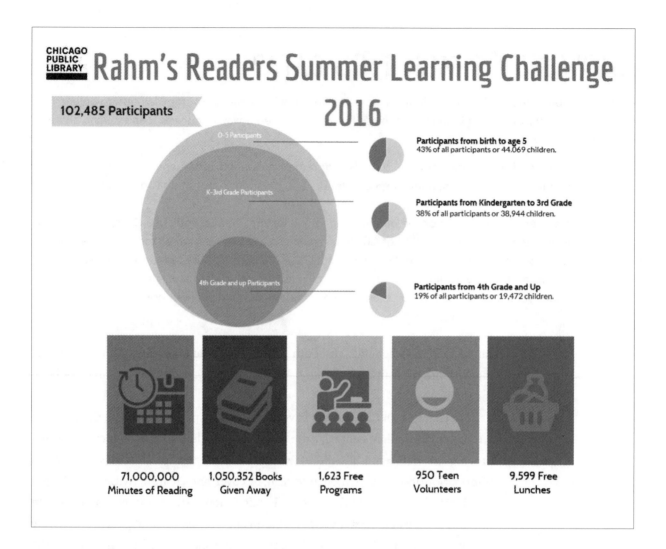

CHICAGO PUBLIC LIBRARY Rahm's Readers Summer Learning Challenge
2016

102,485 Participants

0-5 Participants

K-3rd Grade Participants

4th Grade and up Participants

Participants from birth to age 5
43% of all participants or 44,069 children.

Participants from Kindergarten to 3rd Grade
38% of all participants or 38,944 children.

Participants from 4th Grade and Up
19% of all participants or 19,472 children.

71,000,000
Minutes of Reading

1,050,352 Books
Given Away

1,623 Free
Programs

950 Teen
Volunteers

9,599 Free
Lunches

FIGURE 6.5

Chicago Public Library's 2016 Summer Learning Challenge Infographic

runs itself. In reality, we've learned it's necessary to always work on improving our program for our kids, librarians, and city. By using evaluation and assessment tools, we engage in a continuous improvement process. Continuous improvement is a cycle of assessing, reflecting, and planning in order to target incremental improvements year after year (figure 6.6).

Each year at Chicago Public Library, we work to develop continuous improvement goals to help us administer our Summer Learning Challenge in an effective way. These goals can address any area of improvement we want to support, such as coaching or programmatic enhancements. When developing and revising our continuous improvement goals, we look at results from evaluations and explore program quality assessment.

There are many different assessment tools that can be used in library and other out-of-school-time settings to look closely at the quality of your program. Youth Program Quality Assessment (YPQA), developed by the Weikert Center, is well known and widely used. It is used in many educational settings and is flexible enough

THINK ABOUT IT

Think about what you want to make better in your program and list it in the box below.

FIGURE 6.6

Steps to Continuous Improvement

to meet the needs of many different types and sizes of programs. It can be used throughout the year to get an idea of where your program is at and where it needs to go in terms of youth programming. The National Summer Learning Association worked with the Weikert Center to adapt this tool specifically for use in analyzing summer out-of-school-time programming. There are a lot of options for quality assessment; find the one that works best for you.

Running an effective summer program takes a great deal of planning, assessment, evaluation, and continuous improvement. Everything from developing a logic model

LIBRARIAN'S CORNER
WHAT DO I DO WITH ALL THIS DATA?

There is no use sugar-coating it—detailed, accurate data is time-consuming to collect and enter into our tracking system. However, the information we gather about our participants and their responses to our programs gives me valuable direction and guidance for the future. I firmly believe that the purpose of assessment is to inform practice. To me, the data is not the end point, it is only the beginning. Data enables us to determine and serve the needs of our communities; to assess for the purpose of evaluating and developing library programs; and to enhance and elevate our patrons' use of library services and programming. Evaluating past programs enables us to understand their impact and effectiveness, and ultimately draw conclusions and make informed decisions for next time.

When faced with a tall stack of registration cards, it can be tempting to skip entering some of the details and just record the "power" data—the minutes spent reading, discovering, and

CONTINUED ON FOLLOWING PAGE ▶

► **CONTINUED FROM PREVIOUS PAGE**

creating. I have been thankful time and time again that I have taken the time to diligently capture details like gender, age, school name, and zip code. These details offer unique and invaluable opportunities for planning and marketing our future library programs.

After decades of experience gathered in the field, I often find that the data supports my intuition. However, the more exciting and poignant occurrences are when the data does not support my intuition. I've been surprised to discover the actual breakdown of kids we see from our various schools. For example, I thought we enrolled far more public school kids than non-public school kids, but the truth is we are closer to a 60/40 split between public and private schools. This kind of information will drive my marketing efforts next year. I may be able to identify schools that need "special treatment" from us in order to increase participation. In this instance, and in many others, without those small details that were so painstakingly entered, I would miss out on key information that directly impacts and informs my practice.

Examining data from our past years refocuses our efforts and refines our methods of promoting, scheduling, and evaluating. When planning programs, I can look at each aspect of last year's data to develop a variety of understandings. For example, take my data on audience attendance. If we're getting a big turnout from preschoolers, I may note this patron group as having a high interest and high need, possibly leading me to expand our offerings and provide even more options for that age group. On the flip side, this same data may be used to look at which audiences we are missing and why. Where are all the 11–13 year-olds? What kind of programs can we offer that might pull them into the library? Are they hearing about us? Maybe we need to target those grades during school visits. Are there other opportunities for publicity we are missing? I may also look at the times we get the largest audience size. Of course, I want to schedule programs, staff, and volunteers during those times that our audience is available and already coming in to the library, but I still think about what we can do to encourage participation by other age groups and other times of the day.

Data helps me understand not only *who* our library services impact, but also *how* our library services impact them. While looking at the numbers provides many opportunities for program evaluation and planning, patron surveys can offer an even deeper insight into our programming efforts and their impact on the community. For instance, surveys of program participants and their parents can highlight those components of the program that are most enjoyable or valuable to our patrons. Alternatively, surveys offer the opportunity to glean an understanding of potential areas where further growth, support, or accommodation would be beneficial. Through feedback from "participant reflections forms," we've discovered that our audience doesn't like drop-in, passive programs unless we provide a specific description of the program, a start time and an end time, and details about what we'll be doing. Survey responses can reveal a connection or disconnection between what we thought we were offering and what was perceived by our participants.

—**MS. SHANNON, Woodson Regional Library**

to collecting data to assessing different elements of your program takes time and energy. But once you start, you'll see that your efforts are well worth it because they lead to bigger and better programs that have a community-wide impact. The better your data, the better you can tell your story. Your data will tell your amazing story.

CHAPTER 7

MANAGING CHANGE

The needs of kids have changed, especially in the last fifteen years. To have the most relevant summer program, it's time to make the shift from reading to learning. Shifting from a summer reading program to a summer learning challenge is a big change. Change is exciting, but it can also be scary. How you manage the change, and more importantly, how you help people navigate change is critical to the success of your redesigned program. It affects all stakeholders: staff, youth, families, library leadership, and, in turn, your entire community.

It's often said that change is constant, though many of us do not like change, personally or professionally. Change brings challenges. Change asks us to wade into ambiguity and uncertainty. Change can feel overwhelming, especially when we have run a program like summer reading in one way for so long. Staff, patrons, and administrators all expect the same process and the same results year after year. Change can push us to try new things and to grow in ways we may not have expected. To sum it up: change is hard but necessary. Change responds to a problem and once you know what that problem is, change can help you solve it. Change can make things better. Change allows libraries to respond to nationwide trends and best practices. Change keeps institutions relevant in a changing world.

Can you explain why change is necessary and what changes you want to make? If so, then you are ready to get started. When you manage a large change, like implementing a new summer program, there are important areas to consider.

Research: Rationalize the change you want to make. What evidence do you have that proves this change is the right direction for your program? Doing the research has many benefits. You will likely find yourself even more inspired when you look at concrete outcomes for children in professional papers and studies. Evidence is also important for demonstrating your intent to the administration and staff. Knowing what is happening in the field can help show that this is not a radical change as much as a necessary evolution. By reading this book, you're already on your way.

Plan: What are you going to change? Are you incorporating STEAM into your program? Developing maker activities? Adding play? Whatever you do, you are shifting the paradigm. Make sure you have developed a clear path for your library and that the senior management team is on board with the plan and ready to implement it themselves. Having a plan means that you have considered the impact the change will have on staff, patrons, and the library itself. An effective plan is multi-faceted and considers the full scope of the change. Even if you veer from a plan, it will give you a place to begin this process. Consider these areas:

- How does this change fit into the existing mission of your library?
- How will you organize the staff to brainstorm new ideas?
- How will your library communicate changes to all stakeholders: your community, municipality, partner agencies, governing board, and staff?
- How will you support the staff in making changes?
- How will you handle any dissenting views?
- How will you balance making an institutional change with everyone's day-to-day workload?

Communicate: Once you have a plan, get ready to talk about it all the time. Leaders articulate their vision. Let staff, patrons, and everyone who will be affected know that this change is coming and why it is critically important. It's beneficial to start from the top of your organization. Work with library leadership to share the strategic importance of this change for your library, and then follow through. Stress that the core values at the heart of your library will be retained, but that the practices may begin to look different. Devise a system to communicate to your library effectively. Weekly e-mails, in-person staff meetings, and workshops will show the work you are doing and how it impacts the library.

Communication is a two-way street. The biggest part of communication is not talking; it's listening. Listen to people's suggestions and feedback along with their concerns and fears. Address these issues head-on and let them know that ambiguity is part of this process. Uncertainty is difficult, but it's simply a part of this process. Also, try to pick up on what parts of the change excite staff members and build on that. For example, if staff seem excited about a new STEAM activity you demonstrate, provide supplies so they can try it with kids during the summer.

Collaborate: In order to truly collaborate on a changing summer model, you will have to incorporate other people's ideas into your work. Bring staff into this process as much as possible. Get their advice and feedback and then listen to it. Doing this

Children's Services Staff Attend a Training at the Museum of Science and Industry

means you will have to be flexible and willing to let go of some of your own ideas at some points. On the flip side, you won't always make everyone happy, but by collaborating, you'll know you've weighed every opinion.

Focus Groups: Focus groups bring people together to give advice and feedback. They are intended to get at the core of what people are thinking. People in focus groups are usually asked questions in a group setting so that participants can talk among themselves and bounce ideas off each other. Hosting a focus group allows you to get advice about how to structure and communicate a change. Think about the change you're making and whose perspective may help, then gather the focus group's participants. For example, if you're making a change to an existing program and want community feedback, look for regular users who understand the library and use your programs.

Peer Leadership: Peer-led groups are a great way to give emerging leaders an opportunity to have a leadership role. Creating peer-led leadership teams allows a group of peers to stand up and take responsibility for the program and its design. For example, three staff members may take the lead on developing STEAM activities for everyone. They meet, research, and develop activities and then communicate them back to the larger team. You will be surprised at all the good ideas that are generated this way.

Professional Development (see figure 7.1): The role of professional development cannot be underestimated. It is the formal process for providing ongoing learning for librarians and other youth-serving library professionals. In the public library, professional development allows librarians to grow their skills and practice to create the best outcomes for the children they serve. Continuing to train staff ensures that they are well-versed in best practices, trends in the field, new ideas, and research. When libraries take the time to ensure that their staff are given professional development opportunities, the staffers are able to respond to their users in the most effective way. For example, staff who are trained on the needs of children on the autism spectrum will be stronger when responding to the needs of this user group.

If you are asking staff to try new things, professional development is essential to ensure that staff receive adequate training on appropriate topics. The NSLA cites professional development as one of the indicators for high-quality programming. (National Summer Learning Association 2013). Hosting professional development

LIBRARIAN'S CORNER
WHAT DO THESE CHANGES MEAN FOR THE KIDS I SERVE?

Change is difficult, but change helps us to grow. When we first started discussing changing the way kids reported on books from actual titles to the number of minutes spent reading, I was very skeptical. Questions about how we share books with children began to sprout. How would we know that the kids actually read what they said they were reading? Will kids begin to use a stopwatch to time their reading? Does tracking the amount of time spent reading take away from the blissful joy of getting lost in a book? How would we be able to do reader's advisory if we didn't know what they were reading? Would parents and caregivers be supportive of this change? I had a bundle of questions.

Then I took a step back and really thought about what this change would mean to the kids and families in my library. Some of my kids are struggling readers, and I've always been very flexible about how many titles or what types of titles they had to read to earn the prize. I realized that switching to reading at least twenty minutes a day would not only allow them to read books or other material they can and want to read, but it would instill in them the daily practice of reading and encourage them to develop the habit of reading. It also helps those struggling readers reach the same benchmark, and that is great for their self-esteem. This also helped families to get into the routine of setting aside time at home for family quiet reading that extends beyond summer reading.

Children still come to me to report on what they are reading, and they seem more engaged in their reading because they don't feel the pressure to finish 10–25 books in the summer. They are sharing new and interesting facts that they read in magazines, which prompts them to want to read more about it in books. Reader's advisory has never been as much fun. It has become a family affair as parents, caregivers, and children partake in the joy of looking for books and other materials that they will relish. They even ask me what books I've read and enjoyed. This change has helped me share the love of reading with even more children and families, turning what was a chore for some children into a welcomed choice that is adored by the whole family. The moral to the story is: we embraced a big change and made a great difference for our kids.

—MS. TINA, Blackstone Branch

on a topic doesn't mean everyone will leave as an expert on the topic. For example, attending a workshop to learn how to host a paper airplane program won't make you a pilot or a physics teacher. But you will leave with an introduction to the concepts of flight and ideas for how to make it work as a program. Just as our ultimate goal as librarians is to spark curiosity in kids, professional development inspires librarians in new and stimulating ways.

Conducting hands-on workshops and professional development is also important for communicating programmatic changes to the non-children's staff. When other segments of the staff learn about the changes you're making in your summer program, and why you're making them, they are more likely to get on board.

Finding the right trainer is critical to the success of your work. Partners make natural trainers (see figure 7.2). They are subject experts who can communicate well about the content you are developing. You can also recruit trainers from conference sessions you attend, from people in the field, and from authors of books or articles you respect.

Professional development can take many forms, including:

- Workshops with an expert guest facilitator
- Small-group work
- Webinars
- Online peer-led learning circles
- Team meetings to work on a specific goal

Program Sustainability: Managing change effectively helps to ensure that your program will be sustainable. When managing a large-scale change, keep in mind the strategies that can maintain your program's continued long-term success. When programs are forced to shut down because of loss of funds or support, it can feel as if the entire project—and your time—was wasted. Building in a plan to sustain your program can help you alleviate this. In order to help in the maintenance and growth of your program, you need to think about how to first make your program sustainable and then how to assess that sustainability.

Organizational Capacity: Do you have enough people, space, and materials to support your new program? Consider your library's ability to staff service points; conduct programs; manage, order, and disseminate materials; and support the program from an administrative role.

Funding: Before you ask for funding to support your new program, you will need to have a rock-solid plan backed up with evidence so that you can show your intent, measure your success, and adjust in response to challenges. Funding sources are wide and varied.

- Your library may be qualified to apply for a variety of grants as well as money from local municipalities.
- Partnerships within the business community can lead to sustained giving and in-kind donations that can help your program grow over time.
- Think about what goals of your program might correlate to the goals of an organization. For example, if your program highlights early literacy skills and a local individual donor is interested in supporting that type of initiative, be prepared to specifically highlight this component of your program.

HOW TO DETERMINE YOUR STAFF'S PROFESSIONAL DEVELOPMENT NEEDS

If you are going to commit resources to effective professional development, it's good to start with a baseline: where your staff are, what they know, and what they need to be successful in making change. Here are some questions to guide your planning:

- What subjects have they been trained on in the last several years?
- What is their self-reported level of comfort with key concepts such as STEAM content and programming, twenty-first-century skills, or child development?
- What do you observe when you watch the staff conduct programs? Do you see areas that need strengthening?

The NSLA's planning guide "Summer Starts in September" is a great resource that offers a comprehensive list of elements to include in effective training. Make sure that your training plan is flexible enough to meet the needs of your staff as you make change. See appendix C for a sample of a survey we use to have CPL librarians assess and evaluate trainings.

- Individual donors can also be cultivated for program growth. In fact, sometimes individual donors or small foundations like to give money for start-up programs.
- Consider civic groups such as the Kiwanis, Rotary, or the Chamber of Commerce as potential partners in funding an aspect of your program.

Partnerships: Partners also help you advocate for your program and can provide a point of entry for other city or business entities. (See chapter 3: "Partnerships: Stronger Together.")

Program Evaluation and Adaptation (see figure 7.3): Evaluation helps keep you on track with your goals and can help you change your path if you find you are not seeing the results you want. Program evaluation helps you build the case for sustained financial support.

Communicating Success: When you have a successful program, more people want to come on board. Broadcasting your intentions invites people to participate and allows you to increase the support of the program. Broadcasting your successes may draw in new participants, funders, and partners.

At Chicago Public Library we've worked hard to make our program sustainable, and in the eyes of Rhona Frazin, president and CEO of the Chicago Public Library Foundation, it's been invaluable. "The vision and creativity of the library team in transforming the Summer Learning Challenge has ignited a spark in the private funding community. Companies, foundations, and families have been eager to jump on board to partner with the Chicago Public Library Foundation and the library to create wonder and discovery opportunities for Chicago's children."

PUTTING IT ALL TOGETHER

There's no one way to manage change. At Chicago Public Library, we used the strategies outlined in this chapter and we learned a lot. We began by defining the problem and pulling together research about trends in the field and outcomes for children in summer, all of which you can find in chapter 1. Once the rationale for change was clear, we created a plan encompassing the steps described below.

We started with communication from the top of our organization. Our library commissioner articulated the goals for transforming summer reading into summer learning. He demonstrated support by attending meet-

Ground rules make a focus group successful. Everyone has different opinions; sometimes they are passionate, but none of them are wrong. A healthy group process means that everyone is able to speak but everyone understands that it's not feasible to utilize all opinions. Chicago Public Library's focus-group ground rules include

- Respect everyone's opinions
- Tell us what your community needs
- It's important to say what you think
- Understand that stating your opinion doesn't mean it can necessarily be incorporated
- It's important to know even if your decision isn't the one we go with, you have been *heard*

ings and trainings of the children's librarians. Although Children's Services took the lead on developing the plan for change, the commissioner participated in content development meetings. He was always the first in line to build a catapult, make a bridge, or design a solution to a children's literature-based design challenge, and he still is! This obvious enthusiasm not only helped communicate change, but modeled a positive attitude toward the change we were making. Our senior management team was always right behind him, supporting changes big and small. Together, they continue to lead by example and show everyone that executive-level staff support our work.

When we began making the change, we formed a focus group of children's librarians from across our system. This focus group included seasoned children's librarians with years of experience and new librarians with different perspectives. They met monthly to tackle solutions to issues that arose during the redesign. The focus group explored various areas of program design, including

- How to incorporate STEAM content and maker/art content
- How to track reading, STEAM content, and maker/art content
- The role of play in the program
- How to measure the kids' success

Our focus group influenced countless decisions about the Summer Learning Challenge. For example, their recommendations about kid appeal, engagement, and content led us to the current Explorer's Guide format. All of the decisions in this redesign of the summer program, large and small, have been run through this focus

LIBRARIAN'S CORNER
LEADING THE CHANGE AS A COHORT LEADER

Change can be hard for lots of people. I was happy to be a part of the team that led the change for summer because it gave me a chance to not only have a say in how things were going to change, but also to mentor my colleagues through the change. As a cohort leader, I worked closely with Children's Services and the other cohort leaders to transform our summer program to include the many different ways kids can learn during the summer. It was good to have librarians from all over the city because we were able to think of the bigger picture of summer as opposed to just what works at our library branch.

Once we had ideas of how we wanted to change the program, I was able to go to my small cohort of librarians to get their input on how these ideas would work for them. As I reached out to them, I realized that many of them just wanted to make sure they understood the changes properly and needed the reassur-ance of talking through their implementation ideas with someone. Most librarians' fears were calmed as I connected aspects of the new program to features of the past program. Helping them see the connections between the old and the new program left them feeling less over-whelmed.

I tried to reach out to each of my cohort librarians at least once a week during the planning of the first Summer Learning Challenge and also a few times during the summer to see how things were going. These conversations were always helpful for both the librarians and me because we were experiencing the same changes and needed this support. I believe it was invaluable for our whole organization to have cohort leaders who could listen and work through concerns with the many librarians who are part of our large organization.

—MS. SHARON, Dunning Branch

group. This continues to be important to the process as we test, implement, and refine our thinking.

We knew that this change process would require children's librarians to support each other, and we wanted to create small, peer-led networks to help navigate through the first year of the redesign. We asked the librarians in our focus group to pivot and become peer leaders of a group of four to five other children's librarians. We called these our "cohort groups" and the focus group librarians became our cohort leaders.

Cohort leaders interacted with their cohorts in a variety of ways. The cohort leaders met and talked with the librarians in their groups several times before summer. Cohorts worked together as a group in trainings and were able to engage in small-group work specific to their needs and concerns. Cohort leaders ask the following questions when coaching branch staff:

- How are you feeling about the components of the Summer Learning Challenge?
- What support can I give you in understanding the components or planning your program?
- What books are you using to tie into the theme this summer?
- How comfortable do you feel with the STEAM activities?
- Do you need more science background, or do you feel comfortable?
- How is branch decorating going?

Our desire to involve staff extends beyond peer leadership. Our plan includes professional development on a variety of levels for staff across the system, including children's librarians, branch managers, and clerical staff.

Through our partnership with the Museum of Science and Industry, we developed a strong relationship that continues to lead to many different professional development opportunities. These continue to include staff visits to the museum, museum educators training staff at the library, and STEAM coaching. We have found that in order for STEAM learning to be successful, there has to be a methodology to our professional development and it must be sustained over time. These trainings are important for us because they have three specific outcomes: (a) librarians learn new knowledge and skills and reinforce them; (b) librarians use what they learn to improve programming and leadership; and (c) youth learning and achievement increase because of the new rigor in programming. Our long-term partnership with MSI gives our professional development a consistency and clarity that has helped us make the change to a successful twenty-first-century program.

When surveyed, 95 percent of our children's librarians said that the STEAM trainings offered at the Museum of Science and Industry are critical to their ability to successfully incorporate STEAM learning into their library programs. Our professional development successes have reinforced the idea that finding the right partner is critical.

We also offer shorter professional development sessions to branch managers and clerical staff. These sessions include updates on the program, sneak peeks into exhibits at MSI, and special features of the upcoming summer. We are able to reach over two-thirds of our staff during CPL's annual all-staff training day where they get to play with the upcoming Summer Learning Challenge-themed STEAM activities. This serves as a great educational, promotional, and morale-building session for staff whom we otherwise might not have the opportunity to train.

Managing change is never a fast or linear process (see figure 7.4). At Chicago Public Library, we've learned the value of communicating our goals and sharing our plans to make change easier. We strive to be empathetic to the ways in which staff may be feeling or experiencing change and to acknowledge that change is a difficult

Elements of Success in Transitioning Summer Reading to Summer Learning

Supportive administration and leadership

- Messaging comes from leadership that this is supported work to all of the institution
- Leadership is actively engaged in modeling work
- Leadership is a champion for the work and stays involved in all areas of planning, implementation, and evaluation
- Leadership communicates to local municipality and bodies of governance

Highly trained and supported staff

- Staff receives background training and reading on 21st century learning and STEM learning
- Staff is continuously trained on out-of-school-time latest research and findings
- Staff receives a minimum of 8 hours of hands-on experiential learning training each year
- Staff is supported through an internal system (mentors, cohort groups, or learning circles) developed in keeping with the structure of the library system

Effective partnership or access to high quality content

- High-quality content provider is able to share resources and access to partner institution
- Easy curation of materials needed for experiential learning
- Access to partner institution for trainings, visits by families and children

Effective communication plan

- Patrons are aware of changes to program through: flyers, signage, program materials, parent workshops, written literature, and public service announcements
- Schools are communicated to prior to the program through district level meetings, local school visits to faculty, and classroom visits to children and teachers
- All staff are trained in the methodology of the change and able to answer questions

CONTINUED ON FOLLOWING PAGE ▶

FIGURE 7.4

Elements of Success in Transitioning Summer Reading to Summer Learning

► CONTINUED FROM PREVIOUS PAGE

Adequate planning process	• Time allotted to work on theme and content development • Adequate span of time to develop partnership agreement and memorandum of understanding, co-development of work, and agreed-upon schedule of completion • Monthly task list is shared with partners to keep work flow moving
Fun and engaging activities	• Activities are fun and relevant to children in libraries • Activities are open-ended and allow child to discover and iterate solutions • Activities are tied to children's literature • Activities promote family engagement with a focus on parents/caregivers learning together with their children • Activities reinforce concepts learned in school without feeling like more school
System for recognizing successes	• Library system has a way to recognize success by children: wall of fame, hall of completion, etc. • Library system has a way to recognize success of staff: spotlight profile, award, or recognition in newsletter
Effective evaluation	• Evaluation is built into the continuous improvement plan of library and departments • System has a Logic Model or Theory of Change that reflects the key goals, inputs, and outputs, and short, medium and long-term goals upon which it can test successes • Patrons are surveyed for satisfaction • Performance measures are developed and administered
Sustainability plan	• Funding streams are secured by system • Partnership memorandum of understanding consists of replication plan • Leadership of library works to maintain funding priorities • Work becomes institutionalized and is made a priority for sustained support

FIGURE 7.4

Elements of Success in Transitioning Summer Reading to Summer Learning (continued) process. Professional development has helped all staff members build their excitement and their skills. As we've shifted into a dynamic summer learning program, we've found that the feedback and ideas from the staff have been invaluable, and we make a point to always listen to everyone's point of view. Most importantly, we never miss an opportunity to celebrate everyone's successes: our kids', our staff's, and our library's.

LIBRARIAN'S CORNER
SUPPORTING CHANGE AS AN ADMINISTRATOR

Supporting the Children's Services librarians at Chicago Public Library wasn't hard for me to do at all. Given their track record of hard work and creativity, I knew that the children's librarians would have children's best interests at heart. Their plan to revitalize the summer reading program was proved to me through the research they shared, the goals they laid out, and the plan they developed for training the staff. I am happy to help support change when I can see there is a plan that is well thought out and has included the voices of the people who will be asked to make the change. The Summer Learning Challenge did all these things and continues to do so. By sharing the "continuous improvement goals" with me, I could also see that the children's librarians sincerely cared about deepening their work and working with others in their branch library to make this successful, and that goes a long way as a library administrator.

—ANDREA TELLI,
Assistant Commissioner, Chicago Public Library

AFTERWORD

M eet Avery, an avid library user who loves taking part in the Summer Learning Challenge (SLC). Avery reminds me of the boy I met in 2012 who said, "I only want to do what I want to do." Avery's mother homeschools him, and together they use Chicago Public Library (CPL) and the Museum of Science and Industry (MSI) as learning laboratories. We first met Avery during our Explore and Soar summer, when he sent in a video demonstrating one of our suggested activities explaining how craters form on the moon. Avery and his mother's clear love for the Summer Learning Challenge and their enthusiastic participation are a perfect example of how family engagement enhances the SLC. Moreover, they are a great example of how exploring what you want to learn in any way you choose makes a real difference. Avery quickly became CPL's and MSI's informal science ambassador. For Avery, the Summer Learning Challenge gave him a chance to develop his own path to summer learning at the library, the museum, and everywhere he goes.

Avery, his mother, and Mayor Rahm Emanuel

My name is Avery. I'm 9 years old and I love books. I love books because whenever I read, I journey to a new land and embark on great adventures. I've been a superhero, down the rabbit hole, flown to Neverland, met elves, defeated goblins, and fought fierce dragons. Books also help me learn new things like my favorite composer, Mozart, was called Wolfie as a child. And the first free library in Chicago was a result of the Great Chicago Fire.

The Chicago Public Library is one of my favorite places because it is the home to so many great books and programs like the Summer Learning Challenge. Science is my favorite subject, so summers at the library are amazing. In the SLC, I've made things and learned science. I've played transportation trivia, interviewed Captain Jim Lovell, Skyped with NASA, and met one of my favorite authors, Andrea Beaty. I also learned about Bernoulli's principle and worked with a team of students to construct a NASA glider.

I especially like when the Chicago Public Library works with the Museum of Science and Industry to make awesome activities like Summer Brain Games. I love the Museum of Science and Industry and can spend hour upon hour there. In one of my favorite Brain Games, I made a water bottle rocket powered by air pressure and read a book about Sir Isaac Newton and his Third Law of Motion. It was so much fun.

The library is my portal to knowledge and the librarians are the gatekeepers. My librarian is phenomenal. She has taught me math, science, social studies, and art through books and hands-on projects. Plus she's super nice and makes learning anything fun.

The more you read, the more you can learn, and the more you make and do, the more you learn. The library is so important because it houses loads of diverse books and anyone can read as much as they want for free. And there are always lots of cool, free programs in libraries all across our city with librarians who are curious just like I am. That's why the library is one of my favorite places.

Avery is just one of thousands of kids participating in CPL's Rahm's Readers Summer Learning Challenge who has been able to explore in fun and meaningful ways. How many other kids are out there just waiting for an opportunity to have a summer like Avery's?

Think about the kids we all serve. We can help them stem the summer slide. We can spark their curiosity. We can challenge them to see the world in new ways. We can make them global citizens of the twenty-first century.

And we can do it all at the library.

APPENDIXES

APPENDIX A

- - - - - - - - - - - -

SAMPLE GROUP AGREEMENT FORM

GROUP AGREEMENT FORM

The _____ [LIBRARY NAME] _____ and

_____ [GROUP NAME] _____ have

met and planned the following :

_____ [LIBRARY VISITS, PROGRAMS TO ATTEND, ETC.] _____

_____

_____

_____

_____

For _____ [PROGRAM NAME AND DATE] _____, the _____ [LIBRARY NAME] _____

_____ will supply summer program materials for [NUMBER] children by this

date: _____ .

To be eligible for _____ [REWARDS] _____, registration information and logs MUST be

returned to _____ [LIBRARY CONTACT PERSON] _____ by _____ [DATE] _____ .

Signed by: _____ [LIBRARY CONTACT PERSON] _____

Telephone Number _____ E-mail _____

And _____ [GROUP CONTACT PERSON] _____

Telephone Number _____ E-mail _____

Based on a resource originally developed by Chicago Public Library

APPENDIX B

-- -- -- -- -- -- --

SAMPLE BRANCH STAFF EVALUATION FOR SUMMER LEARNING CHALLENGE

CHICAGO PUBLIC LIBRARY
2016 RAHM'S READERS SUMMER LEARNING CHALLENGE
BRANCH STAFF EVALUATION

Evaluation questions are developed based on areas of the logic model, continuous improvement goals, new program features, and opportunities for self-reflection.

BRANCH: _____

STAFF MEMBER COMPLETING EVALUATION: _____

Total Number of Minutes Read: _____

Total Number of Walk-Ins: _____

Total Number of Outreach Group Participants: _____

Total Number of Achieves: _____

Total Number of Volunteers: _____

Thank you for all you did this summer for Chicago's kids!

Please take some time to consider the following elements of the 2016 Summer Learning Challenge, from your own individual program to system wide aspects of the program. Your honest feedback will help us make a better program in 2017!

Please answer all questions. In the event that a question doesn't apply to you, mark "N/A."

TRAINING

1. Consider the training you received leading up to the 2016 SLC. Having completed the 2016 SLC, rate whether you would have liked less, the same, or more focus given to the following training areas:

	Less	Same	More	N/A
Hands-on training opportunities with Brain Games.	❏	❏	❏	❏
Hands-on training opportunities with other programmatic elements.	❏	❏	❏	❏
Training in STEAM concepts relevant to the summer theme.	❏	❏	❏	❏
Visits to partner facilities such as MSI.	❏	❏	❏	❏
Hearing directly from STEAM content experts.	❏	❏	❏	❏
Training connecting summer content to CPL collections.	❏	❏	❏	❏
Training on how to work with and best prepare Junior Volunteers	❏	❏	❏	❏
Training on SLC program components (paperwork, volunteers, standards, etc.)	❏	❏	❏	❏
Training on Cityspan and data collection	❏	❏	❏	❏
Other (please specify)	❏	❏	❏	❏

2. Rank the usefulness of the various SLC trainings you attended throughout the spring. Add any specific comments for each training below.

	Not Useful	Somewhat Useful	Very Useful	Did Not Attend
March 8th SLC Kick-Off Event at Harold Washington Library Center	❏	❏	❏	❏
• Keynote Presentation from Sarah Pitcock of NSLA	❏	❏	❏	❏
• "SLC Expo" with booths from guests and colleagues	❏	❏	❏	❏
• Breakout Session: SLC Brain Games from MSI	❏	❏	❏	❏
• Breakout Session: Data Collection with Chapin Hall	❏	❏	❏	❏
• Cluster Presentations on SLC Topics	❏	❏	❏	❏
March 15 SLC Paperwork Overview and New Staff Orientation	❏	❏	❏	❏
May 10 Cluster Finale at MSI (with Brain Games training)	❏	❏	❏	❏
Other (please specify)	❏	❏	❏	❏

3. Describe one idea, skill, or concept you took away from an SLC training this year.

4. What aspect of the SLC did you feel most prepared to carry out?

5. What aspect of the SLC would you have liked more training on?

EARLY CHILDHOOD COMPONENTS

1. Think about patron response (from both children and parents/caregivers) to the new Early Literacy Guide for participants ages 0–5. Rate patron response to each of the following aspects of this new piece.

RAHM'S LITTLE READERS GUIDE	Negative Response	Positive Response	Did Not Observe
Tips and activities for the five practices.	❑	❑	❑
Log inside the guide	❑	❑	❑
As a whole, how did patrons respond to the guide vs. previous years' place mat?	❑	❑	❑

Do you prefer the early learning pieces to be in one Early Literacy Guide, like this year, or to have separate coloring sheets, like in 2015? Please explain why.

2. Consider the KPMG book giveaway for Rahm's Little Readers.

- How did patrons like the KPMG book give-away?
- Did you notice that patrons were more or less encouraged to sign up for the program with the incentive of a giveaway book?
- Did most 0–5 aged participants get a bag from Bernie's Book Bank AND their KPMG book? How did that process work?
- Share an anecdote about the book giveaway for 0–5 year olds (either walk-ins or outreach groups).

3. We track reading and the other four practices for ages 0–5 (talk, sing, write, and play) instead of discovers and creates. Please choose which ONE of the following two options you prefer:

Keeping the Rahm's Little Learner's Booklet to highlight the five Every Child Ready to Read practices and *track the five practices on the log.*	❑ **This is my preference.**
Continue to highlight the five Every Child Ready to Read practices in the Rahm's Little Learner's Booklet *but track discover and create on the log, the same as we do for older children.*	❑ **This is my preference.**
Why is that your preference?	

4. Our funders love stories about the Summer Learning Challenge. Please share one positive story or experience from a 0–5 aged participant or parent of a 0–5 year-old.

SCHOOL-AGE COMPONENTS

1. What ages did you see using the Explorer's Guide most this summer (mark only one).

   ❑ 0–5   ❑ 6–9   ❑ 10–13

2. What type of activities did kids seem to prefer or gravitate to? (mark all that apply)

   ❑ Puzzles/Word Games
   ❑ STEM-Challenges/problems
   ❑ Creative/drawing activities
   ❑ Fun facts
   ❑ Brain Games

3. Did most participants use the log included in the Explorer's Guide, a separate printed log, or both the log included in their guide AND a separate printed log?

   ❑ log included in Explorer's Guide   ❑ Separate printed log   ❑ Both

4. Rate the following aspects of the Explorer's Guide (1 = none/not at all, 5 = lots/excellent)

	1	2	3	4	5
Kid-appeal	❑	❑	❑	❑	❑
Children enjoyed the activities.	❑	❑	❑	❑	❑
There was a variety of types of activities.	❑	❑	❑	❑	❑
The Explorer's Guide enhances the SLC.	❑	❑	❑	❑	❑

5. What was the most popular activity or page in the Explorer's Guide?

6. Describe how you saw children and/or families using the guide. Did they use it mostly independently, in small groups, or as a family?

7. Share any additional comments or suggestions for the Explorer's Guide.

8. Consider the Bernie's Book Bank giveaway books for participants ages 6–13.

   • How did this age group respond to the book giveaway?
   • Did you notice this age range to be more or less encouraged to sign up for the program with the incentive of give-away books?
   • Share an anecdote about the book giveaway for 6–13 year-olds.

- If you hosted a Bernie's Book Bank community day, please share how it went and any feedback for next year.

TWEEN COMPONENTS

1. What was the most successful program for ages 11–13 at your branch this summer?

2. Think about the Tween Deck for the following questions:

How did you use the Tween Deck during the SLC?	What ages primarily used the Tween Deck?
❑ Passive Programming ❑ Used in a program ❑ Used by junior volunteers to engage children ❑ Other (please describe) ❑ Did not use Tween Deck	❑ Ages 6–8 ❑ Ages 9–10 ❑ Ages 11–13 ❑ Ages 14 & up

What materials did you use to supplement the Tween Deck?

What would have made the Tween Deck more successful at your branch?

Would you be interested in helping to create the Tween Deck next year?   ❑ YES   ❑ NO

Additional feedback about the Tween Deck:

MATERIALS AND RESOURCES

Rate the following materials and resources' overall impact on the program. For each resource, please share either additional feedback on how it can be improved or an anecdote about how it was used in your branch this summer.

	Enhances Program	Helpful but Not Necessary for Program	Does Not Enhance Program (Please Share Why)
Challenge Cards (with Curiosity Kits)	❑	❑	❑

Additional thoughts:

	Enhances Program	Helpful but Not Necessary for Program	Does Not Enhance Program (Please Share Why)
Curiosity Kits	☐	☐	☐

Additional thoughts:

Website	☐	☐	☐

Additional thoughts:

Discovery Cart	☐	☐	☐

Additional thoughts:

Activity suggestions from March 8 meeting + supplies	☐	☐	☐

Additional thoughts:

VOLUNTEERS

1. Number of SLC '16 volunteers who previously VOLUNTEERED for the SLC: _____
   Number of SLC '16 volunteers who previously PARTICIPATED in the SLC: _____

2. For each volunteer training item provided to you on Sharepoint, please rate its usefulness and note whether or not you used it.

	Not Useful	Useful	Did Not Use
Training Checklist	☐	☐	☐
Training PowerPoint	☐	☐	☐
Tabletop "Reporting Table Tips" cards	☐	☐	☐
Reporting Table Scenario Game	☐	☐	☐

3. What is one thing you do to successfully manage volunteers? Where did you get this idea?

4. Did you observe teen volunteers developing and/or using these work readiness skills during the Summer Learning Challenge?

	No Volunteers	Some Volunteers	Most Volunteers	All Volunteers
PROFESSIONAL ATTITUDE				
• Greets SLC participants and families with enthusiasm	❑	❑	❑	❑
• Takes responsibility for his or her actions and does not blame others	❑	❑	❑	❑
• Stays calm, clearheaded, and unflappable during busy times	❑	❑	❑	❑
• Graciously accepts instructions and/or criticism	❑	❑	❑	❑
TEAM WORK ETHIC				
• Actively looks for additional tasks when there are no participants at the reporting table	❑	❑	❑	❑
• Actively looks for ways to help other junior volunteers	❑	❑	❑	❑
PROBLEM SOLVING				
• Unpacks problems into manageable parts	❑	❑	❑	❑
• Generates multiple potential solutions to solve problems	❑	❑	❑	❑
• Identifies new and more effective ways to solve problems	❑	❑	❑	❑
TIME MANAGEMENT				
• Arrives on time and is rarely absent without calling	❑	❑	❑	❑
• Manages time and does not procrastinate when given a task	❑	❑	❑	❑
• Works steadily on assigned tasks	❑	❑	❑	❑

5. Did you see junior volunteers using what they learned from the training over the summer?

	No Volunteers	Some Volunteers	All Volunteers
Using open-ended questions at the reporting table.	❑	❑	❑
Focusing on employment skills	❑	❑	❑
Using STEM facilitation skills	❑	❑	❑

PROGRAMS

Answer the following questions for ALL system-wide programs you hosted at your branch this summer. Mark "did not host" for programs that didn't take place at your branch.

	DID NOT HOST	Was the program appropriate for the SLC/library?	Rate the audience response (1=hated it, 5=loved it)	Did this program create buzz or interest in your community?	Would you host this program again?	Did the program align with SLC themes?
David L. Hoyt Giant Word Winder	❑	❑ YES ❑ NO	❑ 1 ❑ 2 ❑ 3 ❑ 4 ❑ 5	❑ YES ❑ NO	❑ YES ❑ NO	❑ YES ❑ NO
Explain your audience response rating and share any additional feedback:						
Emerald City Theatre's Magic Treehouse with Jack and Annie	❑	❑ YES ❑ NO	❑ 1 ❑ 2 ❑ 3 ❑ 4 ❑ 5	❑ YES ❑ NO	❑ YES ❑ NO	❑ YES ❑ NO
Explain your audience response rating and share any additional feedback:						
Engineering for Kids	❑	❑ YES ❑ NO	❑ 1 ❑ 2 ❑ 3 ❑ 4 ❑ 5	❑ YES ❑ NO	❑ YES ❑ NO	❑ YES ❑ NO
Explain your audience response rating and share any additional feedback:						

	DID NOT HOST	Was the program appropriate for the SLC/library?	Rate the audience response (1=hated it, 5=loved it)	Did this program create buzz or interest in your community?	Would you host this program again?	Did the program align with SLC themes?
Airplanes: Aerospace Engineering	❑	❑ YES ❑ NO	❑ 1 ❑ 2 ❑ 3 ❑ 4 ❑ 5	❑ YES ❑ NO	❑ YES ❑ NO	❑ YES ❑ NO
Explain your audience response rating and share any additional feedback:						
LEGO WeDo Airplane Rescue	❑	❑ YES ❑ NO	❑ 1 ❑ 2 ❑ 3 ❑ 4 ❑ 5	❑ YES ❑ NO	❑ YES ❑ NO	❑ YES ❑ NO
Explain your audience response rating and share any additional feedback:						
FrankenToyMobile	❑	❑ YES ❑ NO	❑ 1 ❑ 2 ❑ 3 ❑ 4 ❑ 5	❑ YES ❑ NO	❑ YES ❑ NO	❑ YES ❑ NO
Explain your audience response rating and share any additional feedback:						

	DID NOT HOST	Was the program appropriate for the SLC/library?	Rate the audience response (1=hated it, 5=loved it)	Did this program create buzz or interest in your community?	Would you host this program again?	Did the program align with SLC themes?
High Touch High Tech Trains, Planes and Automobiles	❑	❑ YES ❑ NO	❑ 1 ❑ 2 ❑ 3 ❑ 4 ❑ 5	❑ YES ❑ NO	❑ YES ❑ NO	❑ YES ❑ NO
Explain your audience response rating and share any additional feedback:						
Jabberwocky Marionettes Travel: A Puppet Show	❑	❑ YES ❑ NO	❑ 1 ❑ 2 ❑ 3 ❑ 4 ❑ 5	❑ YES ❑ NO	❑ YES ❑ NO	❑ YES ❑ NO
Explain your audience response rating and share any additional feedback:						
James Coffey Let's Go Travelin'	❑	❑ YES ❑ NO	❑ 1 ❑ 2 ❑ 3 ❑ 4 ❑ 5	❑ YES ❑ NO	❑ YES ❑ NO	❑ YES ❑ NO
Explain your audience response rating and share any additional feedback:						

	DID NOT HOST	Was the program appropriate for the SLC/library?	Rate the audience response (1=hated it, 5=loved it)	Did this program create buzz or interest in your community?	Would you host this program again?	Did the program align with SLC themes?
Mad Science: Going Places!	❑	❑ YES ❑ NO	❑ 1 ❑ 2 ❑ 3 ❑ 4 ❑ 5	❑ YES ❑ NO	❑ YES ❑ NO	❑ YES ❑ NO
Explain your audience response rating and share any additional feedback:						
The Magic Boat Traveling Show Let's Fly! A History of Air Travel with The Magic Boat	❑	❑ YES ❑ NO	❑ 1 ❑ 2 ❑ 3 ❑ 4 ❑ 5	❑ YES ❑ NO	❑ YES ❑ NO	❑ YES ❑ NO
Explain your audience response rating and share any additional feedback:						
Rick Kelley Travel the World through Music	❑	❑ YES ❑ NO	❑ 1 ❑ 2 ❑ 3 ❑ 4 ❑ 5	❑ YES ❑ NO	❑ YES ❑ NO	❑ YES ❑ NO
Explain your audience response rating and share any additional feedback:						

	DID NOT HOST	Was the program appropriate for the SLC/library?	Rate the audience response (1=hated it, 5=loved it)	Did this program create buzz or interest in your community?	Would you host this program again?	Did the program align with SLC themes?
ScribbleMonster Shake and Groove on the Move! Transportation of Chicago	❏	❏ YES ❏ NO	❏ 1 ❏ 2 ❏ 3 ❏ 4 ❏ 5	❏ YES ❏ NO	❏ YES ❏ NO	❏ YES ❏ NO
Explain your audience response rating and share any additional feedback:						
Slide, Glide and Ride with the Science Alliance	❏	❏ YES ❏ NO	❏ 1 ❏ 2 ❏ 3 ❏ 4 ❏ 5	❏ YES ❏ NO	❏ YES ❏ NO	❏ YES ❏ NO
Explain your audience response rating and share any additional feedback:						
Tiffany Lawson Dance Moving Through Chicago	❏	❏ YES ❏ NO	❏ 1 ❏ 2 ❏ 3 ❏ 4 ❏ 5	❏ YES ❏ NO	❏ YES ❏ NO	❏ YES ❏ NO
Explain your audience response rating and share any additional feedback:						

	DID NOT HOST	Was the program appropriate for the SLC/library?	Rate the audience response (1=hated it, 5=loved it)	Did this program create buzz or interest in your community?	Would you host this program again?	Did the program align with SLC themes?
West Town Bikes Readers and Riders	❏	❏ YES ❏ NO	❏ 1 ❏ 2 ❏ 3 ❏ 4 ❏ 5	❏ YES ❏ NO	❏ YES ❏ NO	❏ YES ❏ NO

Explain your audience response rating and share any additional feedback:

	DID NOT HOST	Was the program appropriate for the SLC/library?	Rate the audience response (1=hated it, 5=loved it)	Did this program create buzz or interest in your community?	Would you host this program again?	Did the program align with SLC themes?
Fold and Fly with Josh Koppel	❏	❏ YES ❏ NO	❏ 1 ❏ 2 ❏ 3 ❏ 4 ❏ 5	❏ YES ❏ NO	❏ YES ❏ NO	❏ YES ❏ NO

Explain your audience response rating and share any additional feedback:

	DID NOT HOST	Was the program appropriate for the SLC/library?	Rate the audience response (1=hated it, 5=loved it)	Did this program create buzz or interest in your community?	Would you host this program again?	Did the program align with SLC themes?
A Traveling Trilogy with Puppets with Marilyn Price	❏	❏ YES ❏ NO	❏ 1 ❏ 2 ❏ 3 ❏ 4 ❏ 5	❏ YES ❏ NO	❏ YES ❏ NO	❏ YES ❏ NO

Explain your audience response rating and share any additional feedback:

	DID NOT HOST	Was the program appropriate for the SLC/library?	Rate the audience response (1=hated it, 5=loved it)	Did this program create buzz or interest in your community?	Would you host this program again?	Did the program align with SLC themes?
Project Syncere	❑	❑ YES ❑ NO	❑ 1 ❑ 2 ❑ 3 ❑ 4 ❑ 5	❑ YES ❑ NO	❑ YES ❑ NO	❑ YES ❑ NO
Explain your audience response rating and share any additional feedback:						

SELF-REFLECTION

Do a self-check on your comfort level with the following components of the program (this feedback will be used to consider future training, preparation, and additional needs based on where staff feel they need help).

	Strongly Disagree	Disagree	Agree	Strongly Agree
I am comfortable talking about the SLC to patrons.	❑	❑	❑	❑
I am comfortable facilitating STEAM programs.	❑	❑	❑	❑
I am comfortable creating or developing STEAM programs.	❑	❑	❑	❑
I feel comfortable incorporating Every Child Ready to Read 2 components into the SLC.	❑	❑	❑	❑
I am comfortable managing teen volunteers.	❑	❑	❑	❑
I am comfortable training teen volunteers.	❑	❑	❑	❑

	Strongly Disagree	Disagree	Agree	Strongly Agree
I am comfortable facilitating the SLC with 0–5 year-olds and their parents.	❑	❑	❑	❑
I am comfortable facilitating the SLC with school-age children.	❑	❑	❑	❑
I am comfortable facilitating the SLC with tweens.	❑	❑	❑	❑
I serve as an ambassador of the SLC to my branch and help the staff in my branch understand the SLC.	❑	❑	❑	❑
I am comfortable going on school visits.	❑	❑	❑	❑
I feel supported by my branch manager to run the SLC at my branch.	❑	❑	❑	❑

OUTCOMES AND DATA

1. Did you meet your personal branch goals for 2016? Please share what you did to reach these goals and why (or why not) you think it worked?

2. Looking at your 2016 goals and over this entire evaluation, brainstorm goals for your branch for 2017.

3. If we are able to make changes, are there any changes you'd like to see in Cityspan?

4. Are you comfortable with recording stats for walk-in participants vs. outreach participants?

5. Is there anything else we should know about the SLC at your branch and your experiences this summer?

APPENDIX C

- - - - - - - - - -

SAMPLE LIBRARIAN
POST-TRAINING EVALUATION

CHICAGO PUBLIC LIBRARY CHILDREN'S SERVICES
ScienceConnections
Training Evaluation
Making and Mechanics for School-Aged Children
Children's Library Staff Training

Please Circle One: **CPL Librarian**   **CPL Associate Branch Manager**   **Other CPL Staff**

Workshop Objectives:

(1) Participants will build on their knowledge of the importance of STEM and maker programs in the library

(2) Participants will learn how to incorporate STEM into school-aged programming at Chicago Public Library.

(3) Participants will learn how to utilize programming kit materials for use in their STEM programming with school-aged children and families.

Please circle the number that most accurately describes your opinion.

Before the workshop, what was your skills and knowledge base? *(1 is low and 5 is high)*

1. My knowledge of the importance of STEM and maker programs in the library.

1   2   3   4   5

2. My knowledge/skills to incorporate STEM into school-aged programming at CPL.

    1   2   3   4   5

3. My knowledge of how to lead a kit-based STEAM program with children.

    1   2   3   4   5

After the workshop, what is your skills and knowledge base? *(1 is low and 5 is high)*

1. My knowledge of the importance of STEM and maker programs in the library.

    1   2   3   4   5

2. My knowledge/skills to incorporate STEM into school-aged programming at CPL.

    1   2   3   4   5

3. My knowledge of how to lead a kit-based STEAM program with children.

    1   2   3   4   5

How likely are you to request a programming kit from Children's Services?
(1 is not very likely and 5 is very likely)

    1   2   3   4   5

How likely are you to attend another optional training on how to use a specific set of programming kits?
(1 is not very likely and 5 is very likely)

    1   2   3   4   5

Please answer the questions below. Describe way(s) in which your knowledge, attitude, skills, and behavior have been or will be changed by something you learned in this workshop.

Attitude: Because of this training, I have changed my way of thinking about . . .

Skills: I have the following new skill(s) to use on the job:

Behavior: I will implement the following new behavior upon returning to my job:

Comments on workshop presenter or content:

APPENDIX D

- - - - - - - - - -

RECOMMENDED RESOURCES

SUMMER SLIDE

"Effects of a Voluntary Summer Reading Intervention on Reading Achievement: Results from a Randomized Field Trial," by James S. Kim (*Educational Evaluation and Policy Analysis*, 2006)

"Lasting Consequences of the Summer Learning Gap," by Karl L. Alexander, Doris R. Entwisle, and Linda Steffel Olson (*American Sociological Review*, 2007)

"Summer Starts in September: A Comprehensive Planning Guide for Summer Learning Programs," https://summerlearning.site-ym.com/

TWENTY-FIRST-CENTURY LEARNING SKILLS

Active Learning
www.fontichiaro.com/activelearning/

"Museums, Libraries, and 21st Century Skills," Institute of Museum and Library Services, https://www.imls.gov/issues/national-initiatives/museums-libraries-and-21st-century-skills

Remake Learning
http://remakelearning.org/

STEAM

Crazy for Science with Carmelo the Science Fellow, by Carmelo Piazza and James Buckley (POW! 2015)

Institute for Inquiry
https://www.exploratorium.edu/education/ifi/inquiry

Iridescent Curiosity Machine
https://www.curiositymachine.org/

James Dyson Foundation Challenge Cards
www.jamesdysonfoundation.com/resource-category/challenges/

Museum of Science and Industry Summer Brain Games
www.msichicago.org/experiment/summer-brain-games/

Next Generation Science Standards
www.nextgenscience.org/

101 Great Science Experiments, by Neil Ardley (Dorling Kindersley, 2014)

PBS Design Squad
http://pbskids.org/designsquad/

"Public Libraries as Places for STEM Learning: An Exploratory Interview Study with Eight Librarians," by John Y. Baek (National Center for Interactive Learning Education, 2013)

STEM Lesson Essentials, Grades 3–8: Integrating Science, Technology, Engineering, and Mathematics, by Jo Anne Vasquez, Michael Comer, and Cary Sneider (Heinemann, 2013)

Teacher Geek
https://teachergeek.com/

Try This! 50 Fun Experiments for the Mad Scientist in You, by Karen Romano Young (National Geographic, 2014)

PLAY

"The Elements of Play: Toward a Philosophy and Definition of Play," by Scott G. Eberle (*Journal of Play,* 2014)

Lego Foundation Play Research
www.legofoundation.com/nl-nl/research-and-learning/foundation-research

The Power of Play: Designing Early Learning Spaces, by Dorothy Stolz (American Library Association, 2015)

FAMILY ENGAGEMENT

"Family Engagement in Anywhere, Anytime Learning," by M. Elena Lopez and Margaret Caspe (Harvard Family Research Project, 2014)

Meaningful Differences in the Everyday Experience of Young American Children, by Todd R. Risley and Louis Bloom (Paul H. Brookes, 1995)

"The Simple Human Interactions That Make Learning Possible" (Pittsburgh's HIVE Project and the Fred Rogers Institute)

APPENDIX E

- - - - - - - - - -

STORE AND VENDOR LIST

American Science and Surplus
sciplus.com

Arbor Scientific
arborsci.com

Carolina Biological Supply
carolina.com

Classroom Direct
classroomdirect.com

Delta Education
deltaeducation.com

Demco
demco.com

Dick Blick Art Materials
dickblick.com

Discount School Supply
discountschoolsupply.com

Dremel
3dprinter.dremel.com

Educational Innovations
teachersource.com

Edvotek, The Biotechnology Education Company
edvotek.com

Fat Brain Toys
fatbraintoys.com

Flinn Scientific
flinnsci.com

Grainger Industrial Supply Co.
grainger.com

Lakeshore Learning
lakeshorelearning.com

Learning Resources
learningresources.com

McMaster-Carr Supply Co.
mcmaster.com

Nasco
enasco.com

Nature Watch
nature-watch.com

Pitsco Education
pitsco.com

S&S
ssww.com

ULINE
uline.com

Vernier
Vernier.com

Ward's Science
wardsci.com

Webstaurant Store
webstaurantstore.com

Woodworks Ltd
craftparts.com

BIBLIOGRAPHY

Alexander, Karl L., Doris R. Entwisle, and Linda Steffel Olson. 2007. "Lasting Consequences of the Summer Learning Gap." *American Sociological Review* 72 (2): 167–80.

American Library Association. 1996–2015. "About Día." http://dia.ala.org/content/about-d%C3%ADa.

Anderson, Richard C., Paul T. Wilson, and Linda G. Fielding. 1988. "Growth in Reading and How Children Spend Their Time Outside of School." *Reading Research Quarterly* 23 (3): 285–303.

Armstrong, Thomas. 2012. "Multiple Intelligences." www.institute4learning.com/multiple_intelligences.php.

Baek, John Y. 2013. "Public Libraries as Places for STEM Learning: An Exploratory Interview Study with Eight Librarians." Boulder, CO: National Center for Interactive Learning Education/Research Report. www.nc4il.org/images/papers/Baek_Public%20Libraries%20as%20Places%20for%20STEM%20Learning.pdf.

Book Industry Study Group. 2016. "BISAC Subject Codes." http://bisg.org/page/BISACSubjectCodes.

Coffman, Julia. 1999. "Learning from Logic Models: An Example of a Family/School Partnership Program." Harvard Family Research Project. www.hfrp.org/publications-resources/publications-series/reaching-results/learning-from-logic-models-an-example-of-a-family-school-partnership-program.

Common Core State Standards Initiative. 2016. "About the Standards." www.corestandards.org/about-the-standards/.

Costa, Arthur L., and Bena Kallick. 2008. "Learning Through Reflection." In *Learning and Leading with Habits of Mind,* edited by Arthur L. Costa and Bena Kallick. Alexandria, VA: Association for Supervision and Curriculum Assessment. www.ascd.org/publications/books/108008/chapters/Learning-Through-Reflection.aspx.

Cunningham, Anne E., and Keith E. Stanovich. 1998. "What Reading Does for the Mind." *American Educator,* Spring/Summer 1998: 8–15.

Duke, Nell K. 2000. "For the Rich It's Richer: Print Experiences and Environments Offered to Children in Very Low- and Very High-Socioeconomic Status First-Grade Classrooms." *American Educational Research Journal* 37 (2): 441–78. www.jstor.org/stable/1163530.

Gardner, Howard. 2013. "'Multiple Intelligences' Are Not 'Learning Styles.'" *The Washington Post,* October 16. https://www.washingtonpost.com/news/answer-sheet/wp/2013/10/16/ howard-gardner-multiple-intelligences-are-not-learning-styles/?utm_term= .41e06fc0f953.

Gelb, Michael J., and Tony Buzan. 1994. *Lessons from the Art of Juggling.* New York: Crown Trade Paperbacks.

Henderson, Anne T., and Karen L. Mapp. 2002. *A New Wave of Evidence: The Impact of School, Family and Community Connections on Student Achievement.* Austin, TX: Southwest Educational Development Laboratory.

Institute of Museum and Library Services. 2009. *Museums, Libraries and 21st Century Skills.* Washington, DC.

Jolly, Anne. 2014. "STEM vs. STEAM: Do the Arts Belong?" *Education Week,* November 18. www.edweek.org/tm/articles/2014/11/18/ctq-jolly-stem-vs-steam.html.

Kim, James S. 2008. *How to Make Summer Reading Effective.* Baltimore, MD: Johns Hopkins University, National Center for Summer Learning.

McCawley, Paul F. 2001. "The Logic Model for Program Planning and Evaluation." Idaho: University of Idaho Extension.

Nagaoka, Jenny, Camille A. Farrington, Stacy B. Ehrlich, and Ryan B. Heath. 2015. *Foundations for Young Adult Success: A Theoretical Framework.* Chicago: University of Chicago, Urban Education Institute.

National Catholic Educational Association. 2016. "10 Characteristics of a STREAM School." www.ncea.org/NCEA/Learn/Resource/Academic_Excellence/STREAM_Science_ Technology_Religion_Engineering_Arts_Math_/10_Characteristics_of_a_STREAM_ School.aspx?WebsiteKey=60819b28–9432–4c46-a76a-a2e20ac11cfd.

National Research Council. 2009. *Learning Science in Informal Environments: People, Places and Pursuits.* Washington, DC: National Academies. doi:10.17226/12190.

National Research Council. 2011. *A Framework for K–12 Science Education.* Washington, DC: National Academies.

National Science Foundation. 2012a. "Graduate Research Fellowship Program." https://www.nsf.gov/pubs/2012/nsf12599/nsf12599.htm#appendix.

National Science Foundation. 2012b. *NSF at a Glance.* Washington, DC: National Science Foundation.

National Summer Learning Association. 2009a. "Income Affects How Kids Use Technology and Access Knowledge." Baltimore, MD: National Summer Learning Association. http://summerlearning.org/wp-content/uploads/2016/06/IncomeAffectsHowKids UseTechnologyAndAccessKnowledge.pdf.

National Summer Learning Association. 2009b. "More Than a Hunch: Kids Lose Learning Skills over the Summer Months." Baltimore, MD: National Summer Learning Association. http://summerlearning.org/wp-content/uploads/2016/06/MoreThanAHunch KidsLoseLearningSkillsOverTheSummerMonths.pdf.

National Summer Learning Association. 2009c. "Summer Can Set Kids on Right—or Wrong—Course." Baltimore, MD: National Summer Learning Association. http://summerlearning.org/wp-content/uploads/2016/06/SummerCanSetKids OnTheRightOrWrongCourse.pdf.

National Summer Learning Association. September 2013. "Summer Starts in September: A Comprehensive Planning Guide for Summer Learning Programs." https://summerlearning.site-ym.com/.

Next Generation Science Standards. 2013a. "Appendix F—Science and Engineering Practices in the NGSS." www.nextgenscience.org/sites/default/files/Appendix%20F%20%20 Science%20and%20Engineering%20Practices%20in%20the%20NGSS%20-%20FINAL%20 060513.pdf.

Next Generation Science Standards. 2013b. "Appendix G—Crosscutting Concepts." www.nextgenscience.org/sites/default/files/Appendix%20G%20-%20Crosscutting %20Concepts%20FINAL%20edited%204.10.13.pdf.

Razzouk, Rim, and Valerie Shute. 2012. "What Is Design Thinking and Why Is It Important?" *Review of Educational Research* 82 (3): 330–48. doi: 10.3102/0034654312457429.

Roman, Susan, Deborah T. Carran, and Carole D. Fiore. 2010. *The Dominican Study: Public Library Summer Reading Programs Close the Reading Gap.* River Forest, IL: Dominican University Graduate School of Library & Information Science.

Sparks, Sarah D. 2012. "New Literacy Research Infuses Common Core." *Education Week* 32 (12): s6,s8,s9. www.edweek.org/ew/articles/2012/11/14/12cc-research.h32.html.

STEAM Education. 2016. "Georgette Yakman and the Development of STEAM Education." https://steamedu.com/about-us/.

STREM HQ. 2016. "Our Vision for Science, Technology, Robotics, Engineering, and Multi-Media." www.stremhq.com/.

W.K. Kellogg Foundation. 2004. *Logic Model Development Guide.* Battle Creek, MI: W.K. Kellogg Foundation.

Wunar, Bryan, and Nicole Kowrach. 2015. "Redefining the Role of Museums in Science Education." In *New Perspectives in Science Education,* edited by Pixel, 224–27. 4th edition. Florence, Italy: Libraria Universitaria.

ABOUT THE AUTHORS

Elizabeth M. McChesney holds BA and MLIS degrees from the University of Wisconsin at Madison, where her graduate work specialized in service to children. She has worked in various capacities of children's librarianship for twenty-eight years, all at the Chicago Public Library, where she is currently the director of System Wide Children's Services. In 2012, along with her team of children's librarians, she led the transformation of Chicago Public Library's summer offerings into a STEAM & Literacy Summer Learning Challenge which the system's children's librarians conduct each summer. This achievement earned her a 2014 *Library Journal's* Movers & Shakers award, the 2015 Founder's Award for Excellence from the National Summer Learning Association, and the 2016 John Cotton Dana Award. McChesney has written and spoken extensively about library service to children, performed as a professional storyteller, and has taught at the Graduate School of Library and Information Studies at Dominican University in River Forest, Illinois.

Bryan W. Wunar has worked in science education for the past twenty-four years. His work and research have focused on bridging informal and formal science education in order to extend learning beyond the classroom. He is currently the director of community initiatives in the Center for the Advancement of Science Education at the Museum of Science and Industry in Chicago. In this role, he leads the museum's strategic efforts to engage youth, families, and communities in science learning experiences. He has served as the associate vice president for education and programs at Chicago's Adler Planetarium, senior director of the Science and Mathematics Curriculum Program at the Education Development Center, and as the director of the Alliance for Community Education at Loyola University in Chicago. Wunar holds a BS degree in biology, an MA degree in curriculum and instruction, and has completed all the coursework toward a PhD in educational psychology, all from Loyola University in Chicago.

INDEX

A
HEART
OF
WINTER

AYAKO MIURA

TRANSLATED BY MARK CAPRIO AND CLYDE MONEYHUN

AN OMF BOOK

© JAPANESE EDITION : MRS AYAKO MIURA

© ENGLISH EDITION : Mark Caprio and Clyde Moneyhun
Published by Overseas Missionary Fellowship (IHQ) Ltd.,
2 Cluny Road, Singapore 1025, Republic of Singapore

OMF BOOKS is a ministry of the Overseas Missionary Fellowship
(formerly China Inland Mission). OMF is an interdenominational
team from East and West called by God for the speedy
evangelization of East Asia. The Fellowship has more than one
thousand missionaries involved in evangelism and church
planting in urban and rural areas, and in a variety of specialist
ministries.

First published 1991

OMF BOOKS are distributed by
OMF, 10 West Dry Creek Circle, Littleton, Co 80122, USA;
OMF, Belmont, The Vine, Sevenoaks, Kent, TN13, 3TZ, UK
OMF, PO Box 849, Epping, NSW 2121, Australia;
OMF, 1058 Avenue Road, Toronto, Ontario M5N 2C6, Canada
OMF, PO Box 10159 Auckland, New Zealand
OMF, PO Box 41, Kenilworth 7745, South Africa
and other OMF offices.

ISBN 981-3009-36-5

Cover photograph by Kevin Morris
Printed in Singapore

CONTENTS

TRANSLATORS' INTRODUCTION

MIURA AYAKO is one of the most popular writers in Japan today. She has been a best-selling author since the publication in 1965 of her first novel, *Hyoten (The Freezing Point)*, which won a prestigious prize for amateur writers from the Asahi Shinbun newspaper company. Another novel, *Shiokari Toge (Shiokari Pass*, OMF, 1974; Tuttle, 1987), was made into a well-received movie.

Miura is one of three widely read Christian novelists in Japan; the others are Sono Ayako and the internationally respected Endo Shusaku. On one level, Christianity is a philosophical given of Miura Ayako's art, central to the psychology and motivation of her characters and crucial to the meaning of the narrative. On a deeper level, Christianity is the fountain of her inspiration to write, the source of her need to bear witness to the truth of the lives she portrays.

A Heart of Winter examines how a person can go from the depths of sin, from beginnings that would seem to preclude faith in God or even simple goodness, to belief in Christ as a merciful Savior. Its protagonist goes from living a life that is the direct antithesis of the example of Christ, through a shattering rebirth, to the "conviction," as Simone Weil says in her own *Spiritual Autobiography*, that "when one hungers for bread, one does not receive stones." It has the tone, common to such works, of awe about the miracle of belief, astonishment at the thought that there was a time when there was no belief. Compare what Kiyomi says on the very first page of her profession of faith to this passage from Thomas Merton's autobiography *The Seven Storey Mountain* (Harcourt Brace Jovanovich, 1976, p. 37):

"I did not even know who Christ was, that He was God. . . . I thought churches were simply places where people got together and sang a few hymns. And yet now I tell you, you who are now what I once was, unbelievers, it is . . . the Christ living in our midst . . . it is He alone who holds our world together, and keeps us all from being poured headlong and immediately into the pit of our eternal destruction."

An important theme in *A Heart of Winter* is a distinctly Christian rather than Japanese idea: redemption through suffering, enlightenment through suffering and even sin itself. In Buddhism, suffering is a result of attachment to the illusion of the material world. The Four Noble Truths tell us that suffering can be avoided. Christianity asserts that suffering can be a principle means to grace. Miura has known suffering first-hand, through the cruel illnesses and deaths of loved ones and through her own long bout with tuberculosis.

Miura is also familiar with the pain of sin. In her "Author's Note" to the Japanese edition she talks about meeting people whose mothers were prostitutes or who were molested by their own fathers. Their "painful confessions," she says, "smoldered" inside her and helped give birth to the novel.

People deeply scarred and twisted by sin, Miura

believes, are the people who provide the best proof of God's love. "Even if our pain or our hatred is deep-rooted," she says, "God will save us. If we had to wait until we were perfect before being saved, then no one would ever find God." This simple idea — the way ordinary, imperfect, and even sinful people discover the miracle of God's love — permeates and gives meaning to all of Miura's fiction.

Another important theme is the way in which people can pass the gift of God's love on to others. *A Heart of Winter* provides several instances of characters who, through their example and their testament, help lead Kiyomi to Christ, among them the saintly Aunt Saori, Akira, and the Reverend to whom her profession of faith is addressed. The character of Akira seems to be a composite of two real people in Miura's life: Maekawa Tadashi, who introduced her to the world of novels, and her husband Miura Mitsuyo, who first read to her from the Bible during one of her prolonged illnesses. *A Heart of Winter* may be seen as an act of homage to all the people who helped Miura find her way to the Savior.

A word about the translation. One of the first things we talked about when we began work on *A Heart of Winter* was the decision to avoid colloquialisms for the most part. Nothing dates a translation or renders it comical more effectively than a sentence like, "Hey, uncle, shake a leg there or this fellow will fly the coop." We also tried to ignore most of the silly or inaccurate "standard translations" of Japanese words and phrases that plague Japanese-English dictionaries, such as "devil's tongue aspic" for *konyaku* and "what a pity" for *kawaisoo*. We chose to leave two small groups of words in transliterated Japanese: words so familiar to English speakers that they appear in some English dictionaries (*kimono, sushi, futon*), and those ubiquitous words used in Japanese for both family members and others — *oba-san* for both real aunts and middle-aged women in general, *oku-san* for both wives and any female neighbors — words whose meanings we hope are clear in context. Except for the author's name on the cover and title page, names are written according to Japanese convention, family name followed by given name.

Many thanks to our editors at Overseas Missionary Fellowship, particularly Fay Goddard, whose help was indispensable.

1 PROFESSION OF FAITH

DEAR REVEREND,

Today, after the service, you stopped me just as I was about to leave the church. You said, "Write out a profession of your faith in about three pages and give it to me." Since you're a minister, I suppose, you said it just that way — as if it were the easiest thing in the world to do.

But can you imagine what it sounded like to me? How can a person say how she came to believe in Jesus Christ "in about three pages"? Maybe other people you've asked can do it, but I can't.

It's not so much that I can't do what you want, but rather that I feel I have to do more, to explain to you, before God and before everyone, the complete life of my soul up to now. I feel I have to do it because there was a time, as you know, when I didn't believe in the existence of my Savior, a time that seems impossible to me now, now that His presence has become indispensable to me.

Reading this, you may think I'm just long-winded, and you may be right. Lately, I've become a little too talkative — but you have to understand, Reverend, that for me this is something to rejoice over, something to be proud of. Ever since I was five or six years old, I've been withdrawn, unfeeling, closed in on myself in a separate world of silence. For years, I barely spoke to anyone. You can imagine the trouble I caused my mother and my teachers. But now I'm overflowing with things to tell. After all that time, just having something to say is hard for me to believe. So please be patient with me.

Reverend, have you ever walked alone at night on a quiet path through a meadow, the moon shining so bright it makes the grass glisten as if it's wet? You know the meadow near my house, don't you? That's where I go. When I walk there, the inside of my soul dampens, and unexpectedly a gentle, yielding feeling comes over me. It's so quiet that I can hear my footsteps in the soft soil. I can feel the moonlight bathing my face, and I experience a kind of reverence for its source.

But then I suddenly remember who I really am, and standing there in the clear moonlight, I can't help being afraid. Memories of my childhood, no matter how I try to shut them out, remain locked inside. Without warning the terrible memories come rushing into my head. I clench my teeth, telling myself that I'll never bring them back again. But as I stand on that damp, moonlit path, they reappear in my mind.

Next month, in July, I'll be twenty-three years old. Reverend, when you hear my name, Hamano Kiyomi, what do you think? Do you know what comes to my mind? Nothing but shame. Every time I hear that name, I can only hate the people who gave it to me. The two Chinese characters that make up "Kiyomi" — "purity" and "beauty" — are supposed to be lucky. But I'd never use the characters that mean "purity" and "beauty" for my child. If I were beautiful, which I'm not, having the character for "beauty" in my name would still be a burden, and if I were really ugly, the shame would be worse.

Even so, if it were only the character for "beauty," it wouldn't be so bad. Having the character for "purity" in my name is more dreadful. I think, Reverend, if you read my life story, you'll come to agree with me.

I doubt that my parents have ever thought about how I would feel about my name. How could they, who lived a life without a bond that was either beautiful or pure, ever appreciate the shame I feel at having to live with a name that means beauty and purity, when nothing could be further from the truth?

I wrote "parents" here. Actually I was brought up without ever knowing my father's face. I was told he was dead. When I was growing up, there was just my mother and me. We lived in the house my father left us, a little box with an entrance hall — a kitchen, a toilet, and three rooms of six, eight, and ten *tatami* mats.

My mother will be forty-three this year. I'm sure you've met her. Because of her fair complexion and good figure, some might think she's beautiful. People remark on her bright, sparkling eyes, though they're usually a little bloodshot. People have also told me how she's always laughing merrily and what a fun person she is.

I can't say that I've seen much of that side of her. Ever since I was four or five years old, in my heart I knew that my mother was different from other mothers. Sometimes men would come to visit my mother. I remember one was tall and pale, another who was red-faced and had a repulsively loud voice. Altogether there were five or six of them, but they always came one at a time. When they came, my mother would say to me, "Kiyomi, go and play outside until I call you. There's a good little girl." Then she'd put a one-hundred-yen bill in my hands.

Whenever a man was coming, my mother was transformed. She would wake up early, throw open the sliding doors to the little porch, and run the vacuum cleaner through the house. My mother is the kind of person who leaves the bed linens out airing all day. Only on those special days did she do housework energetically, as if she were a different person.

Even my mother's clothes were different on those days. Mother liked to wear a dress with large designs on it, and she would spend a long time in front of the mirror putting on her make-up.

Men would come in the morning as well as the afternoon. For some reason they never came at night. As the men entered the house, I would have to leave with my hundred-yen bill in my hand.

Of course, children usually like to play outside from morning to night. Yet if you're forbidden to return home until a certain time, being outside is not much fun any more. The games you like the most — playing hide-and-seek, playing in the sand — become lonely. Sometimes you get thirsty and want to go home for a drink of water, or for some reason your stomach begins to hurt.

Because I was bribed like this with a hundred-yen bill and shut out of my own house, I think I came to feel, even as a child, the bitter feelings of loneliness and abandonment and despair that usually come only to adults. Even if I had a stomachache, I couldn't run home. I couldn't even go home to use the bathroom. Instead, I would hop around, biting my lip to help me bear the pain. When I couldn't stand it any longer, I would run to the house next door, almost in tears, and cry out, "*Oba-san*, let me use your bathroom!"

She would say, "Not again? You poor thing!" She would let me in, her brows knit in kindly concern. She had a son and a daughter, but they had both left home to go to college.

This neighbor lady was always kind to me, but the first time I asked to use her toilet she said, confused, "Why don't you use the toilet in your own house?"

"The door to my house is locked and my mother is out," I lied. It was a very shameful lie.

It didn't take long for the neighbor to figure things out, though. After a while, perhaps thinking that a child couldn't really understand the situation, she started asking in a soft voice, "Well then, who's visiting today?" She never did seem to understand how much that question hurt.

2   THE THOUSAND YEN

I THINK IT was when I was five, at the beginning of June. I remember the month because that's when the Asahikawa festival is held, and colorful painted paper umbrellas were hung up high in front of my house.

Even on the day of the festival, my mother sent me out of the house. The sky was clear blue, and the afternoon glowed with warmth. I was squatting down not far from our house, drawing a picture of a girl in the dirt. The girl I always drew had a ribbon in her hair and was holding hands with her mother. All the children in the neighborhood were being taken to the festival by their parents. I yearned to see the show tent, the circus, and all the booths set up by the shops.

But it was one of those times when my mother had a man visiting her. So I silently drew pictures of girls in the dirt, erased them, drew them again, erased them again.

All of a sudden someone was standing behind me. I looked up to see an elegant lady smiling down at me and saying, "You're Kiyomi, aren't you?" She bent down and put her hand on my shoulder. She was a few years older than my mother, but with fine features and a slender waist. I was surprised; a lady I didn't know, had never even seen before, knew my name.

"Where is your mother?" she asked in a kind voice.

"She's not home," I lied, as my mother had instructed me. Before sending me from the house, she would always say, "Remember, if anyone comes, just tell them I'm not home." Sometimes, though, the visitor's bicycle or car was in front of the house, and the lie wasn't a very good one.

"Oh, she's not home?" the lady said, taking my hand. "Well, why don't you come with me for a while?"

I didn't hesitate to go with her. I didn't yet know that it wasn't safe to go off with a stranger. And, anyway, this lady was wearing a kimono that even a child could tell was of very fine quality. As I recall, it was a patternless reddish-brown, or it might have had a very small pattern. The lady was overflowing with warmth, someone I would never have thought not to trust. "Where are you from, *Oba-san*?" I asked.

She paused and said, "I'm from Sapporo."

I had no idea where in the world Sapporo was.

"*Oba-san*, how did you know my name was Kiyomi?" I asked. I don't remember what she said. All I know was that she came all the way to the meadow near my house, hugged me tightly, and shed streams of tears. I don't even remember now what we talked about or for how long. I remember only the hymn she sang for me. It was "Child's Hymn Number Fifteen," which I know so well now from singing it in church.

"Now, Kiyomi, I'm going to teach you a song. You won't forget it, will you?" the kind lady said.

"I won't forget it," I promised.

I liked the lady. It was a feeling that was different from what I felt toward my mother. It wasn't that my mother was completely cold toward me. Sometimes she held me so close that it was hard for me to breathe, pressed her cheek to mine, and said things like, "Kiyomi is my girl, my cute little girl." Sometimes she made me a hamburger or a sweet rice ball or one of my other favorite foods. Yet, at other times, my mother scolded me with a frightening, scowling face. The worst thing, though, was when a male visitor came and she didn't give me a second thought. The weather on these days wasn't always sunny and fine. Some days it rained, and other days it even snowed. On some days, it was so cold that my eyelashes became frosty. On those days I would go to a friend's house and play for hours.

So it was that in a clear voice the elegant lady sang:

The good Lord up in Heaven above
Gives to all His gentle love.
On the baby sparrow in the eaves,
On the smallest ones, the least of these
He bestows His mercy.

She sang this song over and over again. "I didn't bring you anything; so this song will have to be my present to you," she said.

After she told me this, I wanted to sing the song, and the lady listened happily. Then she took a one-thousand-yen bill from her handkerchief and wrapped it in tissue paper.

"Here's some money for the festival," she said, putting it in my hand.

My face must have beamed with happiness. A thousand yen! I had never received so much money before from anyone. The one time one of my mother's visitors gave me a thousand-yen bill my mother snatched it from my hand, insisting impatiently, "Giving a thousand yen to a child is a waste of money!"

Then the lady left, looking back at me again and again as she walked away. I took the thousand yen from the tissue paper and scampered home, waving the bill in the air. On the way, I ran into Tsujiko, who was returning from the festival.

"Look!" I said, waving the bill in her face.

"Where did you find that?" she asked crossly. Tsujiko was about two years older than I.

"I didn't find it. A lady gave it to me."

"What? A stranger gave you a thousand yen?" She didn't believe me for a minute. "You stole it from a store," she accused. Then she led me by the hand back to my house and yelled out to my mother, "*Oba-san*, Kiyomi took a thousand yen from a store."

As her visitor had already left, my mother immediately ran out from the entrance hall, and as soon as she saw the thousand-yen bill in my hand, she fell into a blind rage and struck me hard on the cheek.

"I didn't steal it. A lady that I met gave it to me," I sobbed.

But my mother wouldn't listen. "A lady gave it to you?" Her face was hard. "Who?"

"I don't know."

"You're trying to tell me that a person you don't know from a place you don't know gave you a thousand yen?"

When I think about it now, it really was a little hard to believe. That was eighteen years ago, 1966, the forty-first year of the Showa era. A thousand yen wasn't something children were given. So I understand now why my mother couldn't believe what I was saying. But at the time I had no way of understanding my mother's distrust. I was so young that the idea of stealing something had never even occurred to me.

Once I found ten yen on the street, but I had immediately looked for a policeman. Holding the little brown coin tightly in my fist, I ran to the police box in the neighborhood next to mine. A young policeman patted me on the head and took the coin, smiling down at me. Then, without the slightest bit of mistrust in my mind, I trotted home.

I wonder now whatever happened to that ten yen. The policeman didn't even ask my name. Just having my head patted and being told I was a good girl was enough to make me happy. I was the kind of little girl who thought that even money found on the street should be taken to a police box; so why would I steal money now?

Nevertheless, my mother believed Tsujiko rather than me. She was furious; what if word got around that her child was a thief?

Since Tsujiko insisted that I had stolen the money from a store, my mother dragged me to a variety store near my house. In my neighborhood, there was only one place that could properly be called a store, a shop that sold such things as bread, ice cream, candy, gum, notebooks, colored paper, and pencils. With things that would capture a child's attention piled up outside, it was a place where children often went when they had money to spend.

When my mother came through the door with the thousand-yen note in her hand to apologize, the lady running the store seemed confused at first, then said quickly, "She's just a child; so don't get too angry at her." She said it in a very kind voice. "With this I can finally relax," she went on with hardly a moment's hesitation. "A customer said that he left a thousand-yen bill on the counter. Because of the festival, children have been running in and out of here all day. I couldn't remember whether or not I had picked up the money."

The lady very quickly took the money for her own. She pushed a few buttons on the cash register, *ching!* the cash register came open, and she put the thousand-yen note in the drawer.

Even now, I can't forget the sound of that cash register ringing. I hadn't been in the store once all day. I suddenly realized that adults could be dishonest, and I hated all of them.

Up until then I had looked up to all adults. I felt that nothing they ever did was wrong, and I believed everything they said. And so, without even knowing why, I would do as I was told and wait outside until my mother's visitors had gone. That was the child in me, the one who trusted adults. Why did the lady at the store take the money as if it were her own? Why didn't she say, "I didn't see this girl today." At least she could have asked, "About what time did you come?" or "What did you buy?" or "Was anyone else in the store?"

From that time on, I was known by my friends, by their parents, by the whole neighborhood, as the girl who stole a thousand yen. I was watched wherever I went.

"Apologize to the lady!" my mother screamed hysterically. But I didn't apologize. I hadn't stolen the thousand yen. I didn't care if they didn't believe me or not. I got it from the kind lady.

My mother took my face in both her hands and shook me. "You're stubborn!"

Tsujiko stared at me, and the other kids stood behind her, staring and yelling things at me.

"It's all right," the store clerk finally said. "Kiyomi, you're only a child, and you don't know whether you've done anything wrong or not. Just don't do it again, okay?" She patted me on the head. I just glared at her.

After we reached home, my mother made me sit in the shed outside our house. "You stubborn little brat," she said. "You're no child of mine! You'll stay in the shed until you say you're sorry." And when I refused to apologize, she closed the door behind her and left.

The festival day was supposed to be a day of happiness. Instead it turned into a day of misery for me. I hated Tsujiko, who had told an awful lie about me. I hated the lady at the store, and I hated my mother. I wanted to hate the kind lady who had given me the thousand yen too, but I couldn't.

I never did apologize to my mother. I outwaited her. When night fell, she let me out of the shed.

"Why won't you apologize?" she asked.

"The lady gave me the money," I repeated. But my mother wouldn't believe me.

The next day when I went outside, the children sang in unison, "Watch out! Here comes the thief!" Right in front was Tsujiko.

That was when I stopped talking. Even though I hadn't done anything bad, I felt, at the age of five, the numbing pain of being known as the girl who had done something awful. I stopped talking because nothing I said changed what people thought.

Every day was dark with hopelessness. I didn't even want to go outside. Still, when my mother had one of her visitors, she chased me from the house. Even when it rained, my mother sent me outside as if there was nothing strange about it. I suppose she thought that, just as before, I would go to a friend's house to play. She didn't realize how cruel a child's world could be. That the neighborhood children's favorite new game was tormenting me never crossed her mind. She never knew.

One rainy day, since I didn't have anywhere else to go, I went to visit the lady next door. But she wouldn't let me in. "Kiyomi, I have to go out now," she said coldly. "Isn't there somewhere else you can go?" This lady doubted me too.

"You don't believe me either?" I might have said. "Please listen to me. I got that money from a lady I met for the first time. It was strange, but she knew my name, and she hugged me tight and she cried. Then she sang a song for me over and over and taught it to me. She wrapped a one-thousand-yen bill in tissue paper and put it in my hand and said that it was a present."

But instead of saying anything, I left the lady's house, filled with the shame of being an outcast. With no place left to go, I went to the shed where I'd been punished to wait for my mother's visitor to leave. Unable to even go home to my own house, I stared absently at the puddle in front of the shed and watched the rain drops fall from the eaves of the house.

After a while, feeling only numbness, I went and stood at the back door. I thought that it would certainly be locked. However, when I pulled on it, the door unexpectedly opened. I tiptoed into the kitchen. Through the kitchen was the living room and then the back room. The sliding door of the back room was open just a little. What I saw through that narrow space, I dare not say. I still didn't know about such things between men and women, but even with the heart of a child, I knew that I had seen something I wasn't supposed to see. Forever after, this thought never left me.

Reverend, when you were a child, were you ever blamed for something you didn't do? Were you ever bullied by other children you thought were your friends? Did all the adults you knew ever look at you with cold, suspicious eyes? Did you ever see your own mother entangled with a strange man?

From the time of the thousand-yen incident, I had to play by myself. Do you know what it's like to play always by yourself? First of all, it means that the length of your days is extraordinarily long. When you play with friends, you forget the time; but when you play alone, it feels like no matter how long a time has passed, the day will never end.

Playing alone is like the silent loneliness you feel when you're under water. You don't talk to anyone; you live a silent life, an eerie, silent movie screen life. You suffer from vague anxieties, uneasy feelings that from somewhere someone is going to come to torment you.

For me the kids around my own age were the biggest threat, with their fearful jeering. "Watch out! Here comes the thief!" When they jeered, my face would involuntarily contort, and using me for their cruel pleasure, they would shower me with insults.

That still wasn't the worst part. Sometimes the kids would get into a game of "cops and robbers," and they would call me to play with them. At such times Tsujiko was always there among her friends. When it was decided who would be the policemen and who would be the robber that the policemen chased, I was always chosen to play the part of the robber. I was a fast runner, but I was still younger than the others. The first and second grade boys would chase me, tie my hands behind me, and throw me into jail. Of course, someone would always come to help me, but having my hands tied like that frightened me.

At first, just to be able to play with everyone, I did everything they told me to do. However, because it disturbed me always to have to play the part of the robber, I stopped coming out to play with them when they called.

One day, though, they came and invited me to play a different game. "This time it won't be cops and robbers." I wanted so much to be part of the gang again that I believed them. That's how painful being alone was for me.

That day I noticed a boy among the children I'd never seen before. Tsujiko called him "*O-nii-san.*" I was puzzled because I'd never known that she had an older brother. Afterwards I found out that Tsujiko's mother was her father's second wife. The boy was the child of the first wife and lived at his grandparents' house. Maybe something had happened in the family, for I gathered that he had come to stay in his father's house for the first time in a long time. In spite of all this, he wasn't one of those dark, gloomy boys. His movements were quick and sure.

"Today we're going to play 'kidnap,'" announced a leader among the children and, pointing his chin at me, said, "You'll be the criminal." At this all the kids clapped their hands and agreed.

Tsujiko's older brother said, "It's strange to have a girl play the part of the criminal."

Akira — that was her brother's name — said it with a glowing dignity. Of course, I didn't think about it that way until after I'd grown up. But the tone of his voice was the kind that made everyone follow him. Tsujiko was in the first grade, Akira in the third grade. That made Akira the oldest one there.

"Yeah, but, Akira, she stole a thousand yen from a store — so she ought to play the part of the criminal," said one of the second graders.

"*O-nii-san*, Kiyomi *always* plays the part of the robber," said Tsujiko.

"Oh, really?" Akira asked, sounding very adult.

I shook my head violently. "No, I didn't steal! I got a thousand yen from a lady. And then Tsujiko asked me where I got it, and I told her I got it from the lady, but she said I stole it." It all spilled out, I suppose, because I sensed the warmth in Akira's voice. I hadn't said so much to anyone for a long time.

Then Akira said, "If she says it isn't true, then it isn't true. This kid isn't a thief."

I couldn't believe my ears.

"Oh, come on, everybody knows she's a thief," said Tsujiko. "Right, everybody?"

"Hey, do you have any proof?" said Akira. "Did you see her steal anything?"

Tsujiko couldn't answer.

"Hey, did anybody see this kid steal anything?"

Silence. He silenced them all. To this day I can still feel the happiness I knew that moment.

From that moment, Reverend, I held on to that happiness from day to day, while it lasted. When Akira said, "If she says it isn't true, then it isn't true. This kid isn't a thief," his words went right into my heart.

The heart of a child has its secret depths, doesn't it? Even the heart of a small child can be pierced by a sadness that can't be described, seared by a pain that nobody can understand. That day, when Akira defended me, the sadness I couldn't describe and the pain no one could understand were eased. I was overjoyed.

My happiness didn't last long, though. Akira stayed at Tsujiko's house for only a week or so. Suddenly one day he went back to Sapporo. I didn't really understand why he had to leave, but Tsujiko said, "When *O-nii-san* was here, Mama couldn't stand it. Mama and Papa started arguing all the time. So Papa took him back to Sapporo."

My spirits sank. The world had suddenly grown darker. Sapporo, a place I'd never seen, was a world away. I had no way of knowing that Sapporo was only two hours from Asahikawa. For a child unfamiliar places may as well be on another planet.

From that time Sapporo became a special place in my imagination. The kind lady who gave me the thousand-yen bill, and then Akira, who protected me by saying that I wasn't a thief — both came from Sapporo. I began to think that the place called Sapporo was filled with only kind people.

I was alone again. Tsujiko and the other kids once again took up their teasing and bullying. When they came to my house and called for me to come and play, I would hide inside, holding my breath. My mother, without knowing what was happening, would say angrily, "Why don't you go out and play?"

When my mother didn't have any visitors, I could just stay home. When a man came, however, I was forced to go outside whether I liked it or not. I would go to the shed and hide.

But Tsujiko would look for me. When she or the other kids found me, they would pretend to be detectives and say, "Here she is! Hiding right here! Let's take her to the police!" Just as before, I was the criminal.

While I still wasn't old enough, Tsujiko and the others attended elementary school. During the long summer vacation, they were absorbed in play from morning to night. They would catch butterflies and grasshoppers, and some-times go down to the river for a swim. In the children's park they played on the swings, the jungle gym, the slide. Yet none of these activities was their greatest pleasure. Tormenting me was. And at least once every day they made time for this delight.

3 THE SECRET

I LONGED FOR the summer vacation to end. Each day was unbearably long. To avoid my tormentors, I searched for my own private places to play.

Finally I found the perfect playground in the dry part of the river bed, at the place where workmen collected gravel, a place where children were told not to go. Here a huge dump truck came and went all day. A bulldozer, lumbering awkwardly, scooped gravel from the river bed and poured it into the dump truck.

Obviously the riverbed was no place for children. The coming and going of the trucks was dangerous enough, but where gravel had been scooped out water seeped in, creating great, deep puddles. Two children had already drowned there.

To get to my riverbed hiding place from home, I had to cross over a wide field. The kentwood trees and cattails grew so thick that if I went through the middle of the field, I could hide myself completely. Sometimes, in fact, when I reached the center, I felt the helpless anxiety of being lost.

I cut across the field anyway and went to the gravel pit at the riverbed — I had to escape from the eyes of Tsujiko and the others.

As the workmen at the site wouldn't let me be near the

dump truck, I climbed the embankment and watched the awkward jerking of the yellow bulldozer. Sometimes a grasshopper flew onto my skirt. I remember watching two white butterflies all tangled together as they flew down the embankment and then back up again. How I envied those two butterflies! How fortunate they were to have each other to play with, so freely and without ever tiring of each other!

I was still lonely, but at least being alone was peaceful. Compared to being teased by Tsujiko and her gang, those times could be called happy.

I would have remembered this particular day if for no other reason than about midday a stray cat, knowing nothing of my story, came and slept in the shadow of my small body. But it was to be a day I would never forget for a far different reason.

The dump truck wasn't at the riverbed that day. The yellow bulldozer sat idle. None of the workmen, or anybody else, was there because of the O-bon festival. Bored, I scrambled down to the embankment, pock-marked with big puddles of water.

My mother, usually so negligent, always warned me never to go into the gravel pit. "Even a small puddle can be deep," she said time after time.

Crossing the dry bank that day, carefully avoiding the water-filled hollows, I came to the flowing water. I stepped into the shallow stream. Just enough water flowed to cover my heels. Even though my mother had warned me never

to go into the river alone, the shining water looked perfectly safe to me.

I had just taken another step into the river when someone behind me called out. I turned, startled. Coming down
the river bank was none other than Tsujiko. She was wearing
a fancy yellow dress that she wore only for special occasions. It was the same dress she was wearing the day she
accused me of being a thief. I ran away from her, toward
the embankment. I sent rocks skidding as I ran, but I flew
over them like a little monkey.

"Wait! Kiyomi! You wait for me!" my enemy demanded.

Suddenly I heard a cry of alarm. I turned and saw it
happen. Tsujiko's body leaned to the left and tumbled
sideways, her scream ending abruptly with the sound of
a splash. In an instant she disappeared. Chasing me, she'd
paid no attention to where she was running and had fallen
into one of the big puddles in the gravel pit.

I ran back to where I thought she'd been, but there was
no sign of her. It seemed to me that the puddle had grown
larger.

I knew I had to tell somebody. I looked up the
embankment, but so many people had gone to visit
the graves of the dead for O-bon that nobody had come
to the river to fish, and no children had come to swim.
There was no sign of life. Not even conscious of what
I was doing, I scrambled up the embankment and ran
down the path. I ran for about two hundred meters,
my heart bursting to call for help. Then I tripped over a
small stone and fell to the ground I didn't really hurt

myself, though my knee throbbed.

Tsujiko's already dead! The thought inspired an inde-scribable fear in me as I brushed myself off. Recalling the thousand-yen incident, I had the feeling that this incident would be no different. Even though I had nothing to do with it, I would be accused of killing Tsujiko. At the very least, my mother was certain to punish me for going where I wasn't supposed to be. "Why did you go to the gravel pit?" she would yell. The grownups would certainly come crowding around me, asking how Tsujiko died. I decided not to tell.

I don't know anything about it, I repeated over and over in my heart. Anyway, I didn't have anything to do with Tsujiko's death. Not really. She chased after me of her own free will, she fell into a water hole, and she died.

I went home, only to find the door to the entrance hall locked. I went to the shed and before long fell asleep. That's a child for you, isn't it, Reverend? I couldn't really grasp the fact of Tsujiko's death as reality.

My mother came and opened the shed door. Just as she shook my shoulders to wake me up, someone came to the front of our house, then spotted us at the shed.

"Good gracious, it's hot!" It was the voice of the lady next door. She'd brought some kind of circular to my mother. By then I was completely awake.

"You poor baby!" she said. "You must be so tired, waiting out here all this time." She complained to my mother, "Why don't you think about the child a little more?"

My mother just laughed. "Have you visited your family

grave yet?" she asked the lady, to change the subject. But the lady pretended not to hear and returned home.

I went inside. My mother gave me some ice cream from the refrigerator to eat. Eating the frozen treat, I wondered what people did when they went to visit the graves of the dead during the O-bon season. I had been told that my father had died, but I had never been taken to visit his grave. There wasn't even a home altar with his picture on it in our house.

About the time my mother started making dinner, we heard a voice call from the entrance hall, "I'm sorry to bother you, but is my little Tsujiko here?"

A cool evening breeze from the entrance hall stirred the lace curtains hanging across the door to the living room.

My mother replied sarcastically, "Your 'little Tsujiko' doesn't hang around here."

But Tsujiko's mother wasn't the type to be intimidated by my mother. "She left the house at ten this morning," she said, "and she's still not home yet. Have you seen her, Kiyomi? Do you know where she is?"

I was hiding behind my mother, peeking out with one eye. "No," I said.

I did know, though. Tsujiko died in a big puddle. I knew it, but I couldn't feel the fact of it as an actual sensation. I knew it as you know things in a dream.

About an hour after Tsujiko's mother left, the president of the neighborhood association came. It was already dark outside.

"Kiyomi, didn't you see Tsujiko at all today? Didn't

you see her anywhere this morning?"

I said nothing, but only shook my head. Since the time Akira had gone back to Sapporo, I had returned to my habit of silence; so people weren't surprised when I didn't say anything.

The man sat down on the step in the entrance hall. There was another man with him, but the man from the neighborhood association said, as if to himself, "You don't think it's a kidnaping, do you?"

His companion said, "My wife said that the little girl's parents had been fighting recently, but . . . . You don't think she went up to Sapporo, do you?" he added in a tone of voice that was concerned, but also, as I remember it, a little strange.

That night I heard the voices of people searching. "Tsujiko! Tsujiko!"

They found her body the next morning. The grownups talked quietly about it here and there around the neighborhood. There was an article in the evening paper, with a picture of the place where Tsujiko had fallen into the water. My mother showed me the picture and admonished me again and again, "You understand now, don't you, Kiyomi? Never go near the river! If you die like Tsujiko did, it won't be my fault."

Needless to say, I knew that I would never go back to the riverbed again. I imagined Tsujiko's hand sticking up out of the water, pulling hard at my wrist.

My mother and the lady next door spent the night of the wake and the day of the funeral helping out at Tsujiko's house. Children from the neighborhood went to the house along with their mothers to pay their last respects to Tsujiko, but I didn't go. The truth that Tsujiko was really gone, in fact, didn't affect me until some days had passed without her appearing to torment me. Akira, since he was the child of the first wife, didn't attend the funeral.

Telling a lie is a very complicated thing, isn't it, Reverend? It makes its demands on spiritual strength. Not only is telling the same lie over and over tiring, but so is trying to convince people that your lie is the truth.

About five days after Tsujiko's funeral, her mother suddenly appeared again at our house. I was shocked. Her eyes were hollow, her cheeks pale. She looked completely worn out. Even my mother was concerned. "Oh, *Oku-san,*" she said. "You look terrible. Are you all right?"

Tsujiko's mother just stood in the entrance hall, staring at me.

"What is it, *Oku-san?*" my mother finally said sharply. "Do you want Kiyomi for something?"

"They found one of Tsujiko's shoes floating in the water," she replied in a monotone. I had overheard that many times from the neighborhood people's conversations. The president of the neighborhood association had come all the way to our house to tell us excitedly that the reason Tsujiko had been found was because of the shoe floating in the water.

"Yes, I know," my mother said.

Then Tsujiko's mother suddenly said loudly, "Kiyomi, you were at the riverbed, too, weren't you?"

For a moment I could hear Tsujiko's domineering voice yelling, "Kiyomi! You wait for me!" Then I could hear her scream, a scream abruptly swallowed up by the water.

"I wasn't there!" I shouted.

"You're lying! Somebody saw you coming home!" she said feverishly.

"Who was that?" my mother demanded.

"The lady who lives next to my mother, Mrs. Kazuki."

"Oh, that old hag! Why did she wait so long before she said anything?"

Tsujiko's mother was lost for an answer.

"That old lady's always getting mixed up," my mother went on. "You can't believe a thing she says. She's always wandering around getting lost, and she'll get up from the dinner table and complain about how she hasn't had a thing to eat."

"It wasn't only the old lady. Her daughter-in-law was there, too."

"Just say what you've got to say," said my mother, now angry and ready for a fight.

Tsujiko's mother glared at me. "You tell the truth now! Didn't you push Tsujiko into the water? Even a child, if you push from behind —"

"Get out of here!" my mother shrieked, jabbing at the woman's chest. "Get out! I won't listen to any more of your lies!"

Just then, from out of nowhere, the lady from next door poked her face into the entrance hall. "What in the world is all this noise about?"

My mother, beside herself with rage, recounted what had happened.

"Really?" the lady said. "That old woman Kazuki and her daughter-in-law?" I didn't find out until much later that Mrs. Kazuki's daughter-in-law was over forty, and that the two women barely even spoke.

"I know better than anyone what Kiyomi was doing that day," the lady went on. "She spent half the day going in and out of that shed, playing. Then she fell asleep in it. I know because I saw her. Isn't that right, Sawae?"

My mother nodded in agreement. "That's right. You even complained about me not taking care of Kiyomi."

"I didn't mean to. It was just that you locked her out of the house and made her sleep in that tiny shed on such a hot day."

At any rate, thanks to the lady next door, for half the day I was proven to be in the vicinity of the house. Tsujiko's mother finally left.

Later that day, two detectives came. The lady from next door was called to our house, too, and the grownups talked it all over for hours. In the end, even though I'd been seen walking on the path, there was no proof that I'd been to the riverbed. When the detectives were about to leave, one of them stroked my head and said, "Did you like Tsujiko?"

I shook my head. "I hated her," I said point blank.

The two detectives looked at each other and nodded in understanding.

"Well, what do you think of her dying? Are you happy? Sad?"

"I don't know," I said coldly.

I didn't learn until much later that my replies gave the detectives the impression that I was being very honest. When this straightforward little girl said she wasn't at the riverbed, they reasoned, then she must have been telling the truth. But that's only an adult's way of seeing things. As far as I was concerned, I could tell the lie about not being at the riverbed, but I wouldn't under any circumstances say that I liked Tsujiko. Even though she was dead, I hated her.

What I saw at the gravel pit remained my secret.

4 O-TOO-SAN

AROUND THE TIME I entered the third grade, the situation in my house changed. Without my really noticing it, the number of men who passed through the house dwindled. There came a time, in fact, when only one man came, a man of medium height and build, with beautifully smoothed-down hair. He was about ten years older than my mother. As she would have been just twenty-nine years old then, he must have been about forty. Of course, he had a wife and family. He lived on the outskirts of Asahikawa and ran a real estate business. His name was Kanazaki Morio.

When Kanazaki came, my mother would greet him, not with a simple "Come in," but instead always with "Welcome home!"

At first, I couldn't bring myself to accept my mother's treating Kanazaki as if he were a family member. When he came to the house, he would immediately change from his suit and tie into a cotton kimono, just like the father of the house. After taking a bath, he would watch television until late at night. He usually stayed several nights.

Kanazaki always brought me a present. One time he brought me a doll, another time some cake, and another time a beautiful outfit.

Sometimes the three of us went out together. As until then I had only gone out with my mother, it felt strange to go out with two people. Looking back on it now, I can see that we were playing a little drama; it all had that kind of feeling. If we went into a small restaurant, the waitresses would say, "Oh, look at that cute little girl. She has her father's mouth."

Kanazaki would happily say, "Yes, she looks just like her father," and like an actor in a movie he would play the part of my father.

Such times only made me more lonely. Though they talked about Kanazaki as if he were my father, there was no way I could put on a happy face like the adults. When the adults put on their smiles, I felt as lonely as they appeared happy.

When I started actually calling Kanazaki "*O-too-san*," my mother scolded me severely.

"What's the matter?" I said, giving my mother an accusing look.

"The matter?" my mother replied, choking.

"Well, he's the father of this house, isn't he?" I said. I had a feeling that I understood the situation, but at the same time a feeling that there were things I didn't understand.

Reverend, can you believe that I called a stranger "Father"? Actually, I learned to call Kanazaki "Father" fairly easily. From the bottom of my heart, even if it weren't true, I wanted someone to call "*O-too-san*." I didn't know what it was like to have a father, but since all of my friends had someone called "Father," I wanted one too.

Also, from the time Kanazaki started coming, that terrible "being sent outside" stopped. At that time, Kanazaki was still not the revolting person he would become. He didn't yell at me, and he never scolded me. For the first time in my life, I had just a little taste of what it was like to have a normal home life.

I think it was on a Sunday night near the end of October. I was watching an animated program on television. Kanazaki and I were lying on our stomachs on the *tatami*. Mother was also close by, watching the show with us. I remember that she hadn't prepared dinner; so maybe we were planning to eat out that day. After a short commercial, an announcer's voice came on: "Today, we visited the Funato house in Sapporo. This is the home of the two Funatos, Nobumasa and Saori, the renowned flower-arranging teachers." Of course, at the time, I didn't pay any attention to the names or what the announcer said. It was only afterward that I learned who the people were.

I wanted to watch another cartoon, so I changed the channel, but my mother quickly reached over and changed it back again. She'd never done anything like that before, and I remember looking up at her in amazement. She just stared at the television screen. Instinctively I understood that whatever was on the television was too important for me to insist on watching my cartoon.

On the screen were a man and two ladies, all dressed in kimonos. Looking at them, I was taken aback as well. I remembered having seen the younger of the two ladies before. No, "remembered seeing her" is not quite accurate. I could never forget her face, even if I tried. The day of the Asahikawa festival when I was five years old she was the lady who had suddenly appeared beside me, gently hugged me, shed soft streams of tears, and in a beautiful, silvery voice sang again and again,

The good Lord up in Heaven above
Gives to all His gentle love.
On the baby sparrow in the eaves,
On the smallest ones . . .

Then she gave me a thousand yen. On that day I was called a thief for the first time, and from that day I was bullied mercilessly by Tsujiko and her friends. I don't know how many times I had thought, *If only that lady would come again!*

Now, there she was on the television screen. Without thinking, I cried out, "*O-kaa-san!* It was her!"

But my words didn't penetrate my mother's ears. When I looked up at her face, I knew I should be quiet. As if she were another person, she stared at the television screen until the program was over. Kanazaki turned off the television, but my mother continued to stare at the screen, biting her lip, as if the program were still on.

"Mama, it was her, it was that lady, a long time ago. She gave me the thousand yen. Don't you remember?"

"A thousand yen?" my mother said. "A thousand yen?" She still wasn't listening to anything that was going on around her. I turned to Kanazaki. If I didn't tell somebody, anybody, I'd never again have a chance to wipe away the shame of being called a thief. Even Kanazaki would do.

"*O-too-san*, that's the lady. Before I ever went to school, the lady who was just on the program, the lady with the kind face, the one on this side," I said, gesturing to show him which one I meant. "One day that lady gave me a thousand yen."

"A thousand yen," he said, nodding, but glancing at my mother. "Really?"

"And Tsujiko said that I stole it, and *O-kaa-san* got very angry."

"I see."

"But I got the money from that lady, that one on television. Don't you believe me?"

"Of course I believe you," he said, humoring me.

"Really? I'm so happy!" And without thinking, I gave Kanazaki a big hug around the neck. I really was happy. Kanazaki was surprised to hear me say so much, since I was usually so quiet. However, though I had no way of knowing it at the time, Kanazaki was thinking about something other than the meaning of what I had said.

At this point I'm puzzled, Reverend. Should I continue writing, or should I stop here? When a person such as I makes a profession of faith, is it really true that she should confess all the sins she has committed? I'm not sure if I understand this. I understand that if you stand before God and your fellow Christians and confess your sins, you will receive forgiveness. But can a sinner like me really tell, with neither exaggeration nor understatement, every sinful thing she has thought, every sin she has committed? And is it really necessary to stand before God, who knows all of our sins anyway, and tell our sins to Him?

You're a minister, Reverend, and though you may have an obligation to confess your sins to God, is it really necessary for me to confess mine to you? Ministers are, after all, ministers and not God. You hear our confessions, you bear the burden with us, you pray for us before God, but is there anything else you can do? I have a terrible urge to lay down my pen.

After writing about that night when we watched television, I thought for a long, long time. After a while, I found the courage to take up my pen again. I do want sincerely to confess the sins of my past to God and to you, Reverend. I think I can do it, but I'll have to work harder to feel again the hand of God as I did before. Please be patient and give me the chance to tell you everything.

After we saw the famous flower-arranging teachers Funato Nobumasa and his younger sister Saori on television, Kanazaki and my mother became more talkative than usual. They took me to a *sushi* shop for dinner. Again I tried to tell my mother about the beautiful lady who had given me a thousand yen.

"Really?" my mother said. "That was the lady who gave you the thousand yen? Why didn't you tell me this before?"

Of course, I'd told her again and again where I got the money, but she hadn't believed me. Now, after years had passed, all she said to me was, "You little fool," blaming me for the whole thing.

My mother didn't apologize, didn't say she was sorry, didn't say she regretted doing what she'd done. She still didn't realize what a trauma it had been for me. When I heard her say "You little fool," I felt anger well up in me, something I hadn't felt toward her before. It was the beginning of a grudge I still bear, though I think it's a terrible thing to hate your own mother.

Just then Kanazaki said, "Why do you say she's a fool? Being called a thief must have been terrible for her."

There in the restaurant I looked up at Kanazaki's face, overwhelmed by the feeling that he really was my father. I wanted to agree with what he'd said, but no words would come out. I burst out crying and buried my face in my hands. My mother looked at me in astonishment.

"Kiyomi," she scolded hoarsely. "You're embarrassing me, crying in a place like this."

But Kanazaki said, "It's okay, it's okay. When you have to cry, it's best to cry as much as you want."

That night, walking home, I gripped Kanazaki's hand tightly. From that time on, I became attached to him. "*O-too-san*," I would say, hanging onto him. He returned my affection, and I even became a little spoiled. He would sit me in his lap and rock me back and forth like a seesaw. When we did this, I would sometimes sing the song I had learned from the beautiful lady who sang it over and over.

The good Lord up in Heaven above
Gives to all His gentle love.

On the baby sparrow in the eaves,
On the smallest ones . . .

Once I asked Kanazaki, "*O-too-san*, what kind of person is God?"

"Well, I've never met Him before; so I really don't know." Apparently my question made him uncomfortable.

"What? You've never met God before? But you're a grownup."

I was surprised. I was really surprised. I thought that adults somehow somewhere met God or Buddha. My mother sometimes said things like, "God is watching," or "Buddha will punish you if you spill your food." It seemed to me that adults were always having conversations with God or Buddha.

"*O-kaa-san* knows God," I said to Kanazaki. "She tells me what He says." Kanazaki hugged me around the waist and laughed.

"Sawae, Kiyomi says that God is a friend of yours," he called out to my mother. Then he said to me, "Kiyomi, nobody knows if there is a God or not. Nobody has ever met God."

"You mean, there are no gods in the shrines?"

"If there were, you could see them," he said, laughing again.

"But, that lady we saw on television, she taught me a song about God."

Kanazaki was silent.

"*O-too-san*, that lady really is beautiful, isn't she? She's so nice, too. Why did she know all about me?"

Kanazaki didn't answer.

My mother wouldn't tell me anything about the lady, either. I felt even in my child's heart that my mother was keeping something from me. Whenever I brought up the subject, my mother's face would turn sour. She would say sharply, "If I said I don't know, I don't know. You're such a pain, sometimes, you know that?" Finally she said, "Kiyomi, I won't put up with you talking about that lady ever again, do you understand? If you do, *O-too-san* will never come here again."

At that I stopped asking about the kind lady. Kanazaki had come to be like an actual father to me. Of course, he wasn't my real father, and I knew there was something different between him and a real father.

At school one day one of my friends said, "Your mother is somebody's *mekake*." I didn't know that the word "*mekake*" meant a mistress, a kept woman. Then, a few days later, I found a piece of paper in my desk with the word's "mistress's child" written on it with a black marker. I was going to show it to my mother, but decided not to. Instinctively I knew that it wasn't something I could show my mother.

That was when I was in the third grade, around the middle of March. How I hate March, Reverend. During March in Asahikawa the beautiful, fresh snow of January and February turns into dirty, sooty black slush.

My memory of another March day is uglier and more wretched than just dirty snow. Snow will always melt away and disappear in time; my memory of that day will be in my heart forever, no matter how hard I try not to remember it. On that day, March 17, to be exact —

But please wait before I tell about that day. First I have to mention something about my mother and Kanazaki. Sometimes — I don't know why — my mother and Kanazaki had arguments. "Sawae," Kanazaki would sometimes say, "I feel like this is the only place where I can really relax." But though he said that, we could never forget that he still had another household, a real family, somewhere far away. When he went back home after a visit with us, my mother would sit near the stove, making no effort to get up and show him out the door, and would say, "You don't need to bother coming back. You have no obligations here." But her remarks didn't seem to ruffle him, even if I was around.

I would cling to him and ask again and again, "When are you coming back? You aren't coming back, are you?"

Then Kanazaki would look at me and say, "As long as you're still here, Kiyomi, even if she says not to come, I'll come anyway." He always made light of the whole thing, and then he went home.

We never knew when he'd be back. Coming home from school, I would think that he would certainly come on that day, but as time went on, he paid us fewer and fewer visits. Sometimes I would sit outside and wait for him to come. Even if I was frozen stiff, even if it was snowing, if I thought that there was the least chance of seeing him, I would fly outside again as soon as I got home from school. He always came by taxi, so if I saw a taxi at all, it would set my heart throbbing with relief. Sometimes I waited outside so long that the tip of my nose became numb, but I would keep waiting.

It was about two months later, in February, on the night of the Setsubun festival. I remember because my mother was roasting beans, and she counted them into my hand, saying, "Eat only as many as your age now. One, two, three . . .," until she'd given me nine. She took beans for her age as well and as she put them in her mouth she said, "Oh, these are hard. I'm going to break a tooth." Suddenly, I don't know why, I remembered the word "*mekake*," which I still didn't know meant "mistress." I felt that I shouldn't use the word in front of my mother, but for some reason, as I was eating the beans, I felt reassured.

"You'll break your tooth? If breaking your tooth is *hakake*, is breaking your eye *mekake*?" I was very proud of my pun.

My mother instantly slapped me hard across the face. I had no idea why she did it.

"How dare you talk like that in front of your own mother!" She slapped me again, two times, three times. "What do you mean, *mekake!* What do you mean!"

"Why are you hitting me?" I cried. "Is it a bad word? What does it mean?"

My mother just glared at me. It was a long, long, piercing look. I had no way of knowing how my words had hurt my mother, but I understood that the word *mekake* was for some reason a terrible word for her. Just after this event, Kanazaki came and stayed with us for a night. The times when he stayed for several days in a row had stopped.

March 17 — that day, my mother went to Sapporo to attend her cousin's wedding. She said that I was old enough to watch the house for one night alone. She offered to leave me with the lady next door, but I enjoyed being alone. When my mother wasn't home, rather than feeling lonely, I was happy and calm. At any rate, my mother wasn't the kind to think twice about going out and leaving a child alone. She carefully put on her make-up and left. Sitting there alone, I had a feeling, for no real reason, that Kanazaki would come. All day I went in and out of the house, waiting for him to come. Even after night had fallen and he hadn't come, I didn't give up. I told myself, *Before I count to a hundred, he'll be here.* I stood in the entrance hall with the door open, watching a light snow flurry, counting: "One, two, three . . . ." When I got to a hundred and he still hadn't come, I started over. I closed my eyes as if praying and started to count again. Before I reached fifty, I heard the sound of a car. I opened my eyes in relief, and standing before me, holding a paper bag of presents in his arms, was none other than Kanazaki.

"*O-too-san!*" I cried and jumped into his arms, so happy I was crying. I pulled Kanazaki into the house by the hand and said, "I knew you'd come before I counted to a hundred." I told him just how long I'd waited to see him.

Kanazaki took off his jacket and said, "Oh, really? Did you really want to see me so much?" He hugged me, pressing his cheek against mine.

"Yes. I waited," I said, pouting like a spoiled child. "I

came home from school, and I went outside again and again to look for you."

"So many times? In this cold?" Kanazaki said, hugging me tightly. "You love your *o-too-san* that much?"

"Yes, I do! I love you more than my mother!" I said. Was it a sin to say so? Kanazaki kissed me again and again on the cheek, as my mother never did, and I returned his kisses. I'd seen it on television and had always been filled with envy at the sight of parents and children exchanging kisses on the cheek. Giving kisses, receiving kisses: I was in heaven.

Somehow Kanazaki must have known beforehand that my mother wouldn't be home. As we had occasionally done in the past, we took a bath together, just like a real Japanese father and child. Then we took what mother had left in the refrigerator for me, along with the *sekihan* rice Kanazaki had brought with him, and had dinner together. But that's where my happiness ended.

That night, he said, "Let's sleep together," and so I got into bed with him. He cuddled me and fondled me in ways too embarrassing to speak of. It was all an obscene trick. The adult I trusted most in the world, Reverend, hurt me in such a way that I might never recover.

Just now I opened the Bible to First Corinthians, Chapter 13 and read. Having just been writing about my experiences as a child, I have the feeling, as I did then, that I'm drowning in a dirty pool, that something heavy is pressing on my chest. Here in First Corinthians the Bible says:

"Love is patient and kind; it is not jealous or conceited

or proud; love is not ill-mannered or selfish or irritable; love does not keep a record of wrongs; love is not happy with evil, but is happy with the truth. Love never gives up; and its faith, hope, and patience never fail."

You told us to change the word "love" in this passage to "I," and to read it again, like this:

"I am patient and kind; I am not jealous or conceited or proud; I am not ill-mannered or selfish or irritable; I do not keep a record of wrongs . . . ."

You told us that if we read it like this, we could measure just how well the word "I" would fit. If there is a person who could read the passage that way and have it be true, then he must be love incarnate. I must say that I've never personally met anybody like that, least of all myself. That's why I laughed when you said to do it. But I remembered what you said, and so I tried it again.

The first words that strike my heart are, "I am not jealous." Jealousy is a terrible feeling. Have you ever been jealous of anyone? I can't judge how I've been tormented by jealousy in my life up to now, but one night in mid-summer, when I was only in the fourth grade, the jealousy that arose and seized my chest was a bitter envy that I had never experienced before.

I just confessed to being fondled by Kanazaki. From that time on, he never showed his face around our house again. I began to hate him. I had learned that he was a vulgar and disgusting man. However, I didn't tell my mother what he'd done.

I don't think my mother ever knew why Kanazaki

suddenly stopped coming. Up to then, even after long intervals began to separate Kanazaki's visits, my mother still waited for him to come. When it was just the two of us at the dinner table, my mother would sometimes stare absent-mindedly into space, holding her chopsticks, and say, "What can you do? 'Life is nothing but goodbyes.'" I learned later that these words were from Dazai Osamu, but I wonder where my mother, who never reads, learned them. At any rate, she would mutter over and over, "Life is nothing but goodbyes."

One day, I came home from school and overheard my mother talking on the telephone as I slipped out of my shoes in the entrance hall.

"I understand," she was saying. "I knew the day would come. I knew we'd break up eventually." And then, "Yes, yes, I'll wait in the hotel lobby."

I knew immediately that the call was from Kanazaki. I had an unexpectedly strong urge to see him. Even though I despised the man,for some reason I just had to meet him.

My mother put down the telephone and just sat there, ignoring me. I don't think she even knew I was there. I put my school books down on the table and left the house without saying a word. I went out to the meadow near our house. In the meadow flowed a narrow stream, no more than a yard wide. The blue sky was reflected in the clear water. On the banks, a flock of blue forget-me-nots trembled in the breeze. As I stared at the flowers, I was filled with terrible memories of being alone.

I was not a child of beautiful feelings, but looking at the flowers comforted me in some way. At times I felt like breaking off a flower and putting it in a vase, but I couldn't bring myself to pick even one flower from a field.

When I was in the fourth grade, I began to draw pictures of flowers. During art period at school, even if there wasn't a flower in sight, I drew them anyway. This is because I would squat in the flower bed and stare at flowers. One time, as I was staring into a flower, it left an amazingly precise impression on me, as if it were exposed on film. When I began to draw nothing but pictures of flowers, my mother for some reason became very gloomy. One time she said, "What? Flowers again? I guess it's in the blood." She intended to mumble those words under her breath, but I heard them very clearly.

A fourth-grader isn't as much a child as adults may think she is. I had begun to secretly read the books and magazines that Kanazaki had left behind. Kanazaki read mostly detective novels, but even detective novels always contain those passages describing the entanglements of men and women. Even on television programs, though I pretended not to watch, I still saw such things. Mother firmly believed that such programs were those which "children wouldn't understand," but I watched and did understand them. I could perfectly understand the meaning of the bedroom scenes, and when I saw them, I couldn't help but think of Kanazaki.

Now what should I write? I intended to write about jealousy. But before I do, I have to mention something about the day my mother went off to the hotel to say good-bye to Kanazaki.

That day all I could think of was hurrying home after school. It was my turn to help with the cleaning at school, but I lied and said I had a stomachache and rushed home as fast as I could. Let me confess just why I had such anticipation. I had an idea that there was a chance of Kanazaki coming home with my mother.

I still hated Kanazaki; I thought he was an awful man. But at the same time, he had always been so kind to me. If it hadn't been for that one terrible incident, he might still have been a father to me. At any rate, I wanted desperately to see his face.

However, my expectations were not to be satisfied. My mother came home alone, and her face wasn't as downcast and depressed as it had been up until the day before. Her cheeks, which had been so pale, were flushed and had turned rosy. I think now that she looked like a woman who had just been flirting with a man. She said cheerfully, "What a beautiful day! How was school today?"

She very rarely asked me about school.

"I guess he wasn't so bad after all," she said to herself. She was walking around, too excited to sit down. "Seven million yen. Do you know how much money that is?"

"No," I said, not really caring.

"Well, I can tell you it's a lot of money," she said. She opened her handbag, took one bill from it and looked it over, then put it back and closed the bag.

About two months later, that night in July came, that

midsummer night that I mentioned earlier when jealousy came to torment me. That evening my mother and I went to town. The sunset high in the sky looked like someone had spilled red wine. My mother was wearing a white dress. Men and women both were struck by mother's beauty, and some of them stopped and stared. I was wearing a dress made from the same material as my mother's, and had my hair in a ponytail, the way my mother liked it. I looked very grown-up for my age.

"What do you want for dinner?" my mother asked. I was at a loss. *Sushi* sounded good, but I also loved hamburgers and omelets. I was greedy.

Choosing can be difficult, can't it, Reverend? When you have to choose just one thing, the more you think about it the more difficult choosing becomes. If merely choosing something to eat can be so hard, choosing the right person to be with or choosing the right path to follow in life can be a life's work.

But I'm getting off the point. Finally I said, "I want *sushi*."

My mother laughed and said, "Good. That's just what I want, too."

We certainly looked like a loving mother and daughter that night, walking hand in hand down the street. I had to say we "looked like" a loving mother and daughter because I can't honestly say that we ever were.

It wasn't because I despised my mother. Well, I do have to admit that I thought, more than once, *Oh! If only my mother were more like So-and-so's mother!* Especially when friends came to visit, I was ashamed of her. I often thought, *Why do you have to do those things!* or *Can't you just shut up!* These feelings of shame must still be deep inside me.

However, compared to other times, my heart that night was at peace. Walking down the street holding hands with my mother was nice. We turned the corner to go to the *sushi* shop where we always ate, and my mother suddenly pulled my hand violently.

"What was that for?" I said, but she had stopped dead in her tracks. The *sushi* shop was still down the street from us. I looked toward it and almost lost my breath in shock. Coming out of the shop were a girl about my age, a boy three or four years older, a slim lady wearing a light green kimono, and Kanazaki. There was a grand black car parked in front of the place, and a chauffeur standing in a bow. Apparently without noticing us, Kanazaki turned, said something to the little girl, and laughed. The boy and girl both clapped their hands and jumped in excitement. A burning feeling rose like a flame in my heart.

Just before he got into the car, Kanazaki glanced in our direction. I held my breath, staring into his face. But then he was in the car, which pulled away and went right by us. Kanazaki, sitting in the back seat, tapped his daughter on the shoulder and she turned around.

Even after Kanazaki's car was out of sight, we still stood on the sidewalk, frozen in amazement. A good bit of time must have passed before I realized that I was trembling.

Of course, it was a shock for my mother as well, but

not, I think, as strong a shock as it had been for me. Until that moment, I had never thought of Kanazaki's having a wife, a daughter, a family, not in reality. When he came to our house, he was mine and mine alone. As far as I was concerned, my mother and I were his only family. I knew somewhere deep inside that the other family existed, but I didn't have the power to imagine it.

I suddenly suffered the violent attack of jealousy I mentioned, a jealousy that refuses to go away. The biggest reason for it, I'm sure, was the little girl about my age, and I directed the flame of my jealousy toward her.

I had never thought of Kanazaki showing love toward anyone but me, but now I could see with my own eyes, feel as an almost physical sensation, that it wasn't true. With a real son and daughter to love, there was no room for me in Kanazaki's life. I had seen a proper family portrait, with a son and daughter clapping their hands in happiness. From the *sushi* shop, Kanazaki would take them to an even better place, and the children and their parents would live like that, in perfect happiness, day in and day out forever.

Surely Kanazaki wouldn't do to his daughter the obscene thing he had done to me. Utterly without hope, I shut my heart against the pain.

A few days later, my mother asked, "Kiyomi, when we saw Kanazaki, weren't you angry?"

"Why should I be?" I said, pretending to be indifferent.

"Kanazaki never once came to this house in his own car — did you know that?"

It was true. He always came by taxi. I had never dreamed

that he could own such a luxurious, chauffeur-driven car.

"And do you know why he never came here is his own car?"

"No," I said, still trying not to listen.

"I'll tell you why. Because he was afraid we might ask him to give us a ride in it."

I had nothing to say.

"He was ashamed of me! Ashamed to be seen with me! Now I see why he never brought his own car!"

I considered my mother's complaints petty. *What a baby!* I thought. It never occurred to me to be upset over not being able to ride in Kanazaki's car. The only thing I cared about was the daughter, the object of my hatred.

"That bastard!" my mother went on. "I wonder what kind of house he lives in! If his car looks like that, can you imagine what his house must be like? And I got excited about seven million yen!"

But my mother's feelings were harmless compared to mine. I thought of something much more frightening. *How could I make myself into Kanazaki's only child?* Satan himself was living in my breast.

5 CHRYSANTHEMUMS

TWO YEARS had passed since Kanazaki cut off his relationship with us. For the first year or so, no men at all came to our house. Perhaps it was because the seven million yen that my mother had received from Kanazaki allowed her to feel secure. She worked part-time at a supermarket that had opened near our house. Because she finally had a respectable job, nobody could point an accusing finger at either my mother or me. Even so, people continued to look at us with suspicion.

Before long, however, Mother began coming home late again. And on those nights she would bribe me by bringing home cake or juice as a present. "When the store is busy," she would say, "I have to stay late."

Oh, really? I would think. As much as I wanted to believe her, I had my doubts.

It was a winter night about a year after my mother had started working at the supermarket. No, saying it was "a winter night" is too vague. It was the day after Christmas. I remember because on my way home from school that day I was attracted by the bright lights of the decorations for the after-Christmas sale at the store where she worked.

Winter vacation began the next day, and because I had received my school grade reports, I really wanted my mother to come home early. Probably because of the relatively stable life we were leading, my grades had noticeably risen. I had A's in Japanese, math, and sociology, all important classes. Even in gym and music, not my strong areas, I had B's.

But there was something else, something that made me even prouder: one of my paintings had been chosen to represent Asahikawa elementary schools in a competition and had been sent to Sapporo. My teacher told me, smiling, "The painting you did received the gold medal! It was wonderful. I think it has a good chance of being chosen as the best in Hokkaido." I wanted to tell my mother right away. Of course, it would be in the newspaper either tonight or tomorrow morning, but I wanted my mother to know before anyone else.

I waited until 7:00, and still my mother hadn't come home. Since the supermarket closed at 6:00, she should have been back by 6:30. After 7:00 had come and gone, I decided to go to meet her at the store.

All of the lights that had decorated the store were out. Inside the store was dark as well. Only two or three cars broke the emptiness of the parking lot. Mother must have already left, I decided. She must have stopped off somewhere.

I turned to go home.

Just then the door of the employees' entrance swung open, and light spilled onto the pavement. From the doorway emerged a tall man. Behind him was my mother. Quickly stepping behind a light post, I watched as the man got into a car and as my mother circled the car and, as if she'd done it many times before, got in on the passenger side. The car sped off into the darkness. I watched until the red tail lights disappeared.

I was alone, but stronger than the loneliness I felt was a wave of what I can only call hatred.

My mother came back home after ten o'clock that evening. She smelled of alcohol.

"Starting tomorrow we have the big end-of-the-year sale," she said. "I'm pooped from getting ready for it." She had brought some sweets for me.

"That busy?" I said and went straight to bed without saying a word about either my good grades or the gold medal I'd won in the painting competition.

Because my mother never read newspapers, she didn't know that my picture of chrysanthemums had been chosen to represent all the elementary schools in Asahikawa until the lady next door said something about it. Even if she read the paper, it was such a small article that she probably wouldn't have noticed it anyway. When my mother said, "Anything interesting in the paper?" she meant a bank robbery, a murder, a hijacking, or something like that.

Reverend, I have to ask, why is it written in the Bible, "Honor your father and your mother"? Must I honor even a mother such as mine, a woman who sells her body?

It wasn't long before Mother quit her job at the supermarket. She didn't bring any men home with her, but she used the apartment that Tachikawa, her boss from the supermarket, had rented as a place for their dates.

Of course, I didn't know this at the time.

If your mother was the kind of mother mine was, Reverend, would you still respect her? I can't. On the contrary, I despise her. I hate her. I'm ashamed to have her as a mother. Would you say that it's awful to feel that way? All the time I was thinking about being baptized, this was the thing that confused me most. Now I realize that a person who can't even love her own mother is deep in sin and must be saved.

If I were an upright person, a person who did only good deeds, had only good thoughts, a person who could respect even a mother like mine, perhaps I wouldn't need to be saved.

My mother's life had become entangled in the life of my soul. If she were chaste, intelligent, elegant, had love and respect for people, it would be easy for me to respect her. In the Bible, though, it is not written, "If your mother and father are honorable, then you should love them." There is no qualifier in the sentence, only, "Honor your father and your mother."

At first, this requirement of God seems unreasonable, but in reality it's a wonderful thing. When I was first thinking of entering the church, I thought of it not from the point of view of religion, but simply as a matter of everyday morality. I just wanted to be able to look people in the eye, but I felt the depth of my sin lying before me like an obstacle.

But here my pen has rushed a little ahead. Before I completed my profession of faith, I wanted to say something about the life of my soul. I wanted you to hear, and I wanted God to listen. I'll get back to my story.

To my surprise, my painting of chrysanthemums won a first prize in Hokkaido.

"First prize in all Hokkaido! I can't believe it!" my mother said when she heard the news. Her eyes registered her delight. Then a cloud darkened her face. "I guess there's really no question about your blood."

That was the first time I'd heard that in a while. Ever since I began to draw pictures of flowers, I'd been hearing things like, "It's in the blood." I had only a vague understanding of what this meant. After all, I was only in the fifth grade.

In my innocence I asked my mother, "Oh, do you like flowers, too?"

She shook her head and said evasively, "No, no, your mother's no good at drawing pictures." Then she said excitedly, "We'll have to go to Sapporo to see the exhibition, won't we? Number one in all Hokkaido! I wonder what I should wear. A dress? Maybe a kimono is better." She was happy, but as usual she was thinking only about herself.

"Either a dress or a kimono is fine," I said.

Really, either would be fine. As long as she didn't open her mouth, my mother was an attractive woman no matter what she wore.

The exhibition was scheduled to take place during the spring vacation in March at a big department store in Sapporo. During the months before we went, my mother continued to go out at night once or twice a week. I bore her behavior as well as I could. In the end, she decided to wear a kimono. She went all out, ordering a new beige kimono with a bright pattern. When it came, she hung it from her shoulders and admired herself in front of the dresser mirror. Then she suddenly said, "Oh, no!"

"What's the matter?" I asked.

"I didn't think about what you would wear," she said, laughing. "I can't believe I forgot!"

Looking at her, I somehow felt very sorry for her. You may think it's odd for a fifth grader to pity her own mother, but sometimes children have the same kinds of feelings that adults have. Children don't remain children forever. Even if nobody teaches them, they pick up some things along the way. It's how we come to see life as it really is. At any rate, I hid my feelings of pity as I looked at my distressed mother.

Not long after, something strange happened. It was a Sunday. We were just about to go out to look for a sweater for me when a registered special-delivery parcel arrived. Though I could read the sender's name, Sugata Haru, I didn't know who it was. The box was wrapped with paper from the very department store where my picture was to be displayed, and inside was a dress for me, a beautiful sky-blue dress. The collar had a black lace border that contrasted nicely with the light blue and gave the whole dress a very sophisticated look, not like a child's dress at all. Since I didn't know who the dress was from, I wasn't sure if it was all right to be happy.

"What a lovely dress!" my mother said, but without enthusiasm.

"But who is Sugata Haru?"

"I don't know," my mother said, avoiding my eyes. "It doesn't matter who it is. Hurry! Try it on."

"But —" I was still hesitant.

"No more buts. You want me to tell you the truth? A long time ago, when you were born, Sugata Haru was the man I was with."

"The man you were with?" Considering this vague connection, when I looked at the name of the sender again, I had no feelings of nostalgia, no feelings of happiness. I knew that in the world of adults many lies were told; so I dropped the issue and put my arms through the sleeves of the dress. To my great surprise, it fit perfectly. In fact, it looked just right on me. I gazed at myself in the mirror. This sky-blue dress fit me better than any dress I'd ever worn. I didn't care who had sent me the dress; I didn't care if it was stolen. I loved it.

The spring vacation and the art exhibition I had been waiting for finally came. In Asahikawa a few patches of dirty snow remained here and there. The trip to Sapporo was my first. My mother had taken me to places like Rumoi and Obihiro, but for some reason never to Sapporo.

A matching cape came with my new blue dress, and I wore that in place of a coat. This gave me a feeling of elegance, though at the time I wasn't the kind to pay much attention to clothes.

From my first sight of Sapporo, I thought it was wonderful. In the middle of the street in front of the train station the tall trees had tight new buds on their bare branches, and the long line they made impressed me deeply.

The day we arrived was the day of the awards ceremony. Only those involved could enter the room. First they called the names of the elementary school winners, and then those from junior high and senior high schools. Wearing the sky-blue dress, I was called before anyone else to receive a certificate and a prize. My mother sat in the seats reserved for family and watched, smiling proudly.

Following speeches by the governor's representative and the mayor, a man dressed in a formal black kimono embroidered with his family crest stepped to the front. I had seen his face somewhere before. The master of ceremonies introduced him as a teacher from the Boryu School of Flower Arranging. In a soft voice he said: "We see beautiful things, we create beautiful things, we introduce beautiful things to the world. I have more respect for these ideas than any of you can imagine. Strive even harder to know art and to study art. No matter how much mathematics and Japanese language you know, if you cannot understand beauty, you cannot become a complete person. Today, from my heart, I offer you congratulations."

As he concluded, his eyes turned in my direction, looking at a spot just above my head for a long time. They were indescribably warm, soft eyes. More than warm, they had a fiery light. Without realizing it, I stared at him. I had a feeling of belovedness. In contrast to Kanazaki's hugging, this was quite different.

When he stepped down from the stage, we were free to go, and I went back to search for my mother. I found that the smile that had been on her face had turned hard. I wondered what could have happened, what could have put her in a bad mood. Even as I wondered, I suddenly remembered: *That was the man who had appeared on television with the beautiful lady who taught me the hymn and gave me the thousand-yen bill.* My heart started beating hard.

Perhaps you know, Reverend, who this man was, this flower-arranging instructor who delivered the final congratulatory address. This refined, quiet-voiced gentleman dressed in a formal black kimono was my father. Of course, I didn't know it at the time. After the awards ceremony, there was a simple party of tea and cake. My mother showed no emotion, the muscles of her face tense as we stood and drank our tea.

Then the man in the kimono approached us. "Congratulations," he said to me. "Your painting is very good."

The picture was a big bouquet of chrysanthemums all crowded together, jostling each other within the confines of the frame. Though my creation looked as if it had no composition, I had painted each flower carefully, down to the tiniest detail. It was just like a Yamashita Kiyoshi painting. In the middle of the picture, I had made one chrysanthemum bigger than the rest, turning its face toward the sky like a sunflower. It was a design that no adult would have conceived, and perhaps this is what attracted the judging committee to it.

"Do you like flowers?" the man asked me. His voice

was warm, as if he were tender-hearted. I had never known a man with such a gentle way of speaking.

"Yes, I do," I said, a little nervous.

My mother kept her vision on the floor. The man said to her, "She's a good girl, isn't she?" My mother didn't say a word. But paying no attention to her ill humor, the man went on, "Watercolors suit her very well." He continued to smile down at me.

"I was given this dress," I said. "It came from somebody named Sugata Haru."

The man nodded his head and said, "I hope you'll show another painting later. Take care," and he left us.

"That man is a flower arranging teacher, isn't he?" I said, sipping my tea. Mother was silent and let out a big sigh.

"*O-kaa-san*, what's the matter? Don't you feel well?"

"No, it's nothing." Mother let out another sigh.

"That was the man on television, wasn't it?"

My mother looked at me, shocked.

"That time we were watching, he was with the beautiful lady, wasn't he?"

"I'd forgotten all about that," she said quickly.

"Oh, really! You couldn't have forgotten. That was the day I told you that I got a thousand yen from the lady on television." I looked around the auditorium. There was nobody else that I knew, nobody else to talk to but my mother.

"The pictures," my mother said, "let's go look at the pictures," and she started to leave the room. Because of my mother's behavior, by the way she avoided talking to me, I had the feeling that something wasn't right. I knew that it was better not to talk about those two people from now on. I was wise for a child only one week away from entering the sixth grade. I wondered who the two people could be, sure that there was some kind of special relationship between them.

The exhibition hall was alive with adults and the children they had brought along. My picture was displayed in the center of the hall. A crowd of people was standing in front of it. My mother's mood had recovered.

"Look at the people, Kiyomi!"

The people looking at the picture made comments such as "Oh, how carefully this is drawn!" and "It must have taken so long to do." I listened, embarrassed but proud. In its frame, it really did look very good.

My mother and I left my picture and made a circle of the hall. All of the pictures were good. More than simply good, some were interesting with bold composition and peculiar colors — pictures, in fact, that made me understand how childish my painting was.

We made a complete circle of the hall and were about to return to my painting when I was taken aback in surprise. In front of the picture was the lady, the one who had hugged me and shed tears, and had sung for me in a beautiful voice, again and again,

The good Lord up in Heaven above
Gives to all His gentle love.

On the baby sparrow in the eaves,
On the smallest ones . . .

She was wearing a powder-blue kimono and had one leg pulled a little behind her, a very beautiful and elegant way to stand. My mother noticed the lady and said, "Kiyomi, let's go home now," and pulled hard on my hand. I shook off her grasp and ran to the lady's side. How I'd yearned for the longest time to meet her again!

"*Oba-san*," I said impetuously.

When I spoke, the lady turned around in surprise, but she said immediately, "Oh! Kiyomi!" and put her hand on my shoulder. Yes, this beautiful lady knew my name. Even the first time we met, she called me by my name.

"You've gotten so big, Kiyomi!"

The lady put her arm around both my shoulders and looked down at me with a face that looked as if she wanted to laugh and cry at the same time.

"Congratulations," she said, almost whispering. "It's such a beautiful picture." I'll never forget that soft, gentle voice.

I often thought that if I ever met her again, I would sing the song she'd taught me and which I still remembered. I started singing in a low voice, "The good Lord up in Heaven above —"

"Oh! You remember!" Tears fell lightly from her eyes. Before I realized it, my mother was beside me. "Sawae," the lady said, "it's been a long time, hasn't it?"

I wondered if they had anticipated meeting here. The lady didn't seem surprised to see my mother.

"Yes, it has been," my mother said flatly. "Thank you so much, Saori, for Kiyomi's dress."

My heart danced. So she was the one who had sent me the dress! But I was sure that the name on the package that the dress came in was Sugata Haru.

"It looks very nice on her," the lady said. "Thank you for letting her wear it tonight. I'm so happy." My mother looked as if she were about to say something when the lady went on, "Why don't we go for some tea?"

I was thrilled to hear that, but my mother answered bluntly, "We're in a hurry."

The lady took both my hands in hers and said, "Kiyomi, take care of yourself, and draw another nice picture. When we meet again, let me hear you sing again, too." She seemed to put all her heart into every word she said.

"*Oba-san*, thank you for the dress." My throat had a lump in it. I didn't want to say goodbye to her ever again.

She stared deeply into my eyes and nodded. She wanted to say something, but her lips only moved. My mother again pulled on my hand, and we hastily left the hall.

It was to be my last parting from the beautiful lady.

That day, on the train going back to Asahikawa, we sat in a sparsely-filled car, and my mother talked to me for a long time, with frequent pauses. Combining what she told me that day with what I've heard since then, I'll try to tell you the whole story.

My mother had a hard childhood. From about the time she entered elementary school, she was raised by relatives, passed around from house to house. Even so, she came out of it all with a bright, outgoing personality. As soon as she had finished junior high school, she ran away and entered the night-life world of bars and cabarets. With her good looks and cheerful disposition, she fit right in. Before long, she was an assistant manager at a cabaret. There, she met a customer by the name of Funato Nobumasa.

This Funato Nobumasa was the flower-arranging teacher we'd seen on television and who gave the congratulatory speech at the all-Hokkaido elementary and middle school painting exhibition. He was already married when he met my mother, but even knowing this, she gave birth to me. She was barely twenty-one years old.

Up until the time I was told, that day in the train, that my father was the man who'd given the congratulatory speech, I'd thought my father was dead. Now I had to face the fact that he was a man who gave my mother a child and didn't even take responsibility for what he'd done.

"That's my father!" I said out loud without thinking about where I was. "That man is really my father?"

My mother tried to calm me.

"You're a liar!" I said. "You said my father was dead. Why did you lie to me?"

I burst into tears. I took it so hard that my mother probably regretted telling me the truth, but after all it was the best thing for her to do.

Mother said that she had vowed to herself never to lay eyes on Funato Nobumasa again, and she left Sapporo, intending never to return. He gave her some money, and she bought the house we were living in, and our strange life together began. There were just the two of us, though you now know that from as early as I can remember, my mother was bringing men home.

From the beginning Aunt Saori gave my mother all her support. My father consulted with her even before he confessed everything to his wife. His father, who was also a teacher of flower arranging, was very strict and severe. Fear of his father's anger kept him from telling his parents. Saori was the first one in the family to meet with my mother. Even to this day my mother says, "She was the only one who was kind to me. She was like an angel." Saori said that since the child my mother was carrying was her brother's child, the baby would be her niece or nephew. Even before I was born, she felt that I was part of her family and wanted to take care of me. She asked for forgiveness for what her brother had done, and she apologized again and again.

My mother replied, however, that the problem, she said, was strictly between Nobumasa and herself, and she refused any help. She didn't want to ruin the peace of another family, and in the end refused even to acknowledge her acquaintance. My father finally did reveal everything to his imperious parents, and even then Saori mediated between them.

Now you see, Reverend, why my mother was always adamant about not stepping even one foot into Sapporo. Never very logical in her reasoning, she said that she considered herself at least half responsible for what had happened and saw no reason to make trouble or try to blame it all on my father.

Mother said she felt she was "destined" to have me and insisted she had me because she wanted to. My father gave her the money that men usually give their mistresses when ending an affair, but it would be absurd to say that this was her original purpose. "When you think about it," mother once told me, "I had a baby by the man I loved. I think I'm the lucky one."

Mother acted quite admirably, actually, don't you think, Reverend? Yet she also told me that my father was dead, and then lived an immoral life right before my eyes. That's why I wondered if she ever really loved me at all.

These are the dreadful things I learned that day in the train on the way home to Asahikawa. Even so, knowing at last that the gentle lady who taught me the song was my real aunt gave me comfort.

As soon as we got into the house, my mother breathed a sigh of relief, and as always, without bothering to take off her coat, turned on the television. She's the kind of person who can't stand peace and quiet, but always has to be entertained.

On the television was the Hokkaido news. Just at that moment, they were showing the awards ceremony held that day. We watched the film of me accepting the award for first prize in the elementary school division. In my sky-blue dress with the black lace collar, I looked like a girl from an ordinary, respectable family. I thought of the soft voice and kindly face of the gentle lady.

The news went on, "Today there were two tragic car accidents. One was at the Mombetsu highway . . ." Paying no attention, my mother said, "Well, didn't you look grand on television!" However, half watching the news show, I suddenly felt my entire body stiffen in shock. On the screen I read, "Funato Saori (33 years old)," and there was a picture of her face.

"*O-kaa-san!*" "Kiyomi!" we shrieked at the same time, as the announcer was saying, ". . . killed instantly . . . ."

She died, Reverend. She died. She was on her way home from seeing my picture at the exhibition. She was crossing the street at a traffic light, and a reckless young driver ran a red light and slammed into her in the crosswalk.

Of course, I'd known death before. The first time was when Tsujiko died. That last moment is still vivid in my mind. She screamed, I looked back, she lost her balance, and then she was gone, down in the filthy water of the pool at the gravel pit. But as shocking as it was, I didn't experience the grief of death. In fact, Tsujiko's death gave me a feeling of liberation. It gave me a feeling of joy. It gave me peace of mind. I felt these things in a heart as cold as ice.

But when Aunt Saori died, only thirty-three years old, I was plunged into grief. I thought of her not as my aunt, but, as my mother had said, as an angel sent to me from heaven. I had no doubt that her kindness and generosity sprang from the very core of her being. I dare to think that she went to the department store for the sole purpose of seeing my picture, and she met with disaster because of it.

No, I should say that she came not to see my picture, but to see me.

I learned later that in order to have my dress made, my aunt had called my homeroom teacher on the telephone and asked for my size. She told my teacher, "I want to surprise her, so please keep it a secret." Her voice and words were so gentle, my teacher said, that she was enchanted. My homeroom teacher was a young woman, not yet thirty.

The name on the package, Sugata Haru, was not that of the man my mother was with when I was born, as she told me, but that of a maid who had worked for the Funato household for many years. She had raised my father and his younger sister. As their parents were very busy with flower arranging, they had no time to look after the children. Because of all this, my mother knew the name Sugata Haru. Many times, during the O-bon season or at New Year's, Aunt Saori sent presents to us under that name; so when the dress arrived, my mother didn't show the least bit of surprise. Later, in fact, she said that she felt almost certain that Aunt Saori would send something for the occasion.

After we learned that Aunt Saori had been killed, I begged my mother to take me to Sapporo.

"I want to go," Mother said, "but . . . ," and she let her words trail off, shaking her head helplessly. Then she repeated the words that she had said to me on the train. "He has a wife there," she muttered.

I had never been to a funeral, but I'd seen them on television dramas. I remembered a scene in which a little boy did a dance that he had learned in kindergarten before his grandfather's coffin. I was moved to tears by the sight, the little boy so adorable and so pitiful at the same time. I wanted to go to Sapporo because I wanted to sing that song for her one last time. I was beginning to realize that it was more than just a song for her, that it had a meaning very important to her. It dawned on me that the song was her legacy to me, the only thing left of the gentle lady who'd come to see me and then died on her way home.

In the end, of course, we couldn't possibly go to Sapporo. I made a secret grave in the grassy field near my house, no bigger than a grave you'd make for a pet goldfish. I drew a small portrait of her, working with all my heart, and buried it there. This was about the time the new school year was beginning. The snow that had covered the field all winter had melted, and the new grass was just sprouting. Whenever I was lonely, I went there and sang.

The good Lord up in Heaven above
Gives to all His gentle love.
On the baby sparrow in the eaves,
On the smallest ones, the least of these
He bestows His mercy.

As I sang, however, I would become angry. *It's a lie!* I thought. *"Gives to all His gentle love. Bestows His mercy." All lies!* I didn't believe in God. If there was a God, why would He let such a gentle person get killed in such a way? She was walking along innocently, and a stupid reckless driver had come along. How did she deserve to die like that? Singing the song that she taught me became painful.

It was around the end of my first semester back at school. My mother was lying on the floor eating *senbei* rice crackers.

"*O-kaa-san,*" I said, "how could such a nice person die like that?"

Mother slowly bit into a hard cracker, breaking it into pieces, thinking. Then she looked me full in the face. Had she noticed that I'd returned to my old silent, sullen habits? Did she realize that Aunt Saori had made such an impression on me that her death had cast a shadow over my heart? She swallowed her cracker with a loud gulp and said, "Maybe, in heaven, there's a shortage of good people, just like there is here. God must have work for her to do."

I looked at her in surprise. I had never thought that words like "God" and "heaven" would come so naturally out of my mother's mouth. She spoke as if heaven were a place she'd seen for herself.

I believed what my mother had said, that God takes good people to do His bidding in heaven. I accepted it, I suppose, because I knew what kind of person Aunt Saori was. I came to believe that there must be a heaven and that she was in it. I was just as certain that Tsujiko wasn't there. Wherever she had gone, it was definitely far different from the place where God had taken Aunt Saori. I came to these conclusions knowing nothing yet about Christianity.

6 A HANDFUL OF WATER

WHEN I STARTED junior high, my new school was only about a quarter of a mile from the elementary school I'd attended. A small stream ran nearby. Covered with grass ten feet tall in places, the banks were a little dangerous. I would cross to the middle of the little wooden bridge that hung over the stream, lean over the railing, and watch the clear water flow by. It comforted me. The white spring clouds drifted by on the surface of the stream. But even at peaceful times like this, memories of my aunt would suddenly come flooding into my mind.

One day, having stayed behind at school to help clean the art room, I was late coming home from school. With the sunlight in May still weak and by this time low in the sky, the early spring breeze was a bit chilly. In spite of the cold, I paused as always on the little wooden bridge, leaned over the railing, and gazed down at the flowing water below and at the reflection of the fading blue sky in it. Suddenly from behind me came the sound of footsteps. When I turned around, I saw a boy perhaps three or four years older than I. He had stopped and stood looking at me, looking as if he knew me. I was so surprised that it seemed as if time stood still, though it all took just an instant to happen. I knew his face, and suddenly remembered everything.

"Akira!" I cried without thinking. It was indeed the same Akira that Tsujiko had called *O-nii-san*.

How could I ever forget the short time that Akira had spent in Asahikawa, when he stayed at Tsujiko's house! I could still hear him saying, "If she says she didn't do it, she didn't do it. She's no thief."

The days that had followed, when Akira was there, were the happiest days of my life. But the time had been short. Within a week Akira had left. I guessed that Tsujiko's mother hadn't been very fond of Akira. His mother was, after all, her husband's first wife.

Akira had never returned to Tsujiko's house again. Even when Tsujiko died, Akira hadn't come. The years passed, and I gradually thought about him less and less. I didn't know that, in the meantime, Tsujiko's mother and Akira's father had separated and that Akira's father had moved to another part of Asahikawa.

When I was in the fifth grade, I had heard that Akira had moved back to Asahikawa. As it was only a rumor, something I heard by chance one day when my mother was gossiping with the next door neighbor, I didn't give it much thought. I never dreamed that Akira actually was a third-year student in the same junior high school as I was, and I certainly never expected to see him there beside me on the little wooden bridge. I'm surprised that I was able to call his name like that. Maybe it was his warm eyes and the kindness in them that went straight to my heart.

Akira scratched his head in an embarrassed way and eased past me on the narrow span without saying a word.

I stood still, watching Akira's back as he walked away.

Across the bridge the road split and went in two directions. Akira took the right fork, which was in the same
direction as my house. My heart throbbed violently. I wanted
to know where he lived, to follow him, but I stood frozen
where I was.

From the beginning I had thought that Akira was big
for his age, but now, though only a ninth grader, he looked
like a high school student. After walking about a hundred
yards Akira suddenly turned right. As he turned, he looked
back at me. Without thinking, I raised my hand and waved,
and to my delight Akira waved back shyly. I was filled with
happiness.

Starting the very next day, going to school became a
joy. There were four hundred first-year students in my junior
school, twelve or thirteen hundred students in all. Since I
was a first-year student and Akira was a third-year student,
we were in different buildings and used different entrances
to the school grounds. If we didn't move between the
science room, the drawing room, the music room and other
classrooms, first-year students and third-year students
wouldn't see each other at all. In the gymnasium we had
our own assigned places to play, and even outside, the
places where we could gather were restricted. I was happy
anyway. Just the thought of Akira being somewhere in the
same school was enough for me.

Sometimes we did pass each other in the hall. We didn't
speak, but we didn't have to. Each time, Akira would look
over at me with those big warm eyes, eyes full of goodness

and kindness; each time, the blood rushed to my face and my cheeks turned bright red.

One day I waited on the little wooden bridge for Akira to pass by on his way home from school. As we had met by chance on a Friday at around 5:30 in the afternoon, I chose that time to stand waiting on the bridge. I think it was around the first week of June.

On the banks of the river, sweet but forlorn little forget-me-nots were in full bloom. Do you like forget-me-nots, Reverend? I like them so much that it makes me want to cry sometimes. I like their soft blue color and their star-like shape, and I like the time of the year when they are in full bloom. But I especially like the name: "forget-me-nots." Do you know the poem about forget-me-nots? Maybe you've heard it before.

On the banks of a flowing stream
the blue of the water
the same clear blue of the sky
A handful of water to cool your face.
Like that handful of water
everything in life passes
and is forgotten.

There's a certain loneliness about this poem, don't you think? At the time, I'd never heard it, but as I waited for Akira to come home from school, studying the forget-me-nots on the banks of the river, I felt the emotion that the poem expresses.

My strategy paid off, and Akira soon appeared. By this time, we had exchanged glances many times in the hall, and unlike the first time we met on the bridge, this time he turned to me warmly. "Well, here we are again," he said.

I was silent and just nodded, but I'm sure he could see the happiness in my eyes.

"You're a first-year student, aren't you? In, I think, Class Two?"

Akira had somehow learned I was in Class Two! Again I only nodded.

"And you're in the art club too."

"Which club are you in?" I finally managed to say.

"I'm in the chess club."

"The *shogi* club?" I said.

"There are only a few members, so it's usually me against the teacher."

We were talking about little everyday matters as if we'd been friends for a long time. No matter what we talked about, I enjoyed it.

Before long, I met another person who was to be important in my life. I don't suppose you have any idea who it is yet, Reverend. Sometimes I wonder if there's a plan for the way people seem to meet by chance. But before I talk about this other person, I want to write a little more about Akira.

Soon I'll be twenty-three years old, but when I think back to the time I was a first-year junior-high student, I can see that my feelings toward the opposite sex haven't changed much since then. Akira and I met by chance on a

Friday afternoon on the little wooden bridge, and I decided to wait for him right there every Friday afternoon at about the same time. I didn't even have to meet him. Just waiting for him was happiness for me. In fact, sometimes when I saw him coming, I left before he arrived, or exchanged only a word or two with him before hurrying away.

Then one Friday, as always, I was hanging over the railing watching the flow of the river. It was the beginning of September, and one group of forget-me-nots was still beautifully in bloom. No matter how many times I stopped to look at them, I never grew tired of watching the little blue flowers as they nodded on their steep bank over the surface of the stream. The white clouds were reflected in the blue water. It was a quiet, late summer evening. My watch told me that it was past 6:30. I was just thinking that I would give up for today and go home when Akira's tall figure appeared beside me. I was so happy that my chest throbbed. Without thinking I blurted out, "I'm so glad! I thought I wouldn't see you today."

Akira looked straight at me. "Me too," he murmured.

Just those two words were enough to tell me everything. I knew that he had been looking forward to seeing me too. I didn't know what to say in reply. I turned away from him, back toward the river and the flowers on the riverbank. "They're beautiful aren't they? The forget-me-nots."

"I'll get you some." Like the expression in his eyes, his voice was warm.

"It's too dangerous," I said, shaking my head, but Akira was already at the top of the embankment.

The forget-me-nots were at the bottom of the six-foot embankment. Slanting at nearly a forty-five degree angle, the embankment was so steep that I feared Akira would slide down and fall into the stream. The stream was shallow and not really dangerous, but he might still get all wet.

As I expected, Akira slipped. "Be careful!" I cried. He caught himself, hung on precariously, and picked a bunch of forget-me-nots before climbing back up again.

"Thank you," I said, feeling real gratitude from the bottom of my heart. "Thank you very much."

Suddenly I remembered. I remembered Tsujiko. I remembered her high-pitched scream as she fell into the black water. Though I was only five years old when it happened, that sound had made such a strong impression on me that I'll never forget it as long as I live. And even though I could hear Tsujiko's family and the people in the neighborhood searching for her everywhere, I didn't tell them that she had fallen into the black pool in the gravel pit.

There were reasons why I didn't, of course, but the memory still burned in my heart. Even if I had rushed up the wide dry riverbed and run across the meadow and found an adult to tell, she still would have died. And then, just as they had with the thousand-yen-bill incident, wouldn't people have suspected the worst, suspected me of pushing Tsujiko from behind? I told you how my trust in people, and especially in adults, had already been destroyed.

As I clutched the precious forget-me-nots that Akira had picked for me, I remembered everything. It occurred to me that if I told Akira about Tsujiko's death, he would believe me. The time when I was blamed for stealing a thousand yen, nobody believed me but him. Thus, I reasoned, if I told him about Tsujiko's death, he would surely believe every word I said.

Yet, as sure as I was that he would believe me, I couldn't help fearing that he wouldn't. Even if he did believe me, there was the possibility that he would at least blame me for not telling someone the place where Tsujiko had died. You can see that, because of everything that had happened to me, I'd become habitually fearful and didn't trust anybody, not even Akira. Though I knew it wasn't true, I had the terrible feeling of having actually committed the crime of murdering Tsujiko. I wanted to confess, to release Tsujiko's name from my throat. Instead I held the forget-me-nots away from me and thanked him again.

After a moment, Akira said, "You remember Tsujiko, don't you?"

I was taken by surprise. I wanted to say no, but answered quickly, "Yes, I remember."

"She fell into a river and died." He seemed to be reporting something he'd heard secondhand.

"A river?" I said. "I heard that she fell into a pool of water in a gravel pit."

"Really?" Akira looked as if he were already thinking of something else. Apparently Tsujiko's death hadn't had the terrible impact on him that it had had on me. Though she was his half-sister, he barely knew her, and was in Sapporo at the time. But she fell into the black water right before my very eyes, and that vivid memory still reached across the distance of time to chill my heart.

Summer vacation came. During the summer break Akira went to Sapporo to stay with his grandparents. His grandfather, a high school teacher, was going to help him prepare for the high-school entrance exams that he had to take the following year.

With Akira gone, I was lonelier than ever. The loneliness was like an emptiness running through my veins. You know the figure of speech in Japanese about wind blowing through your body? It was a much greater loneliness than that. I wanted to go to Sapporo too, but I had no home there to stay in as Akira had. My real father lived there, but he had a wife and family. It was impossible for me even to consider visiting him. If only my aunt were still alive, I was sure she would have taken me in. Suddenly remembering my dead aunt only added to my dreadful loneliness.

Just before he left for the summer, as I was anticipating the long months of loneliness, Akira asked me, "Do you want to bicycle to Arashiyama tomorrow?" You can't imagine how happy those words made me. That night I couldn't sleep for thinking of the next day. Now, thinking back to this time, I can see that this was my first love. There were no men in my house. Maybe it was enough for Akira just to be male for him to capture my heart. There was also no doubt a yearning in me for an older brother to depend on.

That morning I told my mother, "I'm going to Arashiyama by bicycle. With a friend."

"By bicycle? Isn't that dangerous?"

Try to remember that I never went anywhere with friends, since I didn't have any. For the most part, I took my sketch book and went out alone without telling my mother where I was going. Yet when I announced that I was going bicycling with a friend to Arashiyama, a hillside far out in the suburbs, she wasn't even the least bit surprised.

This casual negligence is very much a part of my mother. She was completely insensitive to her own daughter's private life. She had no curiosity about my friendships with classmates. School friends? I wasn't friends with anyone, and my mother was unaware of it. If she had been aware of my friendlessness, she would have been surprised to hear me say that I was going bicycling with a friend. She didn't understand a thing about me. She was worried only about a traffic accident. It never occurred to her that her daughter was living a life of black isolation, almost to the point of wanting to die. Maybe she just couldn't imagine that such a bitter loneliness could live in the heart of a child.

I asked her, "Don't you want to know what kind of friend it is?"

"What kind of friend?" she said, not understanding my question.

"For example, whether it's a boyfriend or a girlfriend."

She laughed out loud. "You're only twelve! Of course it isn't a boyfriend!"

I also laughed. "You're right," I told her. At the time, I felt a kind of affection for her. She didn't doubt me at all. Her foolishness was beautiful in a way. She thought that she knew so much about relations between men and women, but since for her the feeling of being in love and the physical aspects of love went hand in hand, there was a lot she didn't know.

I made some rice balls, gathered up my sketch book and pencils, and left the house. Of course, I made enough *onigiri* for my "friend," too.

Akira and I were to meet at the foot of the Asahi Bridge. As I waited, I watched the two rivers, the Ishimori and the Ushubetsu, flow into each other under the big bridge. Except for a few light clouds, it was a clear July day. Though the water from the Ishimori River was crystal clear, the water from the Ushubetsu was polluted from the wastes of a pulp mill upstream. When the waters of the two rivers met under the bridge, they didn't join right away, but flowed parallel to each other for a while. I watched this phenomenon with interest. Only several hundred yards down the river did the two streams finally mix.

Akira came a few minutes ahead of schedule. "Oh, I thought I'd be the first one here," he said cheerfully.

Have you ever been to Arashiyama, Reverend? I've heard from my teachers that it's a valuable area for botanists. If you climb to the top, you can see the whole city of Asahikawa, as well as the graceful peak of Mt. Daisetsu to the east. Below is the calmly flowing Ishimori, which drinks up the Ushubetsu under the Asahi Bridge and flows into the Nakabetsu farther downstream.

When I was in the fifth grade, my class climbed Arashiyama once on a school outing. Akira said that he came when he was in the sixth grade. He also came sometimes now with friends and sometimes alone.

"Whenever I come, for some reason I get the feeling that this place is a wilderness, not a place for people," Akira said when we reached Arashiyama, our faces flushed from the ride.

"It's so beautiful here," I said.

We sat a little apart on a bench on the lookout platform. Sitting quietly, we studied the city of Asahikawa sprawled out under the blue July sky. The blue and red tile roofs of the neat rows of houses seemed to stretch to the horizon. From our perspective, the town seemed to be asleep. Apart from the flow of the Ishimori, no matter how hard we looked, we could see nothing stirring. It was like a picture. All we could hear was the singing of the cicadas. After a while we began to talk about our families.

Akira said that he remembered when his mother and father got along well together. His father, Nakayama Shozou, worked at an automobile company and was an excellent businessman. His mother, Kikuko, was good at sewing and cooking. He said that his father was forty-four and his mother was forty-one. "I still don't really understand why," he said, "but when I was five, they got a divorce." Then his mother went to dressmaking school in

Tokyo, and he was left with his mother's parents. His grandfather was a sociology teacher.

Akira told me that not long after his parents separated, his father remarried, and his stepmother came to live in the Nakayama house, bringing Tsujiko along with her. Thinking back on it now, I wonder if Akira's father seduced Tsujiko's mother even before his divorce. Then after they were married, maybe he realized how selfish he had been and began to long for his first wife. He must have deeply regretted sending his only son off to be raised by Kikuko's parents. At any rate, all during that first summer when Akira lived in Asahikawa, Tsujiko's mother made both Akira and his father the objects of her anger. The atmosphere in the house was tense.

In the midst of all this came Tsujiko's death.

"It happened so suddenly," Akira said. A shock ran through me, just as it had when Akira mentioned Tsujiko's death while we were standing on the little wooden bridge.

After Tsujiko died, Akira's father and Tsujiko's mother separated. "I really didn't understand that, either," he said. Not long after that, his mother and father started seeing each other from time to time, and three years after Tsujiko's death, when Akira was in the fifth grade, they got back together again.

"Well, now you're happy," I said.

"Happy? I guess you could say that. But if my mother and father hadn't split up before, I'd be a lot happier." Akira gave a sad little laugh. "I'll bet your house isn't as crazy as mine," he said.

I didn't know what to say. Compared to my house, Akira's was quite stable!

"My house . . .," I began, but stopped. I wanted to tell Akira everything. If he wanted to scorn me after he knew everything, then he could. I wanted to try to tell him the secrets that I couldn't tell anyone else. I was in the seventh grade, but compared to my classmates, I was an adult.

Finally, I spoke. I told him about my mother and father's affair and about my father's wife. I told him about how my mother had taken me from Sapporo to Asahikawa to live alone, about my mother's many men friends, and even about Kanazaki, who was my "father" for a short while. I told him that my real father was in Sapporo, and I described how my aunt had died in a traffic accident. I talked about allthese things. Of course, I mentioned the incident of the thousand-yen bill.

After I had finished talking, Akira was silent. He was quiet for a long, long time. We were alone on the lookout platform, surrounded by the loud buzzing of the cicadas. Akira just stared down at the city.

I immediately regretted having told him everything about my mother. Now he would surely shun her, a woman who had given birth to a married man's baby and who entertained men for money in her own house. I had known the risk I was taking, but had I told him everything. Maybe I just couldn't bear it alone any more. Maybe I needed to share my secret misery with someone. I can't really say what my feelings were, but I think I just wanted a friend to talk to, a companion to whom I could say, "Listen to me, listen to my story." But as Akira sat in silence, perhaps shocked or even angry, I began to feel I'd made a mistake.

Then he said in a voice filled with sympathy, "Kiyomi, do you know what a grown-up is?"

I was surprised. He wasn't angry at all. As far as I could tell, his feelings toward me hadn't changed a bit. But his question was too difficult for me; I didn't know what he meant.

"A grown-up?" I said helplessly.

"When I was little, I always thought that grown-ups were our models. But . . ." and here Akira paused, as if to get courage to say what he was about to, then continued, ". . . my mother and father, Tsujiko's mother too, they're not models."

I'd thought the same thing so many times! I couldn't remember ever thinking of adults as my models. I remembered my mother, when her men friends came over, handing me money and saying, "Now be a good girl and don't come back until I call you." I remembered her red-painted lips laughing, a smudge of lipstick on her front teeth, a stain that made her seem dirty to me, even though I was just a child and didn't really understand. I couldn't go so far as to tell even Akira about that.

"Grown-ups say all kinds of things, like 'Answer me properly,' or 'Why don't you study more?' or 'Why don't you settle down?'" He laughed bitterly.

"And even if we become exactly what they want us to be—" I started to say.

Akira cut in, "But that's impossible anyway. Even

children have their own lives and their own ideas. Adults were young once; so they should understand."

"That's right. Parents were young once, too." I hung onto every word Akira said.

"Have you ever heard of Natsume Soseki?" he said.

"Natsume Soseki?" I shook my head. "I've never heard of him." I didn't know whether he was a school teacher, a movie star, or a baseball player. Since my mother didn't read anything that could be called literature, there were no real books in our house, and the names of authors never entered into our conversation. In any event, most junior high school students couldn't be expected to know such things.

On the contrary, in this respect Akira was an adult. Though only a ninth grader, Akira was in essence a high school student. When he was in elementary school, he had hurt his leg and had to take a year off from school. His father liked books, and his grandfather was also a great reader, so by the time he was in the fifth grade he had read books like *Botchan* and *I Am a Cat*. As mature for my age as I was, compared with Akira, I was, in many ways, quite childish.

Akira didn't make fun of me for not knowing who Natsume Soseki was, though. "You don't like books?" he said.

"I mostly paint pictures. There aren't any books in my house."

"Well, if you don't hate them, then you should try to read a bit. I'll lend you a few."

I said that I wanted to borrow some. I would have done anything that Akira thought I should. This was the first time I'd ever had such a feeling. It made me completely happy.

"What do you think of my mother?" I asked in a burst of courage. "You hate her, don't you?"

"I like Dostoevsky," he said, using a word I'd never heard before. He understood my confusion instantly.

"Dostoevsky was a Russian author back when the USSR was known as Russia. He was a Christian, and he wrote the novel *Crime and Punishment*. If you read and understand this book, then you can't look down on girls who have had a lot of boy friends any more. When your mother was young, she loved a married man. She moved to Asahikawa because she didn't want to cause him any trouble. I think I can imagine what's in your mother's heart. I can't hate her."

I was surprised. I'd never even realized that my mother could be thought of in this sympathetic way. I wondered if people who read books were all like this.

"There's another Russian author, Tolstoy, that you should read, too," said Akira. I was a little bewildered by all the strange new names. "He wrote a novel called *Resurrection*. It's about a rich man's son — he's really no good, and he does something bad to the family's young housemaid."

"Something bad?" I immediately thought of Kanazaki.

"The maid's name was Kachusha, and she was still very pure. Afterwards the young man forgot all about Kachusha. And then much later he was on a jury. He was an aristocrat.

In Russia in those days only the nobility could be jurors. Anyway, one of the criminals on trial was a prostitute."

"Kachusha?"

"That's right. He didn't even recognize her at first. As he listened to her story, though, he remembered when he was young how he'd taken advantage of a pure young girl, and he realized that this girl was Kachusha."

"What happened then?"

"He knew that he was the one responsible for what had happened to her, and he was shaken to the core. Kachusha was exiled to Siberia, and he decided to join her there. He hoped for the rebirth of her soul. There's more to the story than that, but I wish that your father could be like that man and recognize that what he's done is a crime. I don't blame your mother. My intuition tells me that your father is the one to blame."

I'll never forget the fervent tone in Akira's voice when he said that. Perhaps because of it, that day I thought of my father as a real person for the first time.

When I got home, my mother said, "You were lucky to have such nice weather." She took some ice cream from the refrigerator and gave me a dish of it. The thoughts that went through my mind as I sat and ate my ice cream are indescribable. My mother watched television, laughing from time to time at something that amused her.

7 FATHER

AT THIS POINT my story skips ahead three years. During those three years, from the time I met Akira again just after entering junior high school, I can't say anything momentous happened to me. However, I did continue to change inside. For one thing, I began to save up my allowance in order to buy books.

My painting changed too. I want to tell you about it because it reflects what was going on inside me.

Up until the time I discovered novels I had devoted myself to painting pictures — but only pictures of flowers. From a very early age, when I looked at flowers, I would sometimes feel something like a sharp ache in my heart. What touched my heart wasn't people, or dolls, or even little animals. It was flowers. It seems that I really did have the same blood in my veins as my grandfather, who raised flowers all his life, and my father, who taught flower arranging. Flowers have shape, they have color. A flower is a complete world in itself, a small splendid universe.

From the time I was in elementary school, when I first began to sketch flowers, I realized one thing, a very ordinary but profound thing: A flower, no matter how beautiful, no matter how splendid, will wilt in the dark. When there is no light, a flower loses its shape and color.

I realized this ordinary truth, and thought of it when my aunt, who was like pure light, died in the traffic accident.

My conversations with Akira gradually began to revolve around what I was reading. I made a discovery similar to the one I'd made about flowers: that to me novels were very rich in color. For example, if an author wrote, "The young girl turned her white cheek and laughed," then, as if the girl was before my eyes, I could envision her glowing red lips, her black hair shining in the sun, the color of her blouse, her skirt, her shoes. Of course, I imagined the colors I liked the most, but from nothing more than a "white cheek," from only one color, I could create the rest. If there was a passage about a young boy walking down a road in a farming village, I could freely imagine the color of the field, the road, the mountains in the distance, the clouds, the river, the dancing of the light in the air. The imaginary world of literature freed my mind to create as many colors as I wished.

During my three years of junior high school, I read Tolstoy and Dostoevsky, and then Andre Gide, Hermann Hesse, Thomas Mann, and many others. I didn't like everything I read. Some of the books, such as Gide's *Lafcadio's Adventures* and *The Immoralist*, were fairly easy reading, but no matter what I read, I felt a dark shadow hanging over me. After all, a shadow is the first natural product of light, isn't it?

During that time I discovered something else: the existence of the Bible. The face of the Bible kept appearing between the lines of the novels I was reading.

Phrases from the Bible even cropped up in the characters' conversations, as if the words were so well-known that everyone knew them.

Gradually I became interested in this book called the Bible. Yet somehow I was uneasy about the idea of reading it. Sometimes I would think to myself, *Well, I guess it won't kill me not to read the Bible,* and I would talk myself out of buying a copy. Somewhere in my heart was the idea that reading the Bible would be troublesome, would in some way create a painful dilemma in my spirit. I think I feared that the Bible had the power, unlike a novel, to enter directly into my soul. *I can live without the Bible,* I would rationalize. Thinking back on it now, I can't believe that I could ever have had such a feeling.

When I started high school, of course I joined the art club. In drawing and painting I was far and away the best first-year student in the club, though in my stubbornness I painted only flowers. Soon, however, I did begin to expand, and experimented with vegetables and fruit, dishes and dolls, and even people.

In painting people, however, I ran into a problem. It's difficult enough to draw the flesh; you must imagine the subject's very skeleton, and draw the muscles and even the blood vessels with painstaking accuracy. But the real problem is trying to draw what lies in a person's heart. In a person's expression, particularly in the eyes, there's a hint of the world of the spirit that I found hard to acknowledge. When I drew only flowers, I couldn't imagine how difficult this would be. I began to fear this quality in people.

It was about this time that I met the important person I mentioned earlier. For some reason she didn't join the art club until a month after school started; so by the time she joined the other members already knew each other. The club advisor, Mr. Ozawa, told us, "As we have a new member today, let's all introduce ourselves." Always cheerful, Mr. Ozawa made the atmosphere of the art club pleasant.

Just as we first-year students had been questioned when we first joined, so now we all turned to the new member with our questions. She was on the short side, and her complexion was a little dark, but her face was open and friendly. In particular, when she laughed, her narrow eyes become merry and kind.

One of the second-year boys said, "I've got a question!" He always asked the same question if the new member was a girl: "Will you model for me?"

"Model for you!" At first she was a bit surprised, but then she said, "I wouldn't mind — if I can keep my clothes on." Everyone laughed.

"In that case, I have a second question." This was from a third-year student, a boy, as you might expect. "What's your name and address?"

"Kanazaki Noriko. The *ka* of Kato, the *na* of Nara, and the *saki* of Nagasaki," she said, explaining the Chinese characters that made up her name, and then she gave her address.

Kanazaki Noriko? My mind raced; my heart throbbed. *Kanazaki? Kanazaki?*

Reverend, don't you think that we're constantly tested,

day in and day out? I think that our lives are a series of confrontations with problems, confrontations that bring us face to face with our true selves.

I hate being reminded of the kind of person I was that day, the day I met Kanazaki Noriko. Like poison filling a glass, malice filled my heart. Not only because of her last name, but also because of her address, I knew who she was.

That night I couldn't sleep. I scribbled my rival's name in my notebook again and again, *Kanazaki Noriko, Kanazaki Noriko,* I don't know how many times. As I wrote, I filled every character with hate, and I thought of ways to deal with her. I kept remembering that summer evening when my mother and I went to eat *sushi,* when in front of the *sushi* bar we saw that beautiful car with the courteous chauffeur, and then the happy family, the Kanazakis and their daughter Noriko and their son.

I'll never forget the violent jealousy I felt toward Kanazaki's children. And then I remembered the unspeakable things that Kanazaki had done to me, things he would never think of doing to his own precious little girl. Meeting Noriko brought all these things back to burn in my heart.

I'll tell her about her father's perversions, I decided maliciously. Noriko had been raised in comfort and gentility, ignorant of what life was really about. She never had to worry about money or about what kind of people her parents were. I couldn't leave her like that. It's shameful, but I cursed her like a jealous demon.

Until that time, in my pride, I thought I'd become a better person than before. Never showing my emotions, I was the quiet, unassuming type, trying always to be accommodating. I lived by avoiding trouble. Generally I hoped for peace and for the well-being of others.

Yet when I found that Noriko was Kanazaki's daughter, I found myself unwilling to let her happiness continue. When I saw her carefree smile and thought about her blissful ignorance, I had an urge to snatch it all away from her forever.

I could do it too. The father she loved had used my mother for years. He had been like a father to me, yes, but he did things that no father should do to a daughter. All I had to do was to tell her, and her happiness would be destroyed. It never occurred to me that it might be a bad thing to do; in fact, I thought that it was quite proper to destroy the contentedness of Kanazaki and his family. Like an avenging goddess, I would expose Kanazaki's true nature and do away with his family's false little heaven.

People always think that they're right. They can always find a way to justify their actions, to rationalize even the most evil tortures.

As I now understand, no matter what her father did, Noriko couldn't be blamed. Sins are the burden of the sinner only. If a person commits a murder, then only he is responsible, not his whole family. Even if you were a husband or a wife, a parent or a child, you wouldn't be put to death in place of the guilty person. Of course I realize that several people can be held jointly responsible for a crime, but for the most part the sin of a crime rests on one person's head.

I wondered what was the best way to get close to Noriko. Of course, since we were in the art club together, it would be easy to become friends. But I didn't want to use the most natural way of getting close to her. I wanted her to seek me out. I even thought of ignoring her, without talking to her at all, until graduation if need be. I held the key to her happiness, Reverend, and I relished the frightful thought of dreaming up different ways to push this innocent girl into a world of misery.

Lord, I pray You'll forget the person I was then. Turn Your eyes away from my sins. I can hardly bear to confront that hideous side of my nature.

At that time I should have talked openly to Akira about my feelings toward Noriko. If I had, he would surely have extinguished the black flame in my heart.

But I didn't tell Akira. Why? As a third-year student he had begun intense study for the approaching university entrance exams. He still set aside one or two hours a week to talk with me, but I thought my problem with Noriko would be too much of a burden for him. This wasn't the kind of thing you discussed with a person absorbed in study.

Art club activities took great chunks of every day now. Older students aiming at entering an art school were busy from seven o'clock in the morning working on sketches. With a charcoal pencil in one hand and an eraser in the other, the third-year students were all seriousness.

For the early months of the school year Mr. Ozawa

refused first-year students the privilege of using colors. "The first semester is a world of black and white," he told us, unwilling to depart from the practice of his own student days at the Tokyo School of the Arts. So sketching with pencil and charcoal, we practiced earnestly day in and day out. In this atmosphere my strong feelings toward Noriko ebbed.

Drawing was for me, besides life itself, the greatest fact of my existence. Like the third-year students eager to go on to study art, I came to school early and studied their sketches over their shoulders. Four seniors who wanted to get into Tokyo School of the Arts had, as may be expected, exceptional ability, even brilliance.

For the first and second-year students, the best third-year students were like celebrities. Unlike the second-year students, they never threw their weight around, yelling things like, "Do you call this room clean?" or "For a first-year student, you've really got a big head." Instead they would turn to their easels with a resigned sigh, or they would tell a joke to the whole room and make everyone laugh. They really had the air of budding artists. One time a second-year student told me, "The third-year students really shine, but only for now. Once they go off to college and return to visit us, most of the time they're disillusioned. They're like little baby chicks out there. Watch and see when they come back next year."

I understood what he meant. When the entrance exam, the one goal before their eyes, had passed, even those who shone brightly would experience a let-down, some even losing their ambition. I felt that I would pass on to adulthood without experiencing even this momentary but brilliant gleam. I had a feeling that Noriko's presence alone would kill my enthusiasm before it was born.

Noriko — who, of course, knew nothing about my feelings — would place her easel right next to mine when she drew. Since we were both first-year students, she was probably trying to express her friendship in a perfectly natural way.

In the beginning my pictures had a passion that Noriko couldn't begin to equal. However, my pictures changed with my disposition. One day, a third-year student, Takii Ichiro, came and stood beside me, silently watching me draw. Then he said, "Your pictures have become so messy." I was taken aback in surprise. Ichiro was practically a student teacher in the club. He had a reputation for reading Okakura Tenshin and for reading not only art books, but also other literature. Mr. Ozawa was rumored to have said, "A Takii Ichiro comes along only once every few years." His guidance of the younger students was sharp and strict, but warm and sincere, so all of the club members admired him.

As I swallowed my breath in surprise, Ichiro continued. "Kiyomi, when I first saw your sketches, I thought your lines were very clean and clear. I thought that we had someone really promising here. Recently your work has been ordinary. No, less than ordinary. Ugly. Dirty."

I held my breath and listened. I could feel the other club members listening. My face was burning in embarrassment. I realized that he had read my heart perfectly.

"I'm only saying this because you really are talented." His voice was warm. "Now don't go jumping off a roof. It's not that important."

"I understand," I said. "Thank you," and I bowed my head low.

When I was walking home that day, Noriko came up to walk beside me. She'd looked as if she were trying to approach me several times before, but I'd always hurried home or purposely changed direction and gone home by a roundabout way in order to avoid her. However, that day, preoccupied as I was by what by Ichiro had told me, I was absent-minded. For the moment, I forgot completely about my feelings toward Noriko. I wanted to avoid her, but I also wanted somebody to be with.

She started off by talking about why she had been late in joining the art club. "As soon as school started this year, I had to have my tonsils out. Have you had your tonsils out? If my tonsils got just a little bit infected, they would swell up like a big white strawberry. Yuk!" Then she giggled merrily.

Noriko laughed about everything, even if it wasn't funny. Ichiro nicknamed her "The Giggling Girl."

"Anyway, do you know why I joined the art club?" She had a habit of putting questions to people in this way, but after asking the question, she didn't wait for a response. "I joined the art club because my older brother advised me to.

"Do you know my older brother? He's going to graduate this year. He's really practical. He said that some people in the art club go the whole year without painting a single picture. He goes only to watch girls. He shows off by talking about theories of art. I thought, *Well, if that's all there is to it, I think I can do it!* The music club is different. Sports clubs, too." She giggled as always.

I was shocked to hear her say this. Before that, I'd thought that she was more grown-up than I was, not the kind of girl who would join the art club just to be looked at. Her sketches were strong, too, not the kind of thing a frivolous girl would draw. If she weren't Kanazaki's daughter, I would probably want to make friends with her.

All I could say was, "Well, I'm glad you're happy in the club," and I turned down the road to my house. Strangely, on that day I didn't want to say goodbye to Noriko. I was hoping that she would comfort me. Surely she understood the pain of hearing Ichiro say that my pictures were dirty.

Do you know why my pictures are dirty? I thought as I turned around and watched Noriko walk away under the evening June sky. *It's because of your father.*

This one idea went around and around in my mind. If I told her what I was thinking, for once she wouldn't have anything to giggle about.

When I got home that night, it was already close to eight o'clock. As soon as I walked in, my mother rushed up to me, demanding, "Where were you all this time?"

Though she had never said anything before when I

was late, this time she came to the door all flustered and red in the face. Without answering, I squeezed past her into the house.

"We're going to Sapporo," she said in an excited voice.

"Sapporo?"

She nodded silently. Her expression told me that it was something serious. "Your father is sick."

"My father?"

"Yes." With that, she turned away and went to the telephone to call for a taxi.

I wanted to say, "I don't have a father." But I was a first-year high school student now. I had been in the fifth grade the only time I ever met my father. The affection in his eyes and the warmth in his voice had enveloped me. I had never doubted that someday, somehow, we would meet again as father and daughter. I was silent.

"It's a hemorrhage of some kind," my mother went on. "They're in the middle of the operation right now. They said that they can't guarantee he'll live."

We got to the station in time for the last express train to Sapporo. My mother and I sat next to the window, facing each other. She sat silently, holding a handkerchief to her eyes. The handkerchief became soggy from her tears. Seeing her cry, I found it hard to hold back and had to wipe away my own tears.

I discovered a new person in my mother that day. True to her promise, she'd abandoned Sapporo, given me shelter, and guarded her secret for all those years. But, though she kept to her promise not to step foot in Sapporo again for a long time, all that time she kept her love for my father locked in her heart.

From the station we rushed to the hospital to find my father was still in the operating room. The red sign, "Operation In Progress," was lit, and outside the operating room a dozen or so concerned people had gathered and were seated in a row on a long bench. I guessed that some were my father's students.

A lady in her forties was sitting on the end of the bench. When she saw us, mother and daughter, she stood and came toward us. At a glance I knew that this was my father's wife. She stopped in front of my mother and bowed slightly. She looked as if she wanted to say something, but instead offered us a place beside her on the long bench. After we sat down she looked into my face and said, "You must be Kiyomi." Then she turned to my mother. "It's been a long time, hasn't it, Sawae? I'm sorry that I had to call you like that."

My mother put her handkerchief to her eyes and only nodded, crying shamelessly.

The lady began to explain calmly. "I think it was a little past five o'clock. He said that he was tired; so I hurried dinner along. Funato—" she broke off, swallowed hard, then continued, "Funato took two or three bites. Then suddenly he dropped his chopsticks on the floor. Before we even had time to be surprised, his body started shaking, and he bent over and threw up his food."

I listened intently, trying to remember what my father looked like.

"His face turned blue, and his hands became ice cold. Then the maid — you remember Sugata Haru — began to help him so that he wouldn't choke on the food. Eventually she even called for an ambulance, since I was too flustered to do anything. Then, as we were waiting for the ambulance, she told me that if anything ever happened, Funato wanted you and Kiyomi to be called. He'd said the same thing to me ... and so — I was sorry to bother you — I called, and—"

"Yes, yes," my mother interrupted impatiently. "What do you know about his condition now?" It was the first time she'd opened her mouth.

"He's been unconscious the whole time. Until we know how the operation turns out, we won't know his prognosis."

"Is he going to live?"

"The doctors say there's hope. That's why they're operating."

As soon as she said this, my mother said, "There's hope! Thank goodness. Kiyomi, she said there's hope." Finally she smiled. The refined composure of my father's wife contrasted sharply with the figure of my mother.

But there was something else about my mother, Reverend, something I sensed deep in my heart. There were times when she disgusted me, times when I thought she was obscene, times when I was ashamed to have her for a mother. Yet in that same person I saw suddenly something pure and clean, pure as fresh snow.

For my mother's sake, I felt an urge to pray for my

father's recovery. His students crowded together now, whispering to each other. Several men were mixed in with ladies in their forties, fifties, and sixties. They all threw quick, curious glances in our direction, and I had the feeling that they knew all about us.

My mother had told me that my father had no other family in Hokkaido and only a few relatives in the Tokyo area. I sat quietly on the long bench. I thought how different the scene would be if my aunt were still alive. With an indescribable longing, I thought, *If only she could be here to sing her song in that beautiful, angelic voice!*

The good Lord up in Heaven above
Gives to all His gentle love.
On the baby sparrow in the eaves,
On the smallest ones . . .

My father's wife said, "It will be a while before the operation is over. Are you going to wait? Or perhaps it would be better to relax in a hotel."

My mother answered sharply, "I didn't come here to stay in some hotel."

Not showing a bit of emotion, the lady replied, "Yes, I suppose that's so." She bowed, then stood and returned to her original seat on the bench.

After a while, I asked my mother, "Does she have any children?"

"She had one, but it died. Then they adopted a child, but I think he left home."

My mother didn't speak to me again that night. She sat with her hands folded, sometimes mumbling something under her breath, sometimes turning her eyes toward heaven. She prayed by turns to the gods and to Buddha.

Watching her pray for my father's life to gods she couldn't see, I wondered if it was right for me to still bear a grudge against my father. Sometimes I hated him blindly. He'd fathered a child with a woman he wouldn't marry. It occurred to me that night that perhaps my mother had never once hated my father for what he had done to her. Perhaps she still reserved a place for him deep in her heart. Even Kanazaki, who had masqueraded as her husband, couldn't fill that place.

When I remembered Kanazaki, I couldn't help thinking about Noriko. *Noriko has a father.* When that thought came to me, I was consumed by the desire for *my* father to survive. No matter what had happened in the past, he had to live — no longer for my mother's sake alone, but also for my own.

I have a father, too. For the first time I clung to the fact that I had a father. I had thought him dead for many years; now he was dying and I desperately wanted him to live.

8 REVENGE

IN THE END my father was saved. Since he had been rushed to the operating table so quickly, the doctors were successful.

I've learned, Reverend, how filled with prejudice our lives are. Before I met Hatsuko, I imagined that my father's wife would be a proud, cold, conceited woman. It's true that she was cool and rational, but not at all cold. Her capabilities were perhaps limited, but suited to helping her husband make a name for himself in the world of flower arranging and to looking after his many students.

Her husband's affair with my mother had happened many years before. However, she couldn't just brush aside her husband's fathering a child with another woman. The Fifty-first Psalm says, "My sin is ever before me." Perhaps she felt, "My husband's sins are always before me." We soon forget our own sins, while the sins that others commit against us aren't so easily forgotten.

Yet when my mother and I hurried to my father's side, his wife didn't greet us coldly or use harsh words with us. And when it looked as if my father's operation was going to be successful, she said, "We owe it all to Haru. If she hadn't been there, he may have choked to death, and the ambulance wouldn't have arrived in time." She even told my mother, "Sawae, your prayers also saved him." My mother shrugged and said, "I think that the one who saved him was himself."

The next night, I met Sugata Haru for the first time. That's when she told me about my aunt. "There's not another person in the world like Saori," she said, and as she spoke, there was a kind of radiance in her face. I realized how much she loved my aunt. "She was such a beautiful girl, Kiyomi, the marriage offers just came pouring in, and there was one boy she was really in love with. But she never paid any attention to any of them, no matter who they were. She even refused to marry the one she loved, so it wasn't hard for her to turn down the rest. She broke hearts all over the place. She had her reasons. She wouldn't tell anybody but me, but she told me everything."

Haru turned to my mother. "What do you think Saori said, Miss Sawae? She said that she wanted to do her little bit to make up for her brother's sin. She said, 'I want to atone for what he did to Miss Sawae and Kiyomi, by not ever marrying. I know it's not enough, but it's what I swore before God I would do,' she said, and she cried and cried. Once you were born, Kiyomi, she just wanted to devote her whole life to you." She finished, and gave herself up to her tears.

I couldn't find anything to say. My mother tried, but couldn't bring herself to speak either.

That's the kind of person Aunt Saori was, Reverend. I remembered the first time I met her. She led me to the meadow near my house, and in the field where nobody could see us, she took me in her arms and wept. I now understood why she held me so tightly, and why she shed tears. She loved me more than people naturally love cute little girls, more than she might love her brother's child. It was a deeper love than I'd ever known. It was a love full of repentance, a love that now spoke to me, saying, "Forgive your father." No doubt she felt that she had no greater gift to offer than to tell me about God's love, and that's what she was thinking when she sang the children's hymn for me.

In the train on the way home from Sapporo, my mother talked about Aunt Saori. As it was already the end of June, the fields we were passing were full of flower-covered acacias. I watched the misty face of Mt. Tarumae grow fainter and fainter in the distance. I felt that something had changed in the deepest part of my heart. I felt that I wanted to be just like my aunt. I longed to be able to love others as she had.

"From the beginning, Saori forgave me," my mother said again, as she had many times before. She recalled something Haru had said. "She told me that your father's wife didn't become so kind until after Saori died." Then she went on, "Before you were born, Saori begged me, 'Please let me take care of the baby.' She really did — she folded her hands and begged. I've told you all this before, but she made it a life-long resolution to be your second mother." As if she couldn't bear to think about it, she pressed a handkerchief to her eyes.

So, Reverend, though my aunt felt sorry for my mother

having to raise a child alone and though she wanted to take me and raise me herself, my mother felt that giving birth to the child of the man she loved made her "the lucky one," and she was delighted. She really was a simple girl, wasn't she?

In using the word "simple," I don't mean to disparage my mother. Perhaps I meant to say "guileless." Yes, I think "guileless" is a more accurate word in this case. She was disingenuous, and she simply loved my father unselfishly and thought that she alone should raise the child of the man she loved. If my aunt had understood this feeling, perhaps she wouldn't have felt it necessary to remain single all her life for the sake of her brother's redemption. In any case, I still feel that her act was, in a way, wonderful.

My change of heart didn't last for long. I didn't forget my resolution. There wasn't a day that I didn't think of my aunt, or that I didn't remember my desire to be just like her. However, when I got back to school after missing several days and saw Noriko's face again, Satan's hand once again took hold of my heart. A heart is a strange thing. The impulses to do both good and evil can live there side by side.

My father was still in the hospital, and I began to work on a picture of flowers to give him. I had to paint it at home since first-year students weren't allowed to use colors at school. On the other hand, I schemed ways to take my revenge on Kanazaki. As hard as we try, we can't escape the evil influences of the world. I began to allow Noriko to come gradually closer to me.

One day it was our turn to clean the art club room. Outside, the clouds hung heavy and low, threatening rain. When I think back on this day, the word "melancholy" comes to mind. We had finished cleaning, and I went to the windows to close them. Though just two or three days before, the white acacia flowers were blooming beautifully and giving off their sweet smell, today, I noticed, their petals had been scattered by the wind. Without wanting to, I found myself staring up at the black rain clouds.

Noriko came back from emptying the water from the mop bucket and said in a cheerful voice, "Ohama, do you want to go get a cup of coffee somewhere?"

Noriko's voice was always cheerful. I wouldn't have been surprised if her teardrops were like little plastic beads, not even wet. I had once imagined just that.

I kept looking up at the clouds. "I'd like to," I replied coldly without turning around, "but —"

"But what?"

"I'm meeting somebody."

It was true. During lunch time, I'd run into Akira in the hall near the washrooms. Whenever we met at school, we acted as if we barely knew each other. We might simply nod to each other, or exchange fewer words than you'd write in a telegram, nothing more than a quick "How are you?" This was my way of not interfering with Akira's preparation for the college entrance exams.

But that day he'd stopped me and said, "I'd like to talk to you. How about after school?" Of course I agreed. There were a lot of things that I wanted to talk to him about too.

Even if I had nothing in particular to say, just sitting by Akira's side was enough. It comforted me.

"In the school yard under the larches," he said, and we parted. Our school yard was quite large, and in one corner a group of five larch trees stood like five good friends. Akira and I liked meeting there.

"Meeting somebody? Really?" Noriko said, her voice tinged with envy and maybe even a little jealousy.

Noriko was so good-natured that she already considered us close friends. Some people think that a few conversations add up to friendship. She had no doubt decided that if she invited me somewhere, I wouldn't say no.

I rarely had much to say when Noriko and I were together, preferring instead to play the role of listener. Her topics were fairly typical for girls our age: her father, her mother, her brother, even her cat, Pink, who was considered part of the family. Fashion and popular singers. Pictures we were both interested in.

Of course, I was most interested in what she told me about her family, in particular about her father, Kanazaki Morio. As I listened eagerly, she took delight in confiding in me about the details of her parents' arguments, about the life-sized nude pictures hanging in her brother's room, and so on.

I'm sure Noriko considered me a special friend. She was special to me, too, but she could never guess in what way. I think that the reason there was a hint of jealousy in her voice was that she was surprised to hear I had another friend besides herself.

Everybody knew I was the kind of girl who didn't have many friends. I'm sure that knowledge was behind the remark in art club one day, when Ichiro joked, "Ohama, you could model for a picture entitled, 'Winter Day.'"

Who started it I don't know, but someone created a nickname for me by taking the "hama" of my last name and adding an "o" to the beginning. Eventually everybody started calling me "Ohama." I didn't really mind. It wasn't exactly a pleasant-sounding name, but for that very reason, it made me feel like an individual.

I said to Noriko nonchalantly, "But I would like to see your house sometime."

"Really?" Noriko jumped up and down in her childish joy. She'd invited me to her house once before, but I flatly refused, saying, "Ever since I was in elementary school, I've hated going to other people's houses." She must have been very surprised, then, to hear me say such an unexpected thing that day.

As I'd said I would, I sat on the roots of the larch trees and waited for Akira. The black clouds that had promised rain were slowly moving east, and I could see blue gradually spreading across the sky. All that blue made me feel strangely lonely; it reminded me of the color of the dress that Aunt Saori had sent to me so long ago. I didn't want to, but I couldn't help bringing to mind the image of my aunt on the day of the exhibition in Sapporo.

Just then I saw Akira coming toward me, taking long strides.

"When did you get so tall?" he said when he reached the trees. He sounded like an older cousin.

I nodded shyly and said, "I'm five feet tall now."

"Five feet? You're a regular grownup." This kind of talk, in fact, made Akira sound like an adult to me.

In the school yard some boys were playing catch. On the tennis courts a few more were hitting a ball around. Others had started a volleyball game. On a patch of grass nearby a boy had covered his face with his notebook and was sleeping. Here and there, we could see boys and girls in couples, like us, engaged in quiet conversation. It was a place where two people could be comfortable together, rather than sticking out conspicuously in a coffeeshop.

"I hope it's all right to ask you —" Akira began, looking me in the eye.

"What is it?"

"Well, a few days ago in the newspaper there was something about a Funato, the flower arranging teacher."

"Oh, that." My father's illness had appeared in an editorial that had explained the importance of prompt treatment for "subarachnoid hemorrhage."

"What happened?" I felt the warmth in Akira's voice, but for some reason I had misgivings. I had talked to Akira about my mother and father. He knew that my father lived with his wife. He should also know that we didn't have any contact at all. Knowing what he did about our relationship, why did he ask, "What happened?" He must have found out somehow about my going to Sapporo.

"Who told you I went to Sapporo?" I asked.

He glanced at me. "Well," he said with a little laugh, "I heard from Noriko. She told me that a relative of yours was in critical condition and that you had gone to Sapporo."

I was confused. I hadn't told anyone that Akira and I were friends. I had no idea that Akira and Noriko even knew each other. I felt that I had been betrayed by Akira.

"How do you know her?" I intended to be firm, but my voice trembled.

"Noriko? Her older brother and I are in the same club, have been ever since we both started high school. I've been to his house before. We're pretty good friends."

I made my face hard. I had talked about Kanazaki with Akira, concealing his real name and the details of what had happened that horrible night.

"But why did you tell her we were friends?"

"I'm sorry. It was about six months ago. She said that she was in the art club, and since you were in the same club, I said that I knew you. I didn't think there was anything wrong with telling her, and anyway anyone who sees us talking like this would know we were friends. I didn't see that there was anything to worry about," he said lightly. Of course, he knew nothing about what a disgusting man Noriko's father was.

Though I tried to put on a cheerful face, I was tense. "Oh, I see, if you put it that way," I said. "Well, my good friends Noriko and Akira are friends. What a small world!"

"Yes. A small world."

"What's Noriko's brother like?" I said, like a girl without a worry in the world. "Introduce him to me, will you?"

"Sure. He says that Noriko is always saying Ohama this and Ohama that. So maybe he's as interested in you as you are in him." He sounded relieved, and that discouraged me. At the same time, I was concealing something of major importance, something terribly serious. I felt that I was betraying his trust. *If you only knew about Noriko's father!* Just the thought terrified me.

"It was a miracle that my father was saved," I said, bringing the topic back to where we had started.

"That's great," he said. "Are you going to see him?"

"I guess, if my mother goes . . ."

"You could go alone."

"Alone? Me?" Until that moment, I'd never thought of going by myself to visit him in the hospital. I'd gone back to feeling that he had no real existence. My feeling was that he had been my mother's lover a long time ago, though his memory lived on in her heart.

But this man was my real father. We were of the same flesh and blood. There was no reason for me not to go see him by myself. It's strange, but it wasn't until he fell ill that I felt close to him at all. Up until then I hated him for leaving my mother. No, for leaving me. Then, when I saw my mother crying for him, when I saw how she loved him, before I knew it I had the feeling for the first time in my life of really being someone's daughter.

"I guess you're right," I said. "I guess I should go and see him, even if I have to go by myself." I told Akira about the picture I was painting for my father, an arrangement of red and yellow roses in a vase. Even to me, the colors were strange and wonderful. My mother said she could almost smell the flowers.

"Let's go together," Akira said, smiling. "I'll go see my grandfather."

I was captivated by his smiling face. I told him what I'd learned about my aunt.

"Really?" he said. "In repentance for a sin, she never married? In repentance for her brother's sin?" Then he was silent for a while. I knew that when Akira was silent, it was time to leave him to his thoughts.

The other people in the school yard had begun to go home. The rain clouds had drifted away, and in the sky above a white moon, like a thin piece of paper, had appeared. As I looked up at the pale evening moon, I thought I could see the profile of my Aunt Saori. I could feel my heart, which had been so full, become quieter and quieter. I knew that I should forget all about Kanazaki. But I had to see Noriko every day, and I knew this would only nurture my hate for Kanazaki.

"Akira," I said, "I'm thinking of quitting the art club."

He looked at me in surprise. "Quit the art club! Why?"

"Because." I couldn't tell him about Noriko, about Kanazaki.

"Kiyomi, do you know what I was just thinking?"

"I have no idea."

"I was thinking about your aunt. Of course I never even met her. Kiyomi, no matter how it turns out, I want you to paint your aunt. That's what I was thinking. Paint the woman who embraced you in the meadow when you were a child, who cried her heart out for you. Paint the woman who begged your mother to let her help. You have an obligation to paint a portrait of her. You said that she got hit by a car while she was going home after seeing your picture." Akira's cheeks were flushed.

I really wanted to quit the art club. I wanted to avoid having to see Noriko. It was only when I saw Noriko's face that I remembered Kanazaki's. Naturally, since Akira had no idea about any of this, he said that I mustn't quit the art club.

"You have an obligation to paint a picture of your aunt." He was firm, and his words pierced my heart. When she saw my prize-winning picture of chrysanthemums, how happy she must have been! Even if I didn't paint her portrait, I had to keep painting.

I was confused. Of course I wanted to keep drawing. It was in many ways life itself to me. Only through drawing could I express my feelings. Since I was no good with words, pictures were the only way I had to express what was in my heart.

But that didn't mean I couldn't quit the art club, I thought. Even if I wasn't active in the art club, I could still paint. On the other hand, the art club in my high school was excellent. Mr. Ozawa's personality was cheerful, his guidance of our technique was clear, and he excelled at bringing out the best in each student. The whole feeling of the club was ideal for nurturing young painters. The flashy third-year students, especially Ichiro, though they could joke around with each other, had amazing persistence and will power as they labored over the canvases. They were an inspiration to the rest of us.

But having to see Noriko's face was anguish. That time when Ichiro told me that my pictures were dirty, I was shocked. He had hit upon my true feelings toward Noriko, or to put it more accurately, my hatred of Kanazaki.

Two or three days after I talked with Akira in the school yard we met again and went for a walk along the banks of the Ushubetsu River, which flowed only a quarter of a mile or so from the school.

"Akira," I said, "there's someone in the art club I can't stand to see."

"Someone you can't stand to see?" Akira asked suspiciously.

"Yes."

"A boy?"

"Yes, a boy," I quickly replied. I surprised myself. I trusted Akira more than anyone in the world, and yet I could so easily tell him a lie.

"You hate him that much?"

"Yes, I do, I hate him." Even as I said this, I realized that I didn't hate Noriko all that much. It was her father I hated. Noriko was just his daughter, a simple, happy, likable girl.

After thinking about it for a while, Akira said, "Kiyomi, you can't live in a place where there are only people you like. I don't think anybody in the world lives in such luxury." His voice was firm. "Look, you can't even like all of the people in your class. That's impossible. When you go to work, you'll have to work with people you can't stand.

When you get married, you'll find a place to live and there will be people there you don't like. Do you think you can just keep running away?"

As I listened, I knew that he was right.

"You say that you want to quit the art club. There are fewer people in the club than in your class, so the boy you hate is going to seem like a bigger problem than he would otherwise."

I understood completely. I really did understand what he was saying. But if he knew about the relationship between Kanazaki and me, I don't think even Akira would say these things.

I didn't want to stain my soul. I didn't want to allow myself to hate another person. Every night, I tried to remember the message of Aunt Saori's love for me. "Kiyomi, don't hate. Forgive. And love." But some things can't be forgotten.

I was frustrated at not being able to tell Akira everything, though I knew that no matter how much you trusted a friend, there were some things that you couldn't tell anybody. Some things we have to bear alone, and we can't ask others to bear the burden with us. I knew that my experiences were something that lived only in my own heart, and that all people had such a secret place in their hearts.

Then, without my willing it, I felt an idea form in my mind. *If I have no choice, there is nothing left to do but love.* Until that moment, I'd never had such an idea. You hate the people you hate, you detest the people you detest, you don't forgive the people you don't forgive: that was the way I thought about it. But when Akira said that I couldn't run away from the people I hated, I had to think of something else to do. In order to escape from hating him, I had no other choice but to love my enemy.

It's a very difficult thing to love your enemy. It means going from intolerance to forgiveness. I tried to imagine what my Aunt Saori would think. I thought of her beautiful, crystalline voice as she sang the children's hymn to me. It was at that moment that I decided I might go visit one of those places called a church. As the evening breeze cooled the banks of the Ushubetsu River, Akira and I walked back and forth in silence.

One day, with summer vacation just around the corner, I was about to leave the art club room when I was assaulted by Noriko's bubbly voice. "Ohama! Ohama!"

"Don't worry!" I put on a smile before I turned around. "I won't forget!"

Behind that smile, I was choking. I'd been invited to Noriko's birthday party. Since the day I was born, I'd never had a birthday party of my own, though I'd been to my friends' parties when I was in elementary school. We would all gather around a big table covered with a white tablecloth. There was always a big birthday cake in the middle with red, yellow, and blue candles. The birthday girl would blow them out, looking so happy and so proud. My feelings about birthday parties were just the opposite.

When Noriko invited me to her birthday party, I answered as casually as I could, "Thanks, I'd like to come." I'd expected to be asked over some time, so I'd prepared in advance what kind of attitude and what words I would use to accept the invitation. "Who's going to be there?"

"Since I'm in high school now, it'll just be a small party. My brother and his friend, and then Mother and Father. Six people in all."

She couldn't have suspected what a shock she'd just caused.

"Your mother and father too?" I surprised myself by being able to control the emotion in my voice.

"Yes, and Akira too. You know him, don't you?"

"Akira? He's busy with entrance exams, isn't he?"

It was hard to accept the fact that Akira had been invited to Noriko's birthday party. I couldn't help suspecting that perhaps Akira was friendlier with Noriko than with me. But far more important than Akira's presence at Noriko's birthday party was the fact that I was going to see Kanazaki's face again.

Noriko's house was much more splendid than I ever could have imagined. The imposing steel gate, the vast lawn inside the fence, the grove in the garden, and the splendid house facing the setting sun: it was all so totally different from the world I lived in. Inside the house, too, was as different from my house as you can possibly imagine. I could hardly believe my eyes as I walked from the parlor to the bright, roomy kitchen.

I'd bought Noriko a white coloring pencil, which I'd

wrapped in paper and a pink ribbon. I'd bought it with my allowance, and it was all that I could afford. At school, a coloring pencil had seemed like a good idea for a birthday present, definitely nothing to be ashamed of. For someone in the art club, it made more sense than a handkerchief or a cake or some other present. But when I gave Noriko her present in that splendid mansion, I was ashamed. When she saw the five-hundred-yen pencil, Noriko said, "Thank you so much!" and hugged it to her chest. "I'll take good care of it. Using a coloring pencil from Ohama I know I'll draw some good pictures." Such a simple thing caused her such pleasure. My own heart ached.

Noriko left to change her clothes, while I followed her instructions to a huge hall with a grand piano in one corner and two gorgeous chandeliers hanging from the ceiling. It must have been five times the size of the living room in my house. As I stepped onto the soft, fluffy carpet and looked up to see Akira and Noriko's brother enter the room, I felt that a page had turned in my destiny.

Noriko's brother didn't look like either his sister or Kanazaki. He looked a little weak, but he had an affable, cheerful face. Akira introduced me to Kanazaki Takuya.

"So you're Noriko's Ohama?" he said, looking me straight in the face.

"That's me," I answered curtly. I took no account at all of Noriko's brother; my mind was focused entirely on the man who was due to make his appearance in only a few more minutes.

Before long, a maid pushed a cart full of food into the

room. Noriko's mother came in wearing a kimono and said to me with a quiet smile, "Thank you so much for coming, and you too, Akira." She started to spread the plates of food around the table. "Noriko is so excited that you could come."

Just then, Noriko herself came in wearing a long pink dress with a matching ribbon in her hair. I was still in my school uniform and looked like a little matchseller visiting the house of a rich young lady.

Dinner began. The table was filled with a large variety of beautiful Chinese food, but I couldn't bring myself to pick up my chopsticks. Kanazaki, who was supposed to eat with us, still hadn't come in.

"Is anything the matter, Miss Ohama?" Somehow Noriko's mother had gotten the idea that my family name really was Ohama. "Please help yourself."

Noriko laughed loudly. "Sorry, Mama. Her real name is Hamano Kiyomi. 'Ohama' is just a nickname."

"Oh, is that so? I thought that these days, with the manners high school girls have, you were calling each other by your last names, just like boys. Noriko just said 'Ohama' all the time. So your name is Hamano Kiyomi. Well, well. Please go ahead."

"But," I whispered to Noriko, who was sitting next to me, "Your father still isn't here."

"Oh, that old goat," she said, using a rough word on purpose. "He's going to be late because he has an appointment at work."

I was relieved. I still had some time before having to

face Kanazaki. Though I was still tense with anticipation, I reached for a small plate of pickled vegetables.

"Noriko tells me you're good at drawing." Noriko's mother seemed to be trying to draw me out. I suddenly remembered that when Kanazaki came to our house, even if he was thirty minutes or an hour later than he promised, I don't think my mother ever went ahead with dinner. "It's only a few minutes," she would say. "We can wait." Of course, Noriko's mother was only being polite to her guests; but that's what I was thinking about as the conversation went on around me.

Takuya spoke up for the first time. "Oh, the name Hamano Kiyomi is quite famous around school, isn't it, Akira?"

"Oh, yes," said Akira, glancing at me. "Everybody knows her for a real genius."

"That's right." Noriko nodded her head happily. "A real genius."

"Well, well, a genius!" said Noriko's mother. "We'll have to commission a painting from her. It'll be worth a fortune some day!" She said it as a good-natured joke, but it made me think that these were the kind of people who converted everything into monetary terms.

Just about the time we finished dinner and were getting ready to light the candles on Noriko's birthday cake, we heard heavy footsteps in the entrance hall.

"Sorry I'm late! Have I missed everything?" With that, the inimitable Kanazaki Morio entered the room.

Akira and I stood up.

"Akira, good to see you again." Kanazaki cast his gaze around the room until it came to rest on me.

"Papa, this is my friend Hamano Kiyomi," Noriko said enthusiastically.

"Hamano Kiyomi?" He was caught completely off guard. His eyes opened wide in surprise, and his mouth foolishly hung open. This was the face I'd imagined seeing again for so long. It seemed to me that a long time passed before he spoke again, though it was probably only a few seconds. Finally he laughed and said, "Oh, Kiyomi. It's been a long time. You've really grown, haven't you? I didn't recognize you." Turning to Akira, he repeated sociably, "Good to see you again."

"Papa, you know Kiyomi?" Noriko asked. She had to repeat her question before he seemed to hear her. "You know Kiyomi?"

"Oh, I think I do, I think I do. I knew her mother and father because of my work. You were in the third grade then, I think. Only about this big." Kanazaki held his hand at the height of the table and laughed.

I didn't think that anyone in their wildest imagination could have guessed from the way he was acting what had gone on in the past. From the words, "I knew her mother and father," nobody could ever suspect the relationship between my mother and Kanazaki. And from the words, "You were a third grader, only about this big," how could anyone ever imagine what had happened between Kanazaki and a child "only about this big"? Why, I couldn't even bring myself to expose the love affair between him and my mother.

"Ohama, you knew Papa?" Noriko said, leaning toward me.

I kept my eyes fixed on Kanazaki. "I was just a little girl then, and . . ."

"You were only a child yourself, Noriko," said Kanazaki's wife, pouring wine into her husband's glass. "There's no reason why you should remember all your father's business friends."

So it seemed to be accepted as a coincidence, and the talk changed to a different topic. I was glad. I had hoped for Kanazaki to be bewildered, to be brought to a standstill. When I saw that moment of astonishment on his face, I was satisfied. He hadn't forgotten that awful night. I was convinced of that. And when I stared at him, I showed with my steady gaze that I hadn't forgotten either.

Kanazaki was a little heavier than he had been before, and his voice boomed impressively. When he came to my house, the gentleness he showed us, the brisk enjoyment in the way he went about his work — those kinds of feelings were missing from this house. The Kanazaki I saw here was different. Maybe that's the way he was in this house. I wondered if the Kanazaki who came to see my mother was the real Kanazaki, or if the real Kanazaki was the one who lived in luxury here in this house. For some reason, I felt a darkness in the heart of the Kanazaki who lived here.

We sat chatting for about ten minutes or so before he left, saying that he had another appointment. After that, we listened to records and talked for a few hours. Akira and I left the Kanazaki house together.

It was a hot, sticky summer night without a breath of wind. Akira seemed lost in thought. When we were alone together, it was always Akira who began the conversation, but tonight he was strangely silent.

We had reached the bus stop, but he kept walking. "Aren't you going to take the bus?" I asked, breaking the silence.

"Are you tired?" he said. "I feel like walking a little farther."

I wanted to walk with him. We didn't have to talk. I just wanted to be by his side. But he was usually so talkative, and his silence made me want to be alone.

"I'm not tired," I said nevertheless. "I feel like walking too."

Akira nodded silently and kept walking at the same pace. I was frightened. He was like a different person.

"Takuya seems nice," I said, but he didn't answer. After a while, I tried again. "Noriko is lucky to have such a nice brother." But as I expected, he remained silent. Finally I said, "Why are you so quiet?"

But as soon as I'd said it, I felt a little shock run through me. Perhaps Akira had realized what went on between my mother and Noriko's father. But how? I'd told Akira everything about my mother, but of course I hadn't mentioned Kanazaki's name. On the other hand, Akira wasn't stupid. He'd learned a lot about people from all his reading, and he had a sensitive personality. He wouldn't have missed the expression on Kanazaki's face.

He probably had a feeling that something was going on. But why was he so silent? Maybe learning that my mother's lover had been Kanazaki was too much of a shock for him. After all, Noriko was a good friend of his. When he found out that her father was my mother's lover, he couldn't bring himself to talk to me.

I'd just reached that conclusion when Akira finally spoke.

"Kiyomi, you once said that you wanted to quit the art club, didn't you?"

I didn't know what to say. This was a subject I hadn't expected.

"There was a boy that you hated so much you wanted to quit, right? You said it was a boy, but . . . it was really a girl, wasn't it?"

I still didn't have an answer.

"Kiyomi, you're more important to me than anybody in the world. That's why I'm asking. Do you remember when you told me about your mother?"

I kept walking, looking at the ground.

"I thought I wanted to help you carry the burden of the trouble you've suffered because of your mother, maybe for the rest of my life."

I was afraid to hear the words that I knew would come next.

"You knew that the man you told me about was Noriko's father, didn't you?" I couldn't speak.

"I can see that you did. And in spite of knowing, you intruded on that family. It's like you invaded them."

The word "invaded" pierced my heart; that's just what I'd done.

"From where I sat, I could see the surprised look on his face. Takuya was sitting next to me, so I'm sure he could see it very well too. Noriko and her mother were sitting next to him, so maybe . . ."

It was worse than I thought.

"Kiyomi, you went to that house anticipating that everyone would see that expression on his face."

He had guessed the truth.

"Why, Kiyomi, why? Why would you do such a thing? Tonight was awful. It was Noriko's birthday, and I was looking forward to helping her celebrate. I even gave up a night of studying for the entrance exams to do it. For Noriko's sake I pretended to be enjoying myself, playing the guitar and singing. But the whole time I was only thinking about you. I didn't want to believe what you were doing. You didn't go to the party to celebrate your friend's birthday — you went to satisfy a grudge. Is my Kiyomi that kind of monster? I just wanted to scream, 'No, no, it isn't true!'"

I had nothing to say in reply. It was simple to me: Kanazaki couldn't be forgiven. Naturally I hated Noriko for living in happiness by his side. Why couldn't Akira understand? Of course, Noriko was too nice a girl to really hate, but —

"From your point of view, I can understand how much you hate Noriko's father. But what crime has Noriko committed? In her innocence, she respects you. You're so talented. She's so happy to be friends with you. She invited you to her birthday party. What kind of heart do you have to trample on her friendship like that?"

He had to pause before he could go on.

"Until tonight I liked you so much. I liked how in spite of what people said about your mother behind your back, you were brave and you just kept going. I don't understand how you could do such a thing to Noriko. Where do those feelings come from? I hate them. I hate the cruelty in you."

We had stopped walking. "Goodbye," he said, and then he turned away from me and ran off into the night.

9 ONE ANOTHER'S BURDENS

I REALLY was despicable, wasn't I, Reverend? I'd never recognized that disgraceful side of myself. I was as foolish as I was ignorant. When Akira pointed all this out to me — my hatred of Kanazaki, my shameful envy of Noriko — I realized for the first time, really, how odious my feelings and my behavior had been.

Still, I couldn't help but feel that it was natural to hate Kanazaki. According to the logic of my heart, it was quite proper to ruin the happiness of his whole family, though it was a logic that made sense only to me.

Even Akira could not accept my point of view, though he said that he liked me, that I was the most important person in the world to him. Perhaps nobody in the world loved me as much as he did. He was certainly the one who understood me the best. He said he saw something ugly in me, something so shameful that it made him say goodbye to me.

Nevertheless, I still believed that I was the one who deserved sympathy and compassion. What was my ugliness compared to Kanazaki's?

In the end I simply couldn't acknowledge what Akira detested in me. Sometimes people are so self-centered that they can't see the unpleasant truth. I lost Akira because of an egotistical attachment to what I merely wanted to believe.

Before this, when my hatred of Kanazaki was at its most intense, I had tried to think of what Aunt Saori would say if she were still alive: "Don't hate. Forgive. And love." Once I even concluded that if I had to face Noriko every day, the only way to escape my hatred was to love. I knew these things, Reverend, but I just couldn't let go of my hate. It came as naturally to me as water flowing down a hill.

Everything about Kanazaki was evil and reprehensible, and I could never forgive him. An ugly thing is ugly, a bad thing is bad and is to be hated. There was no other way to think about it. Aunt Saori's voice, "Love. And forgive," echoed ever softer, ever weaker.

Losing Akira was bewildering. I stopped working on the painting for my father, and the days flowed by without my touching it. Full of ugliness, how could I create beauty?

Before I knew it, my high school days were over. Without Akira to be with, the two remaining years were dull, spiritless, wasted. I went back into my shell. Of course I quit the art club, and lost all desire to read. Still, sometimes I would pick up an ordinary pencil and begin to sketch absent-mindedly in a notebook. When I realized what I was doing, tears would come to my eyes. My very soul wanted to draw, but each time I stopped and cast the desire away from me.

One day in March, the month I graduated from high school, I received a small package from the post office.

There was no return address. Inside I found a small black leather-bound New Testament. I wondered who could have sent it. Opening the cover, I found written on the title page, "Blessed are the pure in heart, for they shall see God." I had a feeling that it was from Akira. The handwriting wasn't his, but he was the only person who would give me such a present and inscribe such words in it. Those words had a strange kind of magical power over me, like water to a withering blade of grass. I resolved then and there to carry it with me for the rest of my life.

If it was indeed Akira who'd given me the Bible, then it was proof that he hadn't completely abandoned me. I was convinced that he was still watching over me. Love gives birth to miracles, doesn't it, Reverend? One withering blade of grass can grow into a whole fresh green field.

I buried myself in the Bible. There was a lot I couldn't understand, but no matter what I read, I thought of it as a present from Akira.

Six months after I first opened the little black New Testament, I came to a passage in St. Paul's Epistle to the Galatians, Chapter Six, Verse Two, where one line had been underlined in red to make it stand out: "Bear ye one another's burdens." I felt like crying.

I was sure then that the Bible was from Akira. "Bear ye one another's burdens." This was the only underlined passage in the entire book. The red line pierced me through to the heart. I kept thinking that the words were a gift from Akira to me. It had been more than two years since he'd said goodbye to me. I thought that he'd abandoned me completely. Yet he'd sent me the New Testament as a graduation present.

While of course I couldn't be absolutely certain that Akira had sent it, I didn't need any more evidence. When I read the inscription, "Blessed are the pure in heart," I took the word "pure" to refer to the Chinese character "kiyo" in my first name and sensed the hand of Akira. I felt it even stronger in the passage from Galatians underlined in red.

Reverend, can you imagine the effect on my spirit when I finally believed that the Bible was a gift from Akira? When I thought that he had abandoned me because of my wickedness, every day was full of darkness, loneliness, pain. I lost the will to live. However, he hadn't given up on me. No, far from abandoning me forever, he was telling me, "Let's carry our burdens together." When I thought of this, I had the glorious feeling of being freed from prison. *He isn't angry. He forgives me!* I cried joyfully in my heart.

About this time I experienced another similar joy. It was when I first read this passage: "Whosoever believeth in Christ shall not perish, but have life everlasting." I knew the joy of absolution from my sin.

I became completely absorbed in reading the Bible. Every day I read the underlined passage, "Bear ye one another's burdens," and thought about Akira. He was attending the university in Sapporo while I went to a junior college in Asahikawa. Wherever I went, the Bible went with me.

It was an early summer evening. The lilacs were in bloom. That day, as always, I'd read the passage from

Galatians. My mother had just come home from work at still another small shop. She drifted from job to job in supermarkets, food shops, even a men's clothing store for a while, always selling something. The reason she had to change jobs so often was always the same: problems with men.

Mother was forty-three years old now, but her round face made her look younger. I don't mean to blame everything on her charming face or good figure. She was just the kind of person who never thought things through or learned from her mistakes. Never bothering her head about things constituted a kind of tranquillity for her, though it was clear that she took no pleasure in the constant attention from men. She was just the kind of woman men couldn't leave alone.

From the time my father was ill I had sensed a change in my mother. However, once a label is pasted on, it isn't easy to tear it off. No matter how many times she came home from work with the sun still high in the sky, the rumors still flew. The sales manager of the supermarket wouldn't leave her alone. The manager of another store called her to his office every day. The store manager of the men's shop took her with him one day on his customer rounds and used all the malicious gossip to try to get at her.

When this kind of harassment finally became unbearable, Mother would quit her job. Sometimes she would be at home for several months.

But she could not get away from her past. People who

had lived in the neighborhood for a long time, for instance, would tell newcomers all about us. "She'll sleep with anybody as long as he's got money in his pocket." The world was a hard place for my mother. No, it's too early to say "was," as if it's all in the past. Life is still hard for her.

Even now, Reverend, I can't accept being the daughter of such a woman. That's my burden. I grew up surrounded by people asking me, "Where's your father? Is he dead? Where is he?" If I'd been stronger, maybe things would have been different, but as it was the pain made me shrink into myself. Or if someone were there to help me "bear my burden," maybe I could have tried harder myself.

However, on that summer evening, with the sweet fragrance of the lilacs on the breeze, I suddenly realized something. I realized that "bearing one another's burdens" also meant my helping to carry other people's burdens. I had thought only of being helped in carrying my burdens.

What might Akira's burdens be? Until that moment, I'd never once considered the question. Reverend, you often say that selfishness is the beginning of sin. But how do we escape from being self-centered? Even in love, we can't get rid of our selfishness. We really are all deep in our sins, aren't we?

That night I felt that I had to write a letter to Akira. "You're the one who sent me the Bible, aren't you?" And also, "I have to let you know how happy I was to get it, and how diligent I've been about reading it." I began again and again, tearing up the pages each time without finishing. In the end, I couldn't write a letter to Akira. And so, another month passed just like all the rest.

Soon after summer vacation began I finally completed the picture I had started for my father when I was in high school. From the night I thought that Akira had abandoned me until I received the Bible in the mail, I hadn't touched my drawing pencils. But, taking the gift as a sign that I'd been forgiven, I threw myself into drawing again.

Not long after I sent the picture to my father in Sapporo, he called. I had just finished breakfast. I think it was before eight o'clock. When my mother heard the telephone ringing, she said, "Who could be calling this early? Must be a wrong number."

As I was closer to the telephone, I picked it up. "Hello, Hamano residence."

"Kiyomi? This is your father. I got the picture you sent."

I was hearing my father's voice over the telephone for the first time in my life. Even over the telephone, his voice was resonant and beautiful.

The hand holding the receiver was shaking. "Oh," was all I managed to say. "I —"

"It's an amazing picture. A masterpiece. You captured the beauty of the flowers so truly . . . I was overwhelmed." His voice trailed off, his breast clearly swelling with emotion. He was the most popular and talented teacher of flower arranging in Hokkaido. I could understand how happy he was that his own child could express the beauty of flowers through drawing.

When my mother realized that the call was from my father, she took the telephone away from me. She didn't speak, but only held the receiver to her ear, bowing slightly and saying, "Yes, yes."

After she hung up she told me, "Kiyomi, he said thank you. Over and over again, he said thank you, thank you."

"Thank you?" I said, but then I understood. He was thanking her for raising a child who understood the beauty of a flower.

Soon we got a very polite letter from my father's wife asking the two of us to come for a visit. My mother said she wouldn't go. It's hard to say how she felt about it. When his life had been in danger, she had rushed to Sapporo to be by his side. Now she said, "It's not like he's sick or anything. There's no reason for me to go bother everybody." Then she added, "But you're his daughter. You go. Your father doesn't want to see me. He wants to see you."

How could I go see him, though, leaving my mother there all alone? I couldn't think of it. Yet, when I remembered that gentle voice, my heart was filled with love for him. I longed to see him. Yes, he had caused my mother to live a painful life. But who was to say? She could have fallen on hard luck even if she'd never met him. Without knowing it, I began to make excuses for him as a way of protecting him.

One day around that time I was barefoot in a summer kimono, and my mother said casually, "Look, your feet are shaped just like your father's. You have a high instep just like he does." My heart gave a little leap. Rather than look like my mother, I wanted to look like my father. This was not because my mother was somehow inferior to my father, or because my father was more refined than my mother. It was just that I'd always been with her; I didn't need any proof of our relationship. However, I'd met my father on only two occasions: once at the picture exhibition when I was in the sixth grade, and another time when I visited his sickbed. I was starving for proof of our connection. Maybe you've never thought about the happiness of having something in common with a father you've hardly ever seen.

And so, filled to overflowing with love for him, I decided to go to Sapporo. I just wanted to live for one day, for two days, under the same sky as my father.

When I arrived at Sapporo station, I was overcome by a feeling of loneliness that is hard to describe. I remember someone describing the sensation as "being alone in a crowd." Planning to call my father when I arrived, I'd memorized his number. I went to the lobby of the Sapporo International Hotel and picked up the receiver of a pay telephone. The first time I tried to call I hung up after dialing the number. I had the feeling that I had committed a crime. The second time I let it ring three times before hanging up again.

I sat in a chair in the lobby. I felt I shouldn't have come. At the front desk a pleasant-looking young man was taking reservations in a polite tone of voice. Perhaps it was his pleasant voice that raised my spirits. I went to the telephone a second time and began to dial. I caught my self thinking that he probably wouldn't answer the phone himself anyway. Probably it would be the maid, or his secretary, or his wife, or one of his students. I became dispirited again and hung up. There were always too many people around him.

I sat down again in the lobby. I wondered if Akira wasn't in Sapporo right now. Surely he'd gone home to Asahikawa. Perhaps in my heart I connected Sapporo with Akira, since he was at the university there now, not even returning to Asahikawa during the spring, summer, and winter vacations. Ever since he'd said he hated me and told me goodbye, I'd thought of him as far, far away. Perhaps if I went home now, he'd be there too.

I looked at my watch. It wasn't yet two o'clock. I suddenly decided to go to the botanical gardens. I had heard that my mother had often gone there with my father. I had also heard that it was close to the train station. The idea of seeing the plant life there brought my energy back. As I stood up I looked into the restaurant next to the lobby. Near the street at the front of the station, the restaurant's tables were lined up along a big plate-glass window.

Then I saw him.

It was definitely Akira, sitting at a table, facing a young girl and laughing at something merrily. Though I could only see her from the back, there was something familiar about her. It was Kanazaki Noriko. My heart went numb.

I was certain that Noriko had entered a college in Tokyo. Since her birthday party, I had distanced myself from her. It happened naturally, since we were in different classes at school, and especially after I quit the art club. We rarely even saw each other. She had invited me out several times, but I would say that I wasn't feeling well and rudely decline. After I felt that Akira had given up on me, I couldn't find a smiling face to show to anyone.

Akira with Noriko! I was overcome by hopelessness, and then anger. What had he said about carrying our burdens together?

I stood and stared straight at him, but then I couldn't stand seeing the two of them together any longer. I turned to leave, but at that moment Akira glanced in my direction and caught sight of me. Surprise flashed across his face. I started toward the escalator, and ended up almost running for it. I thought that Akira would come chasing after me. In fact, I was sure of it. You may think that I felt so certain because I was so conceited, but I don't think that's what it was. Some people are linked in this life by fate. I felt that what was happening was fated, inevitable. I can't express my idea very clearly, but I think you understand.

At any rate, certain that I was being chased, I reached the escalator. In my hurry to get away, I ran down the steps. I wasn't watching where I was going, and when I reached the bottom of the escalator my foot came down heavily on the floor, snapping the heel of my high-heeled shoe. Instantly I lost my balance and, at the same speed that I'd been running down the escalator, pitched forward and hit my head on the floor.

It was so embarrassing. Just from falling down I knocked myself out, was unconscious for two or three minutes, and suffered a mild concussion. In addition, I severely sprained my right foot. It was all so stupid it was laughable, and to my dismay it turned up in the newspaper, in some reporter's column. He happened to be in the All Nippon Airways lobby downstairs and saw the whole thing. "Young ladies, take care on escalators!" My name wasn't mentioned, thank goodness.

As I'd expected, Akira came running after me. When I came to and opened my eyes, his worried face was the first thing I saw. It was just before the ambulance came. And that's the strange way that Akira and I finally had our reunion.

Since I'd hit my head, I was rushed to the X-ray room as soon as we arrived at the hospital. They also checked my heart and measured my blood pressure, asking over and over, "Does your head hurt? Do you feel like throwing up?"

At last the doctor said, "I think you're going to be fine. That sprain is pretty bad, though. I wouldn't suggest going home to Asahikawa just yet. Why don't you stay here for a day or two?"

Akira and Noriko had followed me to the hospital and tried to call my mother in Asahikawa several times, but for better or for worse, she wasn't home.

I was sure that Akira understood the reason I tried to run away. He didn't say a word about it.

Noriko, though, in the same cheerful voice I

remembered from high school, said, "Oh, I run down escalators all the time. You'd have been fine if you hadn't lost a heel." She said it in such a breezy way that I couldn't help being impressed once again by the goodness that was in her. It was only natural for Akira to choose her over me. Her cheerfulness was good, good in every way. If you compared Noriko and me from Akira's point of view, then his choice was clear, and though it made me sad, I was happy for him.

Though it was getting late, there was still some light in the July sky. "I'd better go," said Noriko. "I'd like to stay, but I promised to meet a friend early tomorrow. Sorry, Ohama."

"Thanks for everything, Onori," I said, using a nickname I'd made up for her. "You should go too, Akira."

He'd hardly opened his mouth the whole time. "No, I'll stick around until visiting hours are over," he said in a firm voice.

Noriko looked at him in surprise and said with disappointment in her voice, "You're not going back to Asahikawa tonight?"

"I can go back to Asahikawa any time. Don't lose your train ticket," he added with a friendly smile.

After Noriko had left, taking her cheerful, echoing laugh with her, Akira and I were alone in the hospital room. The patient in the other bed had checked out that day.

"Does your leg hurt?"

"Yes, a little."

"How about your head?"

"I think it's okay."

"Are you nauseous?" He was mimicking the nurses and the doctor.

"No, not at all."

There were so many things I wanted to say, but I didn't even know where to begin. Not even in my dreams could I have imagined meeting Akira again like this, and I really had no idea of what I should say.

Then Akira blurted out, "I wanted to see you so much."

"What?" He wanted to see me? I couldn't believe my ears.

"I wanted to see you," he repeated. "I really wanted to see you."

"But Akira —" I couldn't forget what he'd said to me that night when we were going home from Noriko's birthday party. *Until tonight, I liked you so much. I don't understand how you could do such a thing to Noriko. Where do those feelings come from? I hate them. I hate the cruelty in you. Goodbye.* To me, those words were as final as a death sentence. He wanted nothing more to do with me.

Of course I hadn't forgotten about the leather-bound New Testament I'd received when I graduated from high school. I'd guessed that it had come from Akira. The underlined words in Galatians, "Bear ye one another's burdens," could have only come from him. But in a way, that wasn't a real, flesh-and-blood Akira. He seemed so far away. Now the Akira right in front of me had said, "I wanted to see you."

"But Akira, that time, I thought you never wanted to see me again."

Akira looked deep into my eyes. "No, Kiyomi. If you believe that, then you must think I'm very shallow."

"Then . . . what was —"

"Everybody says things they don't mean sometimes. What I said about you invading Noriko's house and not wanting to believe you were that kind of girl, that was true. But I never expected things to end like that, the way they did that night." A shadow of what might have been shame passed across his face. "I couldn't bring myself to see you again, or even write to you. But all that time, you don't know how I waited for a letter from you. I don't even remember taking the entrance exams. Kiyomi, the only thing that kept me going was the thought that if I passed the exams and was accepted into a university, I would receive a letter of congratulations from you."

"Akira, really?"

"If I passed, I was sure I'd get a letter from you, and then we'd have a chance to make up. The announcement was in the newspaper, and for days and days I looked for a letter. In the end, I didn't get so much as a post card."

I hung my head in shame. It's amazing, isn't it, Reverend, how little we understand each other's feelings? I'd had no doubt that I'd been completely rejected. Of course I knew about Akira's passing the entrance exams, but I didn't think I was worthy to write and congratulate him. If I did, I thought he might just mark it "Return to Sender" and send it back to me.

"Then you graduated from high school," he said, "and I wanted to give you something —"

"So you sent me the Bible."

"Kiyomi, you knew?"

"I could guess."

"After that I waited again. I was sure you'd know that it was me who sent it. I guess that was complacency."

"But the writing inside wasn't your handwriting."

"No, I didn't write it. When I sent it, I was in the hospital myself. I had appendicitis, and it ruptured before they operated."

"Oh, Akira! I had no idea!"

"My blood pressure dropped way down and I had peritonitis. It was really serious. I started to wonder if I'd hear from you before I died, and so I sent the Bible."

"It was that bad?"

"It was."

"Then who —"

"Noriko's brother Takuya wrote it."

I was taken by surprise. Akira was close to death, and who was with him but Takuya, and probably Noriko as well.

"Akira, I'm so sorry. I didn't have the faintest idea. I didn't think I had any business even writing a thank-you note, and I wasn't completely sure who sent it. So I didn't write. If I'd known you were sick —"

"It was my fault for not writing my name. But I thought you'd know it was me. I thought you'd write. I was stupid to assume so much." He turned toward the window and looked up at the darkening sky.

"Akira, I suppose this means you've forgiven me?"

"Forgiven you? I should be the one asking for forgiveness. Even though I knew what you were going through, I said those cold things to you. Forgive me, Kiyomi."

He turned back toward me. I couldn't answer him. I thought that only I was guilty of a sin, and that I just had to make things right with Akira. Now it was clear that I'd been forgiven.

Forgiveness. It's a beautiful thing, isn't it, Reverend? I have experienced the beauty of being forgiven.

After learning that I'd not only received the Bible and guessed that it was from him, but also tried to read a little bit every day, Akira squeezed my hand in joy. I could count the times that he and I had touched hands before. This time, it meant something. It was symbolic of the joining together of our hearts.

Then I remembered Noriko. I thought that there was a good chance that Akira and Noriko were more than just friends. As for Akira and me, what we were to each other was quite different from what the world calls lovers. Could we be called passionate friends? It wasn't the kind of love accompanied by thoughts of kisses or any kind of physical fulfillment, but a quieter, stronger, deeper, and richer love.

"Thank you for forgiving me. Thank you." I took my hand from Akira's. Then I said prosaically, "It's getting late. You ought to go. Anyway, I'm hungry."

Akira was quiet for a moment, and then from the small

bag he was carrying he took out a Bible.

"I thought that if I ever saw you again, I'd read the Bible with you. I'll read from the Epistle to the Galatians. Do you know this passage?"

I nodded. "Bear ye one another's burdens," I said.

"Yes, carrying our burdens together, to me that's us, Kiyomi, you and me. I'm so glad you remembered those words."

"Of course I do. I've been trying to live them. But when I saw you and Noriko eating together, so happily, I thought that she was the one you'd chosen to share your burdens with, not me. So —"

"So you ran down the escalator? Oh, Kiyomi, no." He laughed tiredly. "Noriko is nice, but we have hardly anything in common. She doesn't read books, and for a person like me who loves reading, there's just not that much to talk about with her. You should've known that."

Then he began to read. "Brethren, if a man be overtaken in a fault, ye which are spiritual, restore such a one in the spirit of meekness; considering thyself, lest thou also be tempted. Bear ye one another's burdens, and so fulfill the law of Christ."

After he finished, my heart was filled with tranquillity. It was the most profound sense of serenity that I'd ever experienced.

"Thank you, Akira. Thank you for forgiving me."

"Kiyomi, you may not yet believe in Christ, but I do. I believe that Jesus Christ died on the cross for the sake of all people, so that everyone might be forgiven, even me. If I know that I'm forgiven, how can I withhold forgiveness from anyone?"

At that time I didn't really understand about Jesus Christ or the meaning of His death on the cross. Still, I thought that when my leg got better, the first thing I would do was use it to take myself to a church.

I was released from the hospital after three days and went home to Asahikawa. My sprained ankle was quite serious, and it took another three weeks before I had completely recovered. My first summer vacation from college was spent in physical therapy.

Before I go into detail about how I first began to attend church, I want to tell how I chose to go to a junior college to become a nutritionist.

You can guess, Reverend, that I really wanted to study art at a university. I wanted to learn drawing and painting. But the economic situation in our house wouldn't allow me to go to Tokyo to study. Not much of the seven million yen that we'd received from Kanazaki years before remained, and on my mother's income it was difficult just to get me through high school. If I tried to go to art school, where would we ever find the money? My mother thought that even if I didn't go to a university, I could still paint pictures. I also thought that whatever it was that drove me to paint was something besides a formal education. And so I gave up on the idea of studying in Tokyo.

A junior college in Asahikawa was all that we could afford, and anyway there were good programs there in welfare and child education. I knew I wasn't very good at handling people, but I didn't mind cooking; so I chose nutrition.

I've made it sound as if my decision was made solely because of money. However, that's not quite the truth. I was also uneasy about leaving my mother alone. If she and I lived apart, she might not be able to stand the loneliness, and I was afraid that she would revert to her old habits. I felt I couldn't trust a woman who had put a few coins into her daughter's hand and ordered her outside to play while men were visiting. It was sad, but if I could have trusted my mother, I might have worked part-time while studying art at a university.

And so I quietly went to school in Asahikawa, and during that first summer vacation clumsily injured myself in Sapporo, thanks to which I was able to have a reconciliation with Akira. After talking to him that day in the hospital, I resolved to start going to church.

Yet for a while I still hesitated to attend a Christian meeting. Why? Well, I felt that my motives for wanting to go to church weren't pure. I felt that the real reason for my wanting to go wasn't that I had a burning desire to study the Bible. I realized that it was because I just wanted to live in the same world as Akira.

On the road that the bus took to get to my school, there was a small church with a red roof. Each time I saw the white cross on top of the steeple glittering in the morning sun, I thought how much I wanted to go inside. But I told myself that if I couldn't go for the right reasons, I would never go.

I got letters from Akira once or twice a month, and sometimes he called me on the telephone. And when he called, I would have to confess that I still wasn't going to church. I was ashamed to have to say it. But Akira would say, "When the time comes for you to go, you'll go. The Bible says that 'there is a time for every purpose,' doesn't it?"

I finally went inside a church for the first time at the beginning of my second year of college, in April. The minister was you, Reverend. Both you and your wife seemed so gentle, with your bright, smiling faces.

To tell you the truth, I was a little put off at first. This is very rude, but I somehow got the feeling that your smile was only for show and that if I touched it, it might break like a fragile little glass trinket.

When I heard your sermon that day, though, my distrust disappeared. It wasn't as if I understood everything you said, but I was made to feel that there was a side to you that was sharp and strict, but at the same time very, very kind. Watching your face as you preached up on the podium, I thought that it was truly the face of a man of God.

I've had so many teachers in elementary school, junior high, high school, and junior college, some of them enthusiastic and hard-working. But there was something about the way you preached that was lacking in all those other teachers. There was an intensity that amounted almost to desperation. I remember an urgency that made the things you said seem to be a matter of life and death.

Your words went straight to my heart.

Starting then, I went to church every Sunday, and except for the times I was sick, I never missed a single week. I joined the youth group and went to the annual summer camp, where we talked and sang hymns around the campfire late into the night. From all of this, I learned that although all people are full of sin, God forgives us. Jesus Christ bore the sins of all mankind. He atoned for them by dying on the cross in our place, and then after three days He rose again from the dead.

My second year in college was filled with church activities. However, when fall came, something significant happened. I use the word "significant," but actually it was much more of a blow than that word implies.

Fall is the season for job interviews. My school recommended me for an interview at a local hospital. I went with several other students, all of us looking for positions.

Three doctors sat stiffly behind a big table, facing us. My companions chatted with each other, laughing about something now and then. I didn't open my mouth. I couldn't help staring at one of the doctors, the one who sat between the other two. He was over fifty, but still in very good shape. An unusual scar stood out on the right side of his chin. I was sure it wasn't the first time I'd seen that scar. And that rather high-pitched voice, with its characteristic crack — I'd heard that before too. Who was he?

When I remembered, all I wanted to do was stand up

and leave the room at once. He was one of the men who had come to my house when I was in elementary school. As soon as I knew who he was, I could clearly see him opening the front door, and later walking away from the house.

Without showing the least sign of recognition himself, the doctor said, "The quiet one, you're . . .," he looked at my resumé, "Hamano Kiyomi?"

I couldn't make myself answer. Apart from Kanazaki, probably none of the other men who sometimes showed up at my house ever knew my name. I was still afraid that my family name would jog his memory. On the other hand, for a doctor, who comes in contact with so many people every day, the name "Hamano" must be an extremely common last name.

"I see you have only your mother for family —"

There was no sign of surprise on his face as he looked at the column for the names of family members. To this man, Hamano Sawae was no more than a passing pleasure. Perhaps even if he had remembered her name, he still wouldn't have felt a thing. I was shocked by the thought. In spite of everything else I felt toward my mother, I also felt deep pity.

"Did your father pass away?"

I didn't answer, didn't even nod my head yes or no. I've forgotten to mention that after my father had recovered from the hemorrhage, he openly acknowledged me as his daughter. If he hadn't gotten so sick, his wife might not have allowed him to do it. However, whether he acknowledged me or not, my situation was still pretty much the same. In the eyes of the world, I was still different, a special case, an outcast. Ever since I can remember, people have been asking those questions.

"Is your father dead?"

"What was your father's name?"

"Do you remember what your father looked like?"

"What did your father do?"

They were perfectly innocent questions, but nobody ever knew how they pierced me to the heart.

I had absolutely no desire to work at this hospital. I saw no reason to answer any questions about my father. The doctor looked at me, and then returned to my resumé.

"I see. Your speciality in school is art and your hobby is reading. But you're too quiet. You should learn to relax!" he said, and laughed in a loud voice.

Yes, sir. Very good, sir. Perhaps if my father lived under the same roof as my mother, perhaps if I'd ever had some semblance of a normal family life, then perhaps I might laugh like you.

After visiting the hospital, I didn't feel like doing much of anything for a while. Men who had come to see my mother so long ago should have become a thing of the past to me, but now I realized that they wouldn't remain in the past. There were men even today right here in this town who had slept with my mother, walking around so full of themselves, so proud of themselves, talking and laughing in big, loud voices. And in their hearts, of the name Hamano Sawae not even a shadow remained.

You may have noticed, Reverend, the melancholy mood I was in at that time. I was so listless that I even began to stay home from church occasionally for no reason.

Even so, I got the job I have now, working at the hospital as a nutritionist. After the job interview, six months passed. The head of the hospital was apparently an unbiased man with no prejudices against my upbringing. Even without connections, I got the job.

In August of the year I started working, I ran across the fifty-first Psalm one day when I was reading the Bible. At the time, it was very comforting, and I often recited it to myself.

Have mercy upon me, O God, according to thy loving kindness; according unto the multitude of thy tender mercies blot out my transgressions.

Wash me throughly from mine iniquity, and cleanse me from my sin.

For I acknowledge my transgressions, and my sin is ever before me.

Against thee, thee only, have I sinned, and done this evil in thy sight.

Behold, I was shapen in iniquity, and in sin did my mother conceive me.

Behold, thou desirest truth in the inward parts, and in the hidden part thou shalt make me to know wisdom.

Purge me with hyssop, and I shall be clean; wash me, and I shall be whiter than snow.

I began to go to church again regularly. From the time of the awful job interview it took me over a year to start again. During that year, I was possessed by the idea that I might meet up with one of the men from my mother's past as I walked around town. The thing I wanted most was to simply disappear from the face of the earth.

Try to understand, Reverend. I had been raised on money that my mother got from men who bought her. Knowing this all my life, having to endure it, was torture. So many times I wanted to say to her, "If that's what you have to do to make money, then I don't want it!" But she did it, and they didn't even remember her name. My heart went out to her.

When I finished junior college and went to work as a nutritionist, my mother quit her job at a men's fashion shop and started working in a laundromat in the next town. Since both of us were bringing money home now, she decided to shorten her working hours. She left the house after I did and came home before, so she took over running the household from me.

There was a bus stop next to the laundromat where she worked. On Saturdays I usually came home earlier than she did, and from the bus I could see her working at the counter. Her crisp white jacket suited her, and standing at the counter she looked as bright and clean as her uniform. She still had the same outgoing personality she'd always had, and her laughing and talking made her seem healthy and strong.

It made me happy to see my mother that way. At the

same time I felt pity for her. If she hadn't met my father, wouldn't her life have been a normal, happy one, in which she could raise her voice in laughter like other people?

From the time I started going again, I went to church regularly and lived a relatively quiet life for two years. My mother and I had long talks and became close in a different way, like sisters. The head doctor and head nurse were very kind to me, and I made friends among my fellow workers. We went out to lunch together, and sometimes I was invited to the head doctor's house for dinner. Every Sunday, after coming home from church, I sat down at my easel. My friendship with Akira gradually deepened into complete trust.

During that time you invited me to be baptized several times, but I hesitated. Finally I decided that the time would be right on Easter of next year.

Before that, however, on a day in December when I was twenty-two years old, something happened that I could never have imagined.

10   THE LEAST OF THESE

IT WAS THE MORNING of the second Sunday in December, close to Christmas. As usual, I was reading the morning paper before going to church.

"Anything interesting today?" my mother asked. She was stirring *miso* into a pot of soup on the stove. She hadn't changed a bit in the last ten years — at least when it came to newspapers. Stories about murder, kidnaping and scandal were still the most interesting part of the newspaper to her.

I picked up the section that always featured such stories. As I turned the pages, one of the headlines leaped out at me: "Kanazaki Industries Bankrupt." The article said that the whereabouts of the president of the company, Kanazaki Morio, were unknown.

At first I was simply shocked, but then my heart was crowded with a surge of emotions. I'm ashamed to say that the strongest one was a vindictive feeling that Kanazaki had finally gotten what he deserved.

I'm sure that my face betrayed what I was thinking.

"What is it?" my mother said. "Something good?" She put the bowl she was holding down on the table, and I handed her the paper without a word. "Bankrupt!" my mother cried. She sank into a chair and read the article quickly. "'Whereabouts unknown?' You don't think he's... dead, do you?" She put her hand over her mouth in alarm.

At that moment I understood the difference between my mother and myself. The person that she loved most in the world was undoubtedly my real father, Funato Nobumasa. But in her own way I think she loved Kanazaki too. Of course, when they had been together, she had received money from him every month. But I think that there were times when she loved him simply for himself. When their affair was over, he had done the honorable thing, as indeed my father had, by paying a sum of money to make a formal end of it. Even now, though she yearned only for my father, I think she still had a place in her heart for Kanazaki. Seeing the tears on her cheeks as she read the article again made my heart ache.

Reverend, when I read about Kanazaki's bankruptcy and disappearance, my only thoughts were, "Now you've got what you deserve," and "Now the score is even." With their luxurious mansion and fancy limousine, the Kanazakis basked in the sun while we crouched in the shadows. In addition to bearing a grudge against Kanazaki for his unforgivable behavior, I was jealous of Noriko and of the charmed life she led.

A few days after we read about Kanazaki's bankruptcy, I asked my mother if she weren't just a little glad that he'd gotten what was coming to him. She was appalled.

"Glad? How can you say such a thing? We ate together as a family with him! Now he's in such deep trouble that he's gone off somewhere and might even be dead. What is there to be glad about?"

Some time before learning of Kanazaki's bankruptcy, I was reading a book called *Three Minutes of Meditation* by Simone Weil. I ran across a passage I couldn't understand: "A constant awareness of the misfortune of the wretched is a rare and unhappy talent." I had trouble understanding what she meant because it seemed obvious to me that people naturally sympathized with the misfortunes of others. If we see someone injured by the side of the road, we stop and call an ambulance, or if someone is campaigning to help people who are starving, then our natural instinct is to join the campaign. Even if our sympathies are somewhat misplaced, I couldn't imagine anyone casting a cold eye on people in distress.

When confronted by my spiteful reaction to Kanazaki's disaster, however, when I realized what I really was in the depths of my heart, I was shocked. I doubted that baptism was really meant for a person like me.

I also realized that I had pathetically little sympathy for the misfortune of the one and only family member I had, my mother. Her parents had died when she was young, and she had been raised without knowing the warmth of a loving home. She had loved my father, Funato Nobumasa, but when she became pregnant, she had been thrust alone into the world. She had raised me by submitting to the embraces of men she didn't even know. And I hated and scorned her.

Mired in self-pity for my own misfortune, I never once

considered sympathy for hers. As I've said, my mother is a cheerful, outgoing person, and can be quite charming — if she only keeps her mouth shut. The first time you came to visit my house, Reverend, do you know what I said to my mother? "*O-kaa-san*, when the minister comes, don't talk too much, okay? You know how you go on sometimes." That's what I said. And when you were leaving, you said, "Your mother is so nice, Kiyomi, and Mrs. Hamano, you have a lovely daughter. You're both very fortunate." My mother bowed deeply and said graciously, "Thank you very much." After you'd gone, she threw herself into a chair with a big sigh of relief and said, "My feet are killing me." I was so glad that she'd been able to keep from acting like that in front of you.

I had no regard for my mother's feelings, for the loneliness she must have felt. She loves to talk, but for me that day she held her natural warm talkativeness in check. She knew how ashamed I was of her, but she hid her pain and welcomed you cheerfully with tea and cake. She never held me to account for my cold-heartedness. Moreover, it wasn't just that one day. For my whole life, I had been ashamed of my mother, without ever realizing the afflictions she suffered herself. Now that I do, as Simone Weil said, I feel her misery as my own.

Even though I realize this now, Reverend, I must admit that I still can't respect her. Is a daughter who can't even love her own mother really worthy of being baptized? The Bible tells us to love our neighbors as ourselves. How can a person who can't even love her own mother love others?

Christ said, "Love your enemies, bless them that curse you, do good to them that hate you." When I first read these words, I thought immediately of Tsujiko. There's been no greater enemy to me than she was. She was the one who labeled me as a thief in front of everyone, and she bullied me mercilessly every chance she got. She was almost solely responsible for my spending day after day alone and in virtual silence. That day at the river, when she let out that strange shriek, she burned into my mind forever the image of the black water closing over her head. What a heavy burden she gave me to bear! I must have felt some natural sorrow at the death of someone I knew, but not a scrap of compassion. Even after she died, my heart was still gripped by fear and hatred of her. Does such a person have the right to be baptized?

I confronted Akira with all this. I confessed everything that I'd withheld before about Tsujiko's death.

"Do you think that a person like me has the right to be baptized? Hating people, scorning my own mother?"

It was a cold, snowy day in the middle of February. We were drinking hot coffee together in a coffeeshop in Asahikawa.

Akira just listened for a long time, nodding. Then he said, "You're ready to be baptized. Really, you are."

His words were simple, but I was still puzzled. "Akira, I can't forgive people. I can't even respect my own mother."

"Now listen. What do you think a Christian is? Someone who doesn't ever hate anybody?"

I was silent.

"Who never feels contempt for anybody?"

Still I had no answer.

"Did you ever hear your minister say that if you don't love everybody all the time, then you can't be baptized? Did he ever say that you couldn't be a Christian if you didn't learn to respect your parents?"

"Not in so many words, but —"

"I don't think you'll ever hear him say anything like that. Yes, the Bible says, 'Love your neighbor,' and 'Honor your mother and father.' But Jesus never said that if you didn't, you wouldn't be saved. We are all sinners, and not one of us isn't. He'll save us anyway. All we have to do is humbly believe in His forgiveness, and we'll be saved."

"But even though I know that I'm a sinner, I still can't repent. Doesn't true repentance mean not committing the same sin again?"

Akira laughed. "Kiyomi, do you know anybody who can avoid committing the same sin twice? It isn't human. Sinfulness is the very basis of human nature. We may at any moment have the pure heart of an angel, and a moment later the same heart may be touched by evil. That's the way we are. And that's why God sent His only Son, our only hope, to bear our sins, to die for us."

On that cold, snowy day I finally accepted the salvation of Christ. I could never do anything myself to atone for the depth of my sin. I felt I heard the Savior whispering to me, "I love you just as you are," and I believed Him.

My long profession of faith is over. Thank you for

taking the trouble to read it, Reverend. I have an image in my mind of Christ bearing on His back all of the ugliness I've written here, taking it all with Him to the cross, where He suffered for my sins in my place.

That night I had a dream. Aunt Saori was in a beautiful, beautiful flower garden, singing a song to herself. She was alone, surrounded by nothing but flowers that stretched as far as the eye could see. The dream glowed with the natural colors of the flowers. The song she was singing was, of course, the one she'd taught me:

The good Lord up in Heaven above
Gives to all His gentle love.
On the baby sparrow in the eaves,
On the smallest ones, the least of these
He bestows His mercy.

That crystalline voice could be no other than my aunt's. I wanted to go to her, but when I tried, she suddenly disappeared. In her place, two sparrows flew over in the shining sky.

Soon after having the dream, I started a picture of flowers and sparrows. It was my aunt who led me to draw a picture with a baby sparrow in it. It was not the beautiful lady in the dream who inspired me, but the woman who had lived her life in this world, believing in Christ with a pure faith.

I think I'd always had, deep in my heart, a fear of living things, things that moved, even tiny insects. They could attack, they could hurt. Somehow, the fear in my heart was replaced by something else. I resolved to draw a picture with both sparrows and flowers, and while I was drawing it, a strange sensation took hold of me. Almost of their own accord, the words from the Gospel according to Matthew, "Behold the fowls of the air," came into my mind.

When Akira saw the finished picture, he said, "This sparrow looks like it's going to fly right out of the picture. And look at these flowers, don't they look as if they're glowing with life!"

Reverend, that picture is also my profession of faith. The love in my heart that I used to devote only to flowers was turned first to little sparrows, and now includes people as well.

As I was painting, I could feel God's love even for sparrows. If He didn't love them, why would He have created so many? More than the spectacular peacock, more than the dignified crane, I felt that He loved the humble sparrow: the beak, the eyes, the head, the tail, the swelling of the breast, the perfect rightness and balance. Making sketches for my painting, as I watched the sparrows flit about, I was overcome by a love that moved me to tears.

I'm thinking now of Tsujiko, I'm thinking of my mother, and I'm thinking of Kanazaki. I'm thinking of myself, their companion. I'm thinking of Akira. I'm thinking of all the people in the church.

I pray that God will hold us in His hands as we worship Him in the coming celebration of Easter.

Hamano Kiyomi

OTHER BOOKS IN ENGLISH BY AYAKO MIURA
PUBLISHED BY OMF BOOKS

SHIOKARI PASS

From the day they first met as children, Nobuo and Fujiko
fell for each other. With unusual skill, Ayako Miura follows
them through life. Her understanding of adolescents and
her ability to carry her reader into a close affinity with the
characters, accounts for the popularity of this book. In
Japan, it is acclaimed for dispelling prejudice against
Christianity. It gives a rare insight into Japanese life. The
unfolding flower of love opens to full bloom in the snows
of Shiokari Pass.

Translated by Bill & Sheila Fearnehough
ISBN 9971-972-23-9

THE WIND IS HOWLING

In this autobiographical account of her own life in Japan's
turbulent post-war period. Mrs Miura explains her pathway to Christianity. The book reveals the Japanese attitude
to life and helps an understanding of their poetic imagination and their courtesy in personal relationships. But
the deepest and most lasting impression is that of Christ
Himself, patiently leading, prompting, pursuing; in the
deepest and starkest crises of life, of human love and
relationship, in serious illness and suffering and loss.

Translated by Valerie Griffiths
ISBN 997-972-89-1

OTHER BOOKS ABOUT ASIAN CHRISTIANS
PUBLISHED BY OMF BOOKS

AS THE ROCK FLOWER BLOOMS
Rosemary Watson

The inspiring story of the transformation that took place in a Lao village when Peng, the son of a spirit priest, became a Christian.

MORE THAN SKIN DEEP
Margaret Armitage

Lamon, a leprosy sufferer in Thailand, was beautifully transformed from the inside when she met Christ.

GOLD FEARS NO FIRE
Ralph Toliver

The gripping, panoramic story of the Lee family and their life in Communist China between 1949 and 1979. Fiction based on fact.

WITHOUT A GATE
Jean Nightingale

Through the eyes and feelings of A Tsa and his wife A Peh you will experience the trauma and freedom that comes when Christ and His Church enter an Akha village in North Thailand.